MW00951525

The Ultimate Plant-Based
Cookbook For Beginners

1000 Days of Flavorful, Nutrient-Rich Dishes for a Sustainable and Healthy Lifestyle Including a 30-Day Meal Plan

Patricia P. Locke

Copyright© 2023 By Patricia P. Locke

All rights reserved worldwide.

No part of this book may be reproduced or transmitted in any form or by any means, electronic or mechanical, including photo- copying, recording or by any information storage and retrieval system, without written permission from the publisher, except for the inclusion of brief quotations in a review.

Warning-Disclaimer

The purpose of this book is to educate and entertain. The author or publisher does not guarantee that anyone following the techniques, suggestions, tips, ideas, or strategies will become successful. The author and publisher shall have neither liability or responsibility to anyone with respect to any loss or damage caused, or alleged to be caused, directly or indirectly by the information contained in this book.

Table of Contents

Chapter 5 Beans and Grains 34

Chapter 6 Snacks and Appetizers 43

Chapter 7 Vegetables and Sides   56

Chapter 8 Stews and Soups   67

Chapter 9 Desserts — 80

Chapter 10 Salads — 89

Chapter 11 Basics — 98

Chapter 12 Staples, Sauces, Dips, and Dressings 105

INTRODUCTION

Welcome to the world of plant-based eating, where the veggies are abundant, the fruits are sweet, and the health benefits are out of this world! If you're here, it's because you're ready to join the #plantgang and start living your best life with the power of plants. And hey, do we have a treat for you!

This cookbook is not just a collection of recipes, it's a journey into a healthier, more sustainable way of living. I wrote this book because I believe that the food we eat has a profound impact on our health, the environment, and the welfare of animals. By choosing to eat plant-based meals, we can make a positive difference in all three areas.

But don't worry, this cookbook is not about deprivation or sacrifice. On the contrary, it's about discovering the incredible variety of flavors, textures, and colors that plant-based ingredients have to offer. You'll find recipes for every occasion, from quick and easy weeknight dinners to show-stopping desserts. And you'll be surprised by how simple and satisfying plant-based cooking can be.

Now, let me introduce you to this amazing cookbook. This cookbook is jam-packed with delicious and nutritious plant-based recipes that will leave your taste buds dancing with joy. From mouth-watering breakfasts to hearty mains and even sweet treats, this cookbook has got you covered.

One of the standout recipes is the "Powerhouse Protein Shake". It is loaded with all the good stuff, like green apples, pineapple, and fresh kale. Plus, they're so easy to make that even your cat could do it (okay, maybe not your cat, but you get the point).

Another recipe that's sure to impress is the "Creamy Curried Potatoes and Peas". This dish is a real crowd-pleaser, and the creamy sauce is perfectly stirred. It's like a big hug in a bowl, but without all the calories and awkward small talk.

One of the philosophies that I want to express in this book is that plant-based eating is not an all-or-nothing proposition. You don't have to give up meat or dairy completely to enjoy the benefits of plant-based meals. Every plant-based meal you eat is a step in the right direction, and you can tailor your diet to your own preferences and lifestyle.

So whether you're a seasoned vegan or just curious about plant-based cooking, this cookbook is for you. Get ready to taste the rainbow and discover a whole new world of delicious, nutritious food!

Chapter 1 Eating and Human

What is the Essence of Eating

Eating is at the core of human survival and overall health. The essence of eating can be understood from multiple perspectives, encompassing various aspects of human life. Here are some fundamental aspects that capture the essence of eating:

1. Nourishment: Eating provides the essential nutrients, vitamins, and minerals necessary for the body to function optimally. Food supplies the energy needed for physical activity, growth, and repair of tissues, as well as the maintenance of overall health. Eating a balanced and varied diet is important for maintaining good health and preventing chronic diseases such as diabetes, heart disease, and obesity. Also the body's metabolism converts the nutrients from food into energy that can be used by the body. The body breaks down food into small molecules that can be absorbed and used to fuel the body's functions.

2. Sustenance: Eating sustains life by satisfying hunger and providing a sense of fulfillment and satisfaction. It supports our basic survival needs and ensures our well-being.

3. Cultural and Social Significance: Food plays a crucial role in cultural identity and social connections. Sharing meals with others fosters bonds, strengthens relationships, and forms a foundation for communal experiences. It allows people to come together, celebrate traditions, and express hospitality.

4. Pleasure and Enjoyment: Eating can be a source of pleasure, enjoyment, and sensory delight. The taste, texture, aroma, and presentation of food can evoke positive emotions, stimulate the senses, and enhance the overall dining experience. The food we eat can also affect our mood and mental health. Eating a healthy diet can improve our mood, while a poor diet can contribute to depression and anxiety.

5. Rituals and Symbolism: Throughout history, eating has been associated with rituals, ceremonies, and symbolic meanings. Food rituals can have religious, spiritual, or symbolic significance, representing concepts such as abundance, gratitude, or the cycle of life.

6. Exploration and Adventure: Exploring different cuisines and flavors allows us to broaden our horizons, expand our culinary knowledge, and experience new tastes and textures. It can be a form of adventure, discovery, and a way to appreciate the diversity of cultures around the world.

7. Mind-Body Connection: Eating mindfully and paying attention to the nourishment we consume can foster a deeper connection between our mind and body. It encourages us to be aware of our eating habits, make conscious choices, and develop a balanced approach to nutrition.

In summary, the essence of eating encompasses nourishment, sustenance, cultural and social significance, pleasure, rituals, exploration, and the mind-body connection. It is an integral part of our lives that goes beyond mere sustenance, providing a gateway to nourishment, enjoyment, and connection with ourselves and others.

What Elements Do Human Need to Intake

Human beings require a diverse range of elements to maintain optimal health and well-being. A balanced and varied diet that includes a variety of whole foods is important for meeting the body's nutritional needs. These elements can be broadly categorized into macronutrients, micronutrients, and water. Here is a detailed explanation of each:

Macronutrients:

a. Carbohydrates: Carbohydrates are the primary source of energy for the body. They are found in foods such as grains, fruits, vegetables, and legumes. Complex carbohydrates, like whole grains, provide a sustained release of energy, while simple carbohydrates, like sugars, provide quick energy boosts.

b. Proteins: Proteins are essential for growth, repair, and maintenance of body tissues, as well as the production of enzymes, hormones, and antibodies. Good sources of protein include meat, fish, poultry, dairy products, legumes, nuts, and seeds.

c. Fats: Fats are a concentrated source of energy and are vital for the absorption of fat-soluble vitamins, cushioning of organs, and insulation. Healthy fat sources include avocados, nuts, seeds, olive oil, fatty fish, and plant-based oils.

Micronutrients:

a. Vitamins: Vitamins are essential for various bodily functions, such as supporting the immune system, maintaining healthy skin, and aiding in the metabolism of macronutrients. There are two types of vitamins: water-soluble (e.g., vitamin C and B vitamins) and fat-soluble (e.g., vitamins A, D, E, and K), each with its own roles and food sources.

b. Minerals: Minerals are necessary for the formation of bones and teeth, maintaining proper nerve function, regulating fluid balance, and facilitating enzyme activity. Examples of important minerals include calcium, iron, potassium, zinc, and magnesium, which can be obtained from foods like dairy products, leafy greens, meat, legumes, and whole grains.

Water:

Water is vital for numerous physiological processes, such as temperature regulation, digestion, nutrient absorption, and waste removal. It helps maintain the balance of bodily fluids and supports overall hydration. It is recommended to drink an adequate amount of water daily, which varies based on factors like climate, physical activity, and individual needs.

It's important to note that individual requirements for these elements may vary based on factors such as age, sex, activity level, health conditions, and specific dietary needs. A balanced and varied diet that includes a combination of these macronutrients, micronutrients, and sufficient hydration helps ensure proper nutrition and overall well-being. Consulting with a healthcare professional or registered dietitian can provide personalized guidance based on individual circumstances.

This cookbook provided you recipes with necessary ingredients. So don't worry! Everything you need is in it!

Diet and Human Evolution

The relationship between diet and human evolution is complex and multifaceted, and has been the subject of much research and debate among scientists and anthropologists.

The human diet has evolved over millions of years, from the early hominids who ate primarily plant-based diets to the emergence of Homo erectus, who began incorporating animal protein into their diets. With the advent of agriculture and animal domestication, humans began consuming more grains, dairy, and processed foods.

The development of agriculture and the domestication of animals allowed humans to consume more calories and nutrients, leading to population growth and the development of complex societies. However, these changes also led to increased consumption of processed foods, refined grains, and sugar, which can contribute to chronic diseases such as obesity, diabetes, and heart disease.

In modern times, the abundance of processed and convenience foods, as well as the overconsumption of animal products, has led to an increase in chronic diseases and environmental concerns. As a result, many people are turning to plant-based diets as a way to improve their health and reduce their environmental impact.

Overall, the evolution of the human diet has been shaped by a variety of factors, including environmental pressures, technological innovations, and cultural practices. Today, the challenge is to find a diet that is both healthy for individuals and sustainable for the planet.

Chapter 2 Step into the Plant- Based World

The Basics of Plant-Based Diet

Plant-based refers to a diet that is primarily based on whole plant foods such as fruits, vegetables, whole grains, legumes, nuts, and seeds. This type of diet typically minimizes or eliminates animal products such as meat, dairy, and eggs, and focuses on whole, minimally processed foods. Plant-based diets have become increasingly popular due to their potential health benefits, including a reduced risk of chronic diseases such as heart disease, type 2 diabetes, and certain types of cancer. Additionally, plant-based diets are often considered to be more environmentally sustainable than diets that rely heavily on animal products. Here are the basics of a plant-based diet:

1. Emphasis on Plant Foods: The foundation of a plant-based diet is plant foods. These include a wide variety of fruits, vegetables, whole grains, legumes (beans, lentils, chickpeas), nuts, and seeds. These foods provide a rich array of essential nutrients, including vitamins, minerals, fiber, and antioxidants.

2. Reduced or Eliminated Animal Products: A plant-based diet minimizes or excludes animal products. Some individuals following a plant-based diet may choose to include small amounts of animal products like fish or dairy occasionally, while others adopt a fully vegan diet and avoid all animal-derived foods.

3. Protein Sources: Plant-based protein sources include legumes, such as beans, lentils, and peas, tofu and other soy products, tempeh, seitan, and plant-based protein powders. These options can provide an adequate amount of protein necessary for the body's needs.

4. Healthy Fats: Plant-based diets typically emphasize the consumption of healthy fats, such as those found in avocados, nuts, seeds, and plant-based oils like olive oil. These fats are beneficial for heart health and provide essential fatty acids.

5. Nutrient Considerations: It's important for those following a plant-based diet to pay attention to specific nutrients like vitamin B12, iron, calcium, omega-3 fatty acids, and vitamin D, as these may require additional attention or supplementation. Including fortified foods or considering supplements can help meet these needs.

6. Whole Foods and Minimally Processed Foods: Plant-based diets often prioritize whole, unprocessed or minimally processed foods. This includes choosing whole grains like brown rice and quinoa over refined grains, and opting for fresh fruits and vegetables rather than canned or processed versions that may contain added sugars or sodium.

7. Variety and Balance: A key principle of a plant-based diet is to consume a wide variety of foods to ensure a balanced nutrient intake. Including different colors, textures, and types of plant foods not only provides a range of nutrients but also makes meals interesting and enjoyable.

8. Sustainability and Environmental Considerations: Many people choose a plant-based diet due to environmental concerns and sustainability. Plant-based diets tend to have a lower carbon footprint and require fewer resources compared to animal-based diets.

It's important to note that adopting a plant-based diet should be done thoughtfully and based on individual preferences, health considerations, and nutritional needs. Consulting with a healthcare professional or registered dietitian can provide personalized guidance and support for transitioning to and maintaining a plant-based lifestyle.

Why Plant- Based?

A plant-based diet can have a wide range of personal and macro benefits, from improved health and weight management to environmental sustainability and animal welfare. Read on and see how it works!

For individuals, plant- based diet can:

♦ Improve health: Plant-based diets are associated with a lower risk of chronic diseases such as heart disease, type 2 diabetes, and certain types of cancer.

♦ Manage weight: Plant-based diets are typically lower in calories and higher in fiber than diets that include animal products, which can help with weight management.

♦ Help better digestion: Plant-based diets are high in fiber, which can help improve digestion and prevent constipation.

♦ Bring more energy: **Plant-based diets can provide all the necessary nutrients for energy, including carbohydrates, protein, and healthy fats.**

♦ Creative positive emotion: **Plant-based diets have been linked to improved mood and reduced symptoms of depression.**

From the macro perspective, it can:

♦ Sustains the environment: **Plant-based diets are often considered to be more environmentally sustainable than diets that rely heavily on animal products, as animal agriculture is a significant contributor to greenhouse gas emissions and other environmental issues.**

♦ Reduce water usage: **Animal agriculture is a water-intensive industry, and a shift towards plant-based diets could help conserve water resources.**

♦ Reduce deforestation: **Animal agriculture is a major driver of deforestation, and reducing the demand for animal products could help preserve forests and other natural habitats.**

♦ Reduce antibiotic resistance: **The use of antibiotics in animal agriculture is a major contributor to antibiotic resistance, and reducing the demand for animal products could help reduce the use of antibiotics.**

♦ Contribute to Animal welfare: **Plant-based diets are a way to reduce animal suffering and promote animal welfare.**

Who Need Plant-Based Diet?

Plant-based diets can be beneficial for a wide range of people, including:

1. Those looking to improve their overall health: Plant-based diets have been linked to a reduced risk of chronic diseases such as heart disease, type 2 diabetes, and certain types of cancer. Therefore, people who want to improve their overall health may benefit from adopting a plant-based diet.

2. Those with specific health conditions: Plant-based diets may be helpful for people with certain health conditions such as high blood pressure, high cholesterol, and inflammatory bowel disease.

3. Athletes and fitness enthusiasts: Plant-based diets can provide all the necessary nutrients for athletes and fitness enthusiasts, including protein, carbohydrates, and healthy fats.

4. Environmentalists: Plant-based diets are often considered to be more environmentally sustainable than diets that rely heavily on animal products, as animal agriculture is a significant contributor to greenhouse gas emissions and other environmental issues.

5. Animal welfare advocates: People who are concerned about animal welfare may choose to adopt a plant-based diet as a way to reduce their impact on animals and the environment.

Overall, plant-based diets can be a healthy and sustainable choice for a wide range of people. However, it's important to make sure that you're getting all the necessary nutrients from your diet, especially if you're eliminating animal products. Consult with a registered dietitian or healthcare provider to ensure that your plant-based diet is nutritionally balanced.

Getting to Know the Plant-Based Food We Eat

It is an important step in adopting a plant-based diet. Here are a few ways to do so:

1. Research: Reading books, articles, and online resources about plant-based foods can help you learn about different types of fruits, vegetables, grains, legumes, and nuts. This can also help you discover new recipes and cooking techniques.

2. Experiment: Trying new plant-based foods and recipes is a great way to get to know them. Visit your local farmers' market or grocery store and pick up some produce that you haven't tried before. Look up recipes online or in cookbooks and try making them at home.

3. Connect: Joining a community of plant-based eaters can provide support and inspiration. Attend local events or join online groups to connect with others who share your interests.

4. Label reading: When purchasing packaged foods, reading the labels can help you identify plant-based ingredients and avoid animal-derived products. Look out for terms such as vegan, plant-based, and vegetarian.

5. Cookbooks: There are many plant-based cookbooks available that can help you learn about different types of plant-based foods and how to prepare them. Look for cookbooks that focus on whole foods and include a variety of recipes.

Overall, getting to know plant-based foods takes time and effort, but it's a worthwhile investment in your health and well-being.

Focus on Plant- Based Diet

Consumers of plant-based food need to focus on ensuring that they are getting all the necessary nutrients from their diet. Here are some key nutrients that plant-based eaters should focus on:

1. Protein: Plant-based sources of protein include beans, lentils, tofu, tempeh, nuts, and seeds. It's important to consume a variety of protein sources to ensure that you're getting all the essential amino acids.

2. Iron: Plant-based sources of iron include dark leafy greens, beans, lentils, tofu, tempeh, and fortified cereals. Consuming vitamin C-rich foods alongside iron-rich foods can help improve iron absorption.

3. Calcium: Plant-based sources of calcium include dark leafy greens, tofu, fortified plant milks, and fortified juices. It's important to consume enough calcium to support bone health.

4. Vitamin B12: Vitamin B12 is primarily found in animal products, so plant-based eaters may need to supplement or consume fortified foods to ensure adequate intake.

5. Omega-3 fatty acids: Plant-based sources of omega-3 fatty acids include flaxseeds, chia seeds, hemp seeds, and walnuts. Consuming these foods regularly can help ensure adequate intake.

6. Vitamin D: Plant-based sources of vitamin D are limited, so it may be necessary to supplement or consume fortified foods.

Except for microelements mentioned above, consumers should also notice the flavor diversity in their daily choices. In the massive plant-based market, there are increasing people who long for plant-based food as alternatives that this trend will keep go on and on.

Chapter 3 Get Ready to Cook

How to Utilize Plant- Based Diet

Plant-based diets can be utilized in a number of ways to promote health and sustainability. Here are some key points on how to utilize a plant-based diet:

1. Focus on whole foods: Choose whole, minimally processed plant-based foods such as fruits, vegetables, whole grains, legumes, nuts, and seeds.

2. Incorporate a variety of protein sources: Include a variety of plant-based protein sources such as beans, lentils, tofu, tempeh, nuts, and seeds to ensure that you're getting all the essential amino acids.

3. Emphasize nutrient-dense foods: Choose nutrient-dense plant-based foods that are rich in vitamins, minerals, and antioxidants, such as dark leafy greens, berries, and cruciferous vegetables.

4. Use healthy fats: Incorporate healthy fats such as avocados, nuts, seeds, and olive oil into your diet.

5. Consider fortified foods: Consider incorporating fortified plant-based foods such as plant milks, cereals, and nutritional yeast to ensure adequate intake of certain nutrients.

6. Plan meals in advance: Planning meals in advance can help ensure that you're getting all the necessary nutrients and can also help save time and money.

7. Experiment with new recipes: Experiment with new plant-based recipes to keep your meals interesting and enjoyable.

8. Supplements: Depending on your individual needs, you may need to supplement your plant-based diet with vitamins such as B12 or D, or Omega-3 fatty acids.

9. Eating out: When eating out, look for plant-based options on the menu or ask for modifications to suit your dietary needs.

10. Sustainability: A plant-based diet can be more environmentally sustainable than a meat-based diet. Consider the environmental impact of your food choices and try to choose locally sourced, seasonal produce when possible.

Overall, utilizing a plant-based diet involves focusing on whole, nutrient-dense plant-based foods, incorporating a variety of protein sources, and planning meals in advance to ensure adequate nutrient intake.

Cooking Know-how

Do you want to be a veteran in the kitchen? Then you have to master some cooking techniques. Cooking techniques for a plant-based diet can enhance the flavors, textures, and overall enjoyment of plant-based meals. Here are some cooking techniques commonly used in plant-based cuisine:

1. Sautéing and Stir-Frying: Sautéing and stir-frying involve cooking small pieces of vegetables or tofu in a small amount of oil over high heat. This method quickly cooks the ingredients while preserving their flavors, colors, and textures. It's a great technique for preparing vibrant and crisp vegetable stir-fries or sautéed greens.

2. Roasting and Baking: Roasting and baking are excellent techniques for bringing out the natural sweetness and flavors of vegetables and fruits. Simply toss chopped or whole vegetables, such as potatoes, carrots, Brussels sprouts, or cauliflower, with a little oil, salt, and spices, and roast them in the oven until they become tender and slightly caramelized. Baking can be used for making plant-based casseroles, muffins, bread, and desserts.

3. Steaming: Steaming is a gentle cooking method that preserves the nutrients and natural flavors of vegetables. It involves using steam to cook food without direct contact with water. Steamers or a steaming basket can be used to steam vegetables, tofu, and grains. Steamed vegetables retain their vibrant colors and crisp texture.

4. Grilling: Grilling adds a smoky and charred flavor to vegetables, fruits, and plant-based protein sources like tofu or tempeh. Marinating the ingredients before grilling can enhance their taste and tenderness. Grilled vegetables, skewers, or veggie burgers are popular choices in plant-based grilling.

5. Boiling and Simmering: Boiling is a technique used to cook grains, legumes, and pasta in a pot of boiling water until they reach the desired tenderness. Simmering, on the other hand, involves cooking ingredients in a liquid at a lower temperature. It's commonly used for preparing soups, stews, and curries with plant-based ingredients like lentils, beans, or vegetables.

6. Blending and Pureeing: Blending and pureeing are techniques used to create smooth textures and combine flavors. They are often used for making creamy soups, sauces, dressings, and smoothies. Blending can be done using a blender or food processor, while an immersion blender can be used for pureeing directly in the cooking pot.

7. Fermenting and Culturing: Fermentation is a traditional method used to transform ingredients like cabbage into sauerkraut or soybeans into miso. Culturing involves using beneficial bacteria or yeast to create plant-based yogurts, cheeses, or fermented beverages like kombucha.

8. Raw and Salad Preparation: Emphasizing raw ingredients in salads and other dishes is a great way to retain their natural textures, flavors, and nutrients. Raw vegetables, fruits, nuts, and seeds can be combined to create refreshing salads, slaws, and raw desserts.

Remember, the choice of cooking techniques depends on personal preferences and the specific recipe. Experimenting with different methods can help you discover new flavors and textures in plant-based cooking.

Kitchenware You Might Need

Cooking plant-based meals at home can be simple and delicious with the right tools in your kitchen. Here are some essential kitchenware that you might need to use.

1. High-Speed Blender: A high-speed blender is perfect for making smoothies, soups, sauces, and dips. It can also be used to grind nuts and seeds for homemade nut butter or flour.

2. Food Processor: A food processor is essential for chopping vegetables, making hummus, nut-based cheeses, and energy balls.

3. Chef's Knife: A sharp chef's knife is a must-have for chopping vegetables, fruits, and herbs.

4. Cutting Board: A sturdy cutting board is essential for chopping, slicing, and dicing fruits and vegetables.

5. Vegetable Peeler: A vegetable peeler is useful for peeling and slicing vegetables and fruits.

6. Non-Stick Skillet: A non-stick skillet is perfect for cooking plant-based proteins such as tofu and tempeh.

7. Cast Iron Skillet: A cast iron skillet is great for cooking vegetables and grains, and can also be used for baking.

8. Baking Sheet: A baking sheet is useful for roasting vegetables, making homemade granola, and baking bread.

9. Steamer Basket: A steamer basket is perfect for steaming vegetables, grains, and legumes.

10. Mason Jars: Mason jars are great for storing homemade sauces, dressings, and smoothies.

By having these essential kitchen tools, you can make delicious and nutritious plant-based meals at home with ease.

More Than Just Food in Your Plate

However, a bowl of vegetables or beans is not enough. There are so many you can do!

First,Exercise regularly. Regular exercise is important for overall health, so make sure to incorporate physical activity into your daily routine. Any type of exercise can be suitable for someone following a plant-based diet, as it largely depends on individual preferences and fitness levels. However, here are some types of exercises that can be particularly beneficial:

1. Cardiovascular exercise: Cardiovascular exercise, such as running, cycling, or swimming, can help improve heart health, boost endurance, and burn calories.

2. Strength training: Strength training, such as lifting weights or using resistance bands, can help build muscle mass, increase metabolism, and improve bone density.

3. Yoga: Yoga can help improve flexibility, balance, and relaxation, as well as reduce stress and anxiety.

4. Pilates: Pilates is a low-impact form of exercise that can help improve core strength, flexibility, and posture.

5. Outdoor activities: Outdoor activities such as hiking, rock climbing, or kayaking can provide a fun and stimulating way to exercise while enjoying nature.

Remember to choose activities that you enjoy and that fit your fitness level and goals. Aim for at least 150 minutes of moderate-intensity aerobic exercise per week, as well as strength training exercises at least twice a week.

Second, get enough sleep. Getting enough sleep is important for overall health and can help regulate your appetite and energy levels.

And, it is recommended to practice mindful eating. Mindful eating involves paying attention to your body's hunger and fullness cues, as well as the taste, texture, and enjoyment of your food.

Let's Get Cooking

So, if you want to join the #plantgang and start living your best life, this cookbook is a must-have. With its delicious recipes and witty commentary, it's basically like having your own personal chef and comedian rolled into one. So grab your apron, turn up the music, and let's get cooking!

30-Day Meal Plan

DAYS	BREAKFAST	LUNCH	DINNER	SNACK/DESSERT
1	Buckwheat Porridge	Red Peppers with Herby Breadcrumbs	Vegan "Toona" Salad	Overnight Cookie Dough Oats
2	Shiitake Bakin'	Green Chile Rice with Black Beans	Detox Salad	Crispy Baked Chickpeas
3	Breakfast Scramble	Berbere-Spiced Red Lentils	Greek Salad in a Jar	Garlic Hummus
4	Polenta with Seared Pears	Orange Quinoa with Black Beans	Caramelized Onion Potato Salad	Baked Vegetable Chips
5	Spiced Sorghum and Berries	Mushroom Risotto	Beet, Cabbage, and Black Bean Salad	Peanut Butter Snack Squares
6	Vanilla Breakfast Smoothie	Chana Masala	Succotash Salad	Protein Power Grilled Veggie and Fruit Skewers
7	Blueberry Scones	Whole-Grain Corn Muffins	Classic French Vinaigrette	Eggplant Caponata Bruschetta
8	Powerhouse Protein Shake	Bulgur Chickpea Pilaf	Dill Potato Salad	Cherry Chocolate Hemp Balls
9	Seeds, Nuts, and Fruit Baked Granola	Spicy Chickpeas and Fennel	Mock Tuna Salad	Nori Snack Rolls
10	Banana-Date Shake with Oats	Quick Panfried Tempeh	Mock Tuna Salad	Green Energy Bites
11	Maple, Apple, and Walnut Great Grains	Spring Steamed Vegetables with Savory Goji Berry Cream	Baked Brown Rice Risotto with Sunflower Seeds	Mexikale Crisps
12	Superseed and Nut Breakfast Cookies	Creamy Curried Potatoes and Peas	Southwest Stuffed Peppers	Avomame Spread
13	Lazy Steel-Cut Oatmeal	Daikon Beet Pickle with Lime	Wild Rice, Cabbage and Chickpea Pilaf	Spirulina-Golden Berry Power Bars
14	Banana and Oat Muffins	Crispy Maple Mustard Cabbage	Baked Tempeh Nuggets	Peanut Butter Chocolate Seed Balls
15	Millet Porridge with Pumpkin and Cinnamon	Sheet-Pan Garlicky Kale	Peanut Butter Tempeh	Strawberry Shortcake Rice Bites
16	Liver Flush Juice	Beet Sushi and Avocado Poke Bowls	Smoky Cajun Bowl	Earl Grey Tiramisu
17	Choco Almond Mousse Pudding	Spicy Miso-Roasted Tomatoes and Eggplant	Chickpea Pâté	Two-Ingredient Peanut Butter Fudge
18	Baked Flaxseed-Battered French Toast	Lemony Roasted Cauliflower with Coriander	Barley and Sweet Potato Pilaf	Peanut Butter Nice Cream

DAYS	BREAKFAST	LUNCH	DINNER	SNACK/DESSERT
19	Irish Breakfast Oats	Glowing, Fermented Vegetable Tangle	Curried Chickpeas and Rice	Banana Bread Scones
20	Cookies for Breakfast	Braised Red Cabbage with Beans	Almost Instant Ramen	Sweet Red Beans
21	Savory Ginger Green Onion Crepes	Sweet Potato, Kale, and Red Cabbage Salad	Shaved Fennel and Lemon Pickle	Cranberry Orange Biscotti
22	Banana, Date and Coconut Muesli	Meyer Lemon Romanesco Glow Salad	Fermented Carrots with Turmeric and Ginger	Mango-Peach Sorbet
23	Stuffed Breakfast Sweet Potatoes	Crunchy Curry Salad	Roasted Carrots with Ginger Maple Cream	Chocolate-Peppermint Nice Cream
24	Savory Oatmeal	Creamy Fruit Salad	Mustard-Roasted Beets and Shallots with Thyme	Walnut Brownies
25	Carrot Cake Oatmeal	Orange, Fennel and White Bean Salad	Roasted Cauliflower Bowls	Pumpkin Bread Pudding
26	Cinnamon Apple Toast	Blueprint: Lifesaving Bowl	Blackened Sprouts	Pineapple Soft-Serve
27	Sunrise Smoothie Bowl	Ancient Grains Salad	Grilled Eggplant "Steaks"	Chocolate Microwave Mug Cake
28	Chickpea and Mushroom Breakfast Bowls	Pineapple Quinoa Salad	Sautéed Collard Greens	Golden Banana Bread
29	Slow-Cooked Steel-Cut Oats	Apple Broccoli Crunch Bowl	Grilled Vegetable Kabobs	Coconut and Tahini Bliss Balls
30	Breakfast Tofu	Peaches, Peas, and Beans Summer Salad	Garlic Toast	Triple Chocolate Icebox Cake

Chapter 4 Breakfasts

Buckwheat Porridge

Prep time: 5 minutes | Cook time: 20 minutes | Make

4 cups

1 cup raw buckwheat groats, soaked overnight in 2 cups filtered water
4 cups filtered water

1 teaspoon ground cinnamon or cardamom
Pinch of fine sea salt (optional)

1. Cook the buckwheat: Drain the buckwheat in a strainer and rinse it thoroughly under running water until it's no longer slimy. Drain well and transfer it to an upright blender. Add 4 cups of water, cinnamon, and salt (if using) and pulse until the grains are cracked. Pour the mixture into a medium pot and bring it to a boil over high heat, whisking frequently. Cover the pot, reduce the heat to low, and simmer for about 15 minutes, stirring occasionally to prevent sticking, until the grains are soft and the porridge is creamy. 2. Serve hot or store for later: Serve the porridge hot. If you have leftover porridge, pour it into a wide-mouthed glass jar or other container and allow it to cool. Cover tightly and store it in the fridge for up to 5 days.

Per Serving:(1 cup)

calories: 40 | fat: 0g | protein: 1g | carbs: 9g | fiber: 2g

Shiitake Bakin'

Prep time: 5 minutes | Cook time: 30 minutes |

Makes 1 cup

1 (3½ ounces / 99 g) package shiitake mushrooms , stems discarded and sliced thinly
1 teaspoon maple syrup (optional)

1 teaspoon reduced-sodium, gluten-free tamari
¼ teaspoon black pepper
¼ teaspoon garlic powder
¼ teaspoon smoked paprika

1. Preheat the oven: Preheat the oven to 375ºF (190°C) and line a baking sheet with parchment paper. 2. Prepare the mushrooms: Combine the shiitakes, maple syrup (if desired), tamari, pepper, garlic powder, and paprika in a medium bowl. 3. Bake the mushrooms: Spread the mushrooms in a single layer on the prepared baking sheet and bake for 30 minutes, tossing every 10 minutes, until the mushrooms start to crisp. 4. Serve or store: Remove the mushrooms from the oven and allow them to cool on the baking sheet before serving. The mushrooms can be stored in an airtight container for up to 3 days.

Per Serving:(1 cup)

calories: 55 | fat: 1g | protein: 2g | carbs: 10g | fiber: 1g

Seeds, Nuts, and Fruit Baked Granola

Prep time: 10 minutes | Cook time: 40 minutes |

Serves 8

7 cups old-fashioned oats (use gluten-free if desired)
1 cup shredded coconut
1 cup sunflower seed kernels
1 cup walnuts

1 cup coconut sugar (optional)
¼ cup chia seeds
1 cup coconut oil (optional)
1 cup raisins

1.Preheat the oven: Preheat the oven to 300ºF (150°C). 2. Mix the ingredients: In a large bowl, mix all the ingredients together except for the raisins. Spread the mixture out in a large baking pan. 3. Bake and stir: Bake for 40 minutes, taking the pan out of the oven every 10 minutes to stir the mixture. Return the pan to the oven. 4. Add raisins: After 30 minutes, add the raisins and stir. Bake for 10 more minutes. 5. Cool and store: Take the pan out of the oven and let the mixture cool. Pack the mixture in an airtight container. It will keep for 4 weeks.

Per Serving:

calories: 566 | fat: 32g | protein: 20g | carbs: 52g | fiber: 16g

Choco Almond Mousse Pudding

Prep time: 5 minutes | Cook time: 0 minutes | Serves 2

2 cups soy milk
1 cup pomegranate seeds
2 peeled bananas
2 scoops soy protein isolate, chocolate flavor

¼ cup almond butter
1 cup water (optional)
Optional Toppings:
Blueberries
Shredded coconut

1. Blend the ingredients: Add all the ingredients to a blender and blend until smooth. Alternatively, blend the bananas, soy isolate, and almond butter until smooth. 2. Add the almond butter mixture: Add a heaped tablespoon of the almond butter mixture to 2 large glasses or Mason jars. 3. Add the soy milk and pomegranate seeds: Add ¼ cup of soy milk and a tablespoon of pomegranate seeds to each glass or jar. 4. Repeat the layers: Repeat steps 2 and 3 until all of the almond mixture, pomegranate seeds, and soy milk have been used. 5. Add toppings and serve: Serve with the optional toppings and enjoy! 6. Store and consume: Store the pudding in an airtight container in the fridge and consume within 2 days. Alternatively, store in the freezer for a maximum of 60 days and thaw at room temperature before serving.

Per Serving:

calories: 596 | fat: 23g | protein: 43g | carbs: 55g | fiber: 12g

Banana and Oat Muffins

Prep time: 10 minutes | Cook time: 20 minutes |

Makes 12

1 ripe banana, mashed
½ cup unsweetened applesauce
¾ cup coconut milk
1 teaspoon baking soda
1 tablespoon lemon juice
½ cup quick-cook rolled oats, uncooked
½ cup whole-wheat flour
2 tablespoons ground flaxseed
1 teaspoon ground cinnamon
1 teaspoon baking powder
⅓ cup chopped pecans, toasted
⅓ cup raisins, no sugar added

1. Preheat the oven: Preheat the oven to 425ºF (220ºC) and line 12 muffin cups with paper liners. 2. Mix the wet ingredients: In a medium bowl, mix the banana, applesauce, and coconut milk. 3. Mix the baking soda and lemon juice: In a small bowl, combine the baking soda and lemon juice. Add to the banana mixture. 4. Mix the dry ingredients: In a large bowl, mix the quick oats, whole-wheat flour, flaxseed, cinnamon, and baking powder. 5. Combine the wet and dry ingredients: In the large bowl, combine the wet and dry ingredients; then add the pecans and raisins and mix thoroughly. 6. Fill the muffin cups: Fill the muffin cups three-quarters full with batter. 7. Bake and store: Bake for 20 minutes or until a toothpick inserted in the center of a muffin comes out clean. Store the muffins in an airtight container or a zip-top bag in the refrigerator for up to 5 days.

Per Serving:

calories: 222 | fat: 12g | protein: 4g | carbs: 28g | fiber: 4g

Lazy Steel-Cut Oatmeal

Prep time: 15 minutes | Cook time: 30 minutes |

Serves 1

1 teaspoon virgin coconut oil (optional)
½ teaspoon ground cinnamon
¼ cup certified gluten-free steel-cut oats
2 tablespoons dried sour cherries or other dried fruit
⅛ teaspoon fine sea salt
(optional)
1 cup unsweetened almond milk, plus extra for reheating if necessary
1 tablespoon pure maple syrup, or to taste (optional)
Chopped fresh fruit, for serving (optional)

1. Cook the oats: Heat the coconut oil in a small saucepan over medium heat. Add the cinnamon and stir until fragrant, about 30 seconds. Add the oats and stir to coat them in the cinnamon. Add the dried cherries, sea salt (if using), and almond milk, and stir. 2. Let the oats soak: Bring the mixture to a boil. After it boils, turn off the heat, remove the saucepan from the burner, and cover with a lid. Leave the oats on the cold stove overnight. 3. Reheat and serve: The next morning, place the saucepan back on the burner over medium heat. Add more almond milk if you like. When the porridge starts to boil, remove from the heat and scrape it into your serving bowl. Top the porridge with the maple syrup and chopped fruit (if using).

Per Serving:

calories: 283 | fat: 9g | protein: 6g | carbs: 35g | fiber: 6g

Superseed and Nut Breakfast Cookies

Prep time: 10 minutes | Cook time: 15 minutes |

Makes 12 cookies

1 tablespoon ground flaxseeds
3 tablespoons water
1 cup whole-wheat flour
1 cup rolled oats
2 tablespoons hemp hearts
2 tablespoons pumpkin seeds
2 tablespoons sunflower seeds
3 tablespoons raisins
1 tablespoon baking powder
1 teaspoon salt (optional)
1 tablespoon ground cinnamon
2 tablespoons chopped walnuts
3 tablespoons coconut oil, melted (optional)
2 tablespoons natural peanut butter
½ cup maple syrup (optional)

1. Preheat the oven: Preheat the oven to 350ºF (180ºC). Line a sheet pan with parchment paper. 2. Prepare the flax egg: In a small bowl, mix together the flaxseeds and water to form a "flax egg." Set aside. 3. Mix the dry ingredients: In a large bowl, mix together the flour, oats, hemp hearts, pumpkin seeds, sunflower seeds, raisins, baking powder, salt (if using), cinnamon, and walnuts. 4. Add the wet ingredients: Add the coconut oil, flax egg, peanut butter, and maple syrup to the flour mixture and stir well until combined. 5. Bake the cookies: Using a spoon, scoop 2 tablespoons of batter per cookie onto the prepared sheet pan, leaving at least 1 inch between them. Bake for 10 to 12 minutes, or until the cookies are firm and golden brown.

Per Serving:

calories: 351 | fat: 16g | protein: 8g | carbs: 49g | fiber: 6g

Maple, Apple, and Walnut Great Grains

Prep time: 10 minutes | Cook time: 3 to 4 hours |

Serves 4 to 6

2 large apples
½ cup quinoa, rinsed
½ cup steel-cut oats
½ cup wheat berries
½ cup pearl barley
½ cup bulgur wheat
1 tablespoon ground flaxseed
2 teaspoons ground cinnamon
½ teaspoon ground or grated nutmeg
7 cups water
⅓ cup maple syrup (optional)
½ cup chopped walnuts
½ cup raisins
Unsweetened plant-based milk, for serving (optional)

1. Prepare the slow cooker: Peel, core, and chop the apples and place them in the slow cooker. Add the quinoa, oats, wheat berries, barley, bulgur wheat, flaxseed, cinnamon, nutmeg, water, and maple syrup (if using). Stir gently. Cover and cook on High for 3 to 4 hours or on Low for 7 to 8 hours. 2. Add toppings and serve: Before serving, stir in the walnuts and raisins. Spoon the mixture into a bowl and add your favorite milk (if using).

Per Serving:

calories: 691 | fat: 13g | protein: 18g | carbs: 113g | fiber: 21g

Spiced Sorghum and Berries

Prep time: 5 minutes | Cook time: about 1 hour | Serves 4

1 cup whole-grain sorghum	milk
1 teaspoon ground cinnamon	1 teaspoon vanilla extract
1 teaspoon Chinese five-spice powder	2 tablespoons pure maple syrup (optional)
3 cups water, plus more as needed	1 tablespoon chia seeds
1 cup unsweetened nondairy	¼ cup sliced almonds
	2 cups fresh raspberries, divided

1. Cook the sorghum: In a large pot over medium-high heat, stir together the sorghum, cinnamon, five-spice powder, and water. Bring the water to a boil, cover the pot, and reduce the heat to medium-low. Cook for 1 hour, or until the sorghum is soft and chewy. If the sorghum grains are still hard, add another cup of water and cook for 15 minutes more. 2. Add the remaining ingredients: In a glass measuring cup, whisk together the milk, vanilla, and maple syrup (if using) to blend. Add the mixture to the sorghum, along with the chia seeds, almonds, and 1 cup of raspberries. Gently stir to combine. 3.Serve: Serve the sorghum mixture topped with the remaining 1 cup of fresh raspberries.

Per Serving:

calories: 289 | fat: 8g | protein: 9g | carbs: 52g | fiber: 10g

Vanilla Breakfast Smoothie

Prep time: 10 minutes | Cook time: 0 minutes | Serves 1

1 frozen banana, sliced	1 tablespoon flaxseed meal
1 cup vanilla almond milk	¼ teaspoon cinnamon
¼ cup old-fashioned oats	3 tablespoons vanilla protein powder
¼ cup raisins	

1. Blend the ingredients: Place all the ingredients in a blender and blend until very smooth.

Per Serving:

calories: 399 | fat: 12g | protein: 26g | carbs: 48g | fiber: 12g

Blueberry Scones

Prep time: 10 minutes | Cook time: 20 minutes | Makes 8 scones

1 cup whole wheat flour	3 tablespoons cold coconut butter
¾ cup old-fashioned rolled oats	¾ cup almond milk
½ teaspoon baking powder	1 tablespoon fresh lemon juice
½ teaspoon salt (optional)	2 teaspoons coconut sugar (optional)
1 cup frozen blueberries, thawed and drained	

1. Preheat the oven: Preheat the oven to 475ºF (245ºC). Lightly grease a baking sheet or use parchment paper. 2. Mix the dough: In a medium bowl, mix the flour, oats, baking powder, and salt (if desired). Add the butter and use a pastry cutter, two forks, or your fingers to mix until well combined. Fold in the blueberries. Add the almond milk and lemon juice and mix with a fork until it forms a shaggy ball of dough; do not overmix. 3. Shape the dough: Split the dough into two balls. Spread one ball of dough into a circle on one end of the sheet. It should be 1 inch thick. Repeat on the other side. Sprinkle one teaspoon of sugar over each circle. Use a knife to cut each circle into 4 wedges. 4. Bake and serve: Bake for 20 minutes, or until a toothpick inserted in the middle comes out clean and the scones are golden brown. Serve warm. (Toast any leftovers before serving.)

Per Serving:(2 scones)

calories: 250 | fat: 8g | protein: 8g | carbs: 45g | fiber: 7g

Powerhouse Protein Shake

Prep time: 5 minutes | Cook time: 0 minutes | Serves 2

2 green apples, peeled, cored, and chopped	rinsed
1 cup fresh or frozen pineapple chunks	1 teaspoon spirulina
1 cup fresh kale, chopped	1 cup coconut water
1 cup spinach, drained and	2 scoops of unflavored vegan protein powder

1. Prepare the drink: Add all the required ingredients to a blender and blend for 2 minutes until smooth. 2.Serve: Transfer the drink to a large cup or shaker and enjoy.

Per Serving:

calories: 257 | fat: 4g | protein: 26g | carbs: 30g | fiber: 5g

Millet Porridge with Pumpkin and Cinnamon

Prep time: 5 minutes | Cook time: 25 minutes | Serves 2

1¼ cups unsweetened plain or vanilla almond milk	no sugar added
½ cup millet	½ cup pumpkin purée
½ cup golden raisins (sultanas),	Pinch ground cinnamon
	Pinch ground nutmeg (optional)

1. Heat the almond milk: In a small pot, bring the almond milk to a boil. 2. Add the millet and raisins: Add the millet and raisins to the pot. Return to a boil; then reduce the heat to a simmer. Cover and cook for 20 minutes until the millet is tender. 3. Add the pumpkin purée: Add the pumpkin purée and cook for 3 to 5 minutes more, just enough time to heat the porridge through.

4. Serve and add toppings: Serve the porridge in small bowls and top with the cinnamon and nutmeg (if using).

Per Serving:

calories: 378 | fat: 4g | protein: 11g | carbs: 79g | fiber: 8g

Cookies for Breakfast

Prep time: 10 minutes | Cook time: 20 minutes | Makes 12 cookies

1¼ cups certified gluten-free rolled oats
1 teaspoon ground cinnamon
½ teaspoon baking soda
½ teaspoon fine sea salt (optional)
½ cup almond flour
¼ cup brown rice flour
½ cup mashed ripe banana

½ cup smooth almond butter, stirred
3 tablespoons pure maple syrup (optional)
2 tablespoons ground flaxseed
3 tablespoons liquid virgin coconut oil (optional)
1 teaspoon pure vanilla extract

1.Preheat the oven: Preheat the oven to 350ºF (180ºC). Line a baking sheet with parchment paper and set aside. 2. Mix the dry ingredients: In a large bowl, stir together the rolled oats, cinnamon, baking soda, sea salt (if using), almond flour, and brown rice flour until combined. 3. Mix the wet ingredients: In the bowl of a food processor, combine the mashed banana, almond butter, maple syrup (if using), ground flaxseed, coconut oil (if using), and vanilla. Process on high until the mixture is smooth. 4. Combine the wet and dry ingredients: Scrape the almond butter mixture into the large bowl with the oats and flour mixture. Stir the mixture with a spatula until you have a unified and very stiff cookie dough. 5. Form and bake the cookies: Drop 2 tablespoons of dough per cookie onto the prepared baking sheet. Flatten each mound of dough with the palm of your hand. Slide the baking sheet into the oven and bake until lightly golden brown, about 15 to 17 minutes. 6. Cool and store the cookies: Cool cookies completely before storing in an airtight container. These will last on the counter for 5 days. You can also wrap each cookie individually with plastic wrap and freeze them.

Per Serving:

calories: 160 | fat: 10g | protein: 5g | carbs: 17g | fiber: 4g

Savory Ginger Green Onion Crepes

Prep time: 5 minutes | Cook time: 20 minutes | Makes 8 crepes

⅔ cup chickpea flour
⅔ cup buckwheat flour
2 green onions, finely sliced
2 teaspoons fine sea salt (optional)
1 teaspoon chili powder

1 piece of fresh ginger, peeled and finely grated
1 tablespoon sesame seeds
1½ cups filtered water
Olive oil spray, for cooking (optional)

1. Preheat the oven and baking sheet: Preheat the oven to 275ºF (135ºC). Place a baking sheet in the oven. 2. Mix the dry ingredients: In a large bowl, combine the chickpea flour, buckwheat flour, sliced green onions, sea salt (if using), chili powder, grated ginger, and sesame seeds. Whisk to combine. 3. Add the water: Add the filtered water to the flour mixture. Whisk the batter until all flour is incorporated. The batter should be thinner than pancake batter, dripping slowly from the edge of a spoon or spatula, but not as thin as almond milk. Add extra water, by the tablespoon, if necessary. 4. Rest the batter: Cover the bowl with plastic wrap and

allow the batter to rest for 30 minutes. 5. Heat the crepe pan: Heat a crepe pan over medium-high heat. If your batter has thickened and seems almost elastic when you drag a spoon through it, add a couple of tablespoons of water and lightly whisk the batter one more time. 6. Ladle and spread the batter: Spray the hot crepe pan with olive oil (if using). Ladle about ⅓ cup of batter into the crepe pan. Holding the pan's handle with your non-ladling hand, quickly use your wrist to shake the pan in a circular motion, distributing the crepe batter into a thin, circular crepe. You can lift the pan right off the stove and shake it in the air to get the batter moving. 7. Flip and cook the crepe: Once the crepe appears dry on the surface and some holes have poked through, flip the crepe over. Cook the crepe another 45 seconds, or until lightly browned and dry on the other side.

Keep the crepes warm: Keep the cooked crepes warm on the baking sheet in the oven while you repeat this process with the remaining batter.

Per Serving:(1 crepe)

calories: 87 | fat: 2g | protein: 4g | carbs: 14g | fiber: 3g

Banana, Date and Coconut Muesli

Prep time: 10 minutes | Cook time: 0 minutes | Serves 2

1 cup rolled oats
¾ cup unsweetened almond milk
½ cup pitted and chopped dates

¼ cup unsweetened coconut, toasted
1 banana, peeled and sliced

1. Mix all the ingredients in a bowl and let them soak for 15 minutes.

Per Serving:

calories: 331 | fat: 7g | protein: 13g | carbs: 76g | fiber: 12g

Irish Breakfast Oats

Prep time: 5 minutes | Cook time: 40 minutes | Serves 4

4 cups water
¼ teaspoon sea salt (optional)
1 cup gluten-free steel-cut oats
1 tablespoon pure maple syrup (optional)

1 tablespoon almond butter
Suggested Toppings:
1 ripe banana, sliced
½ cup sliced almonds
Dash of ground cinnamon

1. Cook the oats: In a 4-quart saucepan, bring the water and salt (if using) to a boil. Add the oats and stir well. Reduce the heat to low and cook for 30 to 40 minutes, or until cooked through. The oats will be chewy, but they should not have any crunch. 2. Add the almond butter and maple syrup: Stir in the maple syrup (if using) and almond butter, then spoon the oatmeal into 4 bowls. 3. Add toppings and serve: If using any suggested toppings, add them now. Serve the oatmeal hot.

Per Serving:

calories: 188 | fat: 9g | protein: 7g | carbs: 28g | fiber: 6g

Chickpea and Mushroom Breakfast Bowls

Prep time: 5 minutes | Cook time: 15 minutes | Serves 4

1 tablespoon extra-virgin olive oil (optional)
1 red or yellow bell pepper, seeded and diced small
8 ounces (227 g) cremini or white mushrooms, cut into ½-inch-thick slices
1 tablespoon low-sodium soy sauce or gluten-free tamari

½ teaspoon garlic powder
½ teaspoon smoked paprika
1 (15 ounces / 425 g) can chickpeas, drained and rinsed
1 bunch kale, stemmed and chopped
1 cup frozen peas
2 tablespoons water

1. In a large saucepan, heat the oil over medium heat. Add the bell pepper and mushrooms and cook, stirring occasionally, until the mushrooms are browned, 4 to 5 minutes. 2. Add the soy sauce, garlic powder, smoked paprika, chickpeas, kale, peas, and water and cook until the kale is wilted and fork-tender, about 5 minutes.

Per Serving:
calories: 205 | fat: 6g | protein: 12g | carbs: 30g | fiber: 9g

Slow-Cooked Steel-Cut Oats

Prep time: 10 minutes | Cook time: 8 hours | Serves 2

1 cup steel-cut oats
2 cups chopped dried apple

1 cup dates, pitted and chopped
1 cinnamon stick

1. Combine the oats, dried apple, dates, cinnamon stick, and 4 cups of water in a 2- or 4-quart slow cooker. Cook for 8 hours, or until the oats are tender. Remove the cinnamon stick before serving.

Per Serving:
calories: 320 | fat: 3g | protein: 10g | carbs: 89g | fiber: 15g

Breakfast Tofu

Prep time: 10 minutes | Cook time: 30 minutes | Makes 12 slices

2 (16 ounces / 454 g) packages sprouted or extra-firm tofu, drained
1 tablespoon reduced-sodium, gluten-free tamari
¼ cup nutritional yeast

1 teaspoon ground cumin
½ teaspoon garlic powder
½ teaspoon ground turmeric
½ teaspoon yellow curry powder
¼ teaspoon black pepper

1. Preheat the oven to 400ºF (205ºC). Line a baking sheet with parchment paper. 2. Slice each package of tofu into six pieces. Pat dry. Drizzle evenly with the tamari. 3. Combine the nutritional yeast, cumin, garlic powder, turmeric, curry powder, and black pepper in a large rectangular food storage container with a tight-fitting lid. Place the sliced tofu in the container and shake gently until all slices are covered. (You might need to open the container and rotate the slices a bit.) Let sit while the oven preheats. (The marinated tofu can be refrigerated for up to 1 day.) 4. Place tofu on the baking sheet. Spread any extra seasoning mix on top. Bake for 30 minutes, flipping halfway through. 5. Serve at room temperature or cold from the fridge.

Per Serving:
calories: 111 | fat: 6g | protein: 11g | carbs: 5g | fiber: 2g

Tropical Smoothie Bowl

Prep time: 10 minutes | Cook time: 0 minutes | Serves 2

2 cups frozen mango chunks
½ cup frozen pineapple chunks
1 frozen banana
½ to 1 cup plant-based milk
2 tablespoons chopped nuts of your choice

¼ cup chopped fruit of your choice
Optional Toppings:
1 tablespoon flaxseed meal
1½ tablespoons coconut shreds

1. Add the mango, pineapple, banana, and milk (1 cup makes it a thinner smoothie and ½ cup makes it thicker) to a blender and blend until smooth. 2. Pour the smoothie into a bowl and top with the nuts and fruit.

Per Serving:
calories: 254 | fat: 5g | protein: 6g | carbs: 50g | fiber: 6g

Baked Flaxseed-Battered French Toast

Prep time: 10 minutes | Cook time: 15 minutes | Serves 4

¼ cup ground flaxseeds
1½ cups unsweetened plant-based milk, divided
Olive oil cooking spray
1 tablespoon ground cinnamon

1 teaspoon vanilla extract
3 tablespoons maple syrup, plus more for serving (optional)
8 slices whole-grain bread

1. Mix the flaxseeds and plant-based milk: In a medium bowl, combine the flaxseeds and ½ cup of plant-based milk. Let the mixture stand for 10 minutes to give the flaxseeds time to absorb the liquid and thicken, which will give them a pudding-like consistency. 2. Preheat the oven: Preheat the oven to 400ºF (205ºC). Spray a sheet pan with olive oil cooking spray. 3. Mix the remaining ingredients and dip the bread: Add the remaining 1 cup plant-based milk, the cinnamon, vanilla, and maple syrup (if using) to the flax mixture and mix until combined. Dip each slice of bread into the flax mixture, making sure to completely cover in the liquid. Let any excess drip back into the bowl and then put the slices on the sheet pan. 4. Bake and flip the bread: Bake for 10 minutes. Using a spatula, carefully flip the bread and bake for 5 minutes. 5.Serve: Serve with maple syrup.

Per Serving:
calories: 272 | fat: 7g | protein: 11g | carbs: 42g | fiber: 7g

Savory Rosemary–Black Pepper Scones

Prep time: 10 minutes | Cook time: 20 minutes | Makes 8 scones

1 cup whole wheat flour	black pepper
¾ cup old-fashioned rolled oats	½ teaspoon salt (optional)
2 tablespoons minced fresh rosemary	3 tablespoons puréed white beans or tahini
½ teaspoon baking powder	¾ cup almond milk
½ teaspoon freshly ground	1 tablespoon fresh lemon juice

1. Preheat the oven to 475°F (245°C). Lightly grease a baking sheet or use parchment paper. 2. Mix the flour, oats, rosemary, baking powder, pepper, and salt (if desired) in a medium bowl. Add the puréed white beans and use a pastry cutter, two forks, or your fingers to mix until well combined. Add the almond milk and lemon juice and mix with a fork until it forms a shaggy ball of dough; do not overmix. 3. Split the dough into two balls. Spread one ball of dough into a circle on one end of the sheet. It should be 1 inch thick. Repeat on the other side. Use a knife to cut each circle into 4 wedges. 4. Bake for 20 minutes, or until a toothpick inserted in the middle comes out clean and the scones are golden brown. Serve warm. (Toast any leftovers before serving.)

Per Serving:(2 scones)

calories: 237 | fat: 9g | protein: 10g | carbs: 41g | fiber: 7g

Nut Butter and Jelly Breakfast Cookies

Prep time: 10 minutes | Cook time: 20 minutes | Makes 12 cookies

¾ cup nut butter	preserves
½ cup berries or 1 small banana, mashed with a fork	1 to 1¼ cups whole wheat flour
¼ cup plus 2 tablespoons fruit	¾ teaspoon baking powder
	⅛ teaspoon salt (optional)

1. Preheat the oven to 350°F (180°C). Line two baking sheets with parchment paper. 2. Add the nut butter, berries, and preserves to a food processor. Pulse until thoroughly combined. Add 1 cup of the flour, the baking powder, and salt (if desired), continuing to pulse until combined. Add additional flour, as needed, until a thick dough forms. The dough should be smooth and glossy (almost greasy), with no visible flour. If needed, transfer to a bowl and knead the dough until the flour is fully incorporated. 3. Divide the dough into 12 pieces, roll each piece into a ball, then flatten into a cookie shape; add the traditional peanut butter cookie hashmarks with a fork if desired. 4. Bake for 17 to 20 minutes, until the tops are golden brown. Allow to cool completely on the baking sheet before serving. Cookies can be stored at room temperature in an airtight container for up to 5 days.

Per Serving:(1 cookie)

calories: 141 | fat: 9g | protein: 5g | carbs: 13g | fiber: 3g

Paradise Island Overnight Oatmeal

Prep time: 5 minutes | Cook time: 0 minutes | Serves 2

2 cups rolled oats	chunks
2 cups plant-based milk	1 sliced banana
½ cup fresh or frozen mango, diced	1 tablespoon maple syrup (optional)
½ cup fresh or frozen pineapple	1 tablespoon chia seeds

1. In a large bowl, mix together the oats, milk, mango, pineapple, banana, maple syrup (if desired), and chia seeds. 2. Cover and refrigerate overnight or for a minimum of 4 hours before serving.

Per Serving:

calories: 510 | fat: 12g | protein: 14g | carbs: 93g | fiber: 15g

Maple-Spice Buckwheat Crispies Cereal

Prep time: 15 minutes | Cook time: 50 minutes | Makes 5 cups

1 cup raw buckwheat groats, soaked for at least 1 hour	(optional)
1 cup sliced almonds	1½ teaspoons ground cinnamon
1 cup large-flake coconut	¼ teaspoon ground ginger
½ cup raw sunflower seeds	¼ teaspoon ground nutmeg
2 tablespoons chia seeds	2 tablespoons liquid virgin coconut oil
3 tablespoons maple sugar or coconut sugar (optional)	¼ cup pure maple syrup (optional)
¼ teaspoon fine sea salt	1 teaspoon pure vanilla extract

1. Preheat the oven to 325°F (165°C). Line a large baking sheet with parchment paper and set aside. 2. Lay out a clean kitchen towel or a couple of lengths of doubled paper towels. In a fine-mesh strainer, rinse the buckwheat groats thoroughly. You're aiming to remove as much of the slimy soaking liquid as possible. Scrape the rinsed buckwheat groats onto the clean kitchen towel and spread them out. Lightly pat the buckwheat groats dry and then transfer them to a large bowl. 3. To the large bowl, add the sliced almonds, coconut flakes, sunflower seeds, chia seeds, maple sugar, sea salt, if using, cinnamon, ginger, and nutmeg. Toss everything to coat. 4. In a small bowl, whisk together the coconut oil, maple syrup, if using, and vanilla, and then pour that over the buckwheat groats mixture. Stir with a rubber spatula to coat. 5. Scrape the wet cereal mixture onto the prepared baking sheet. Flatten and spread everything out with the back of your spatula as much as possible. Slide the baking sheet into the oven and bake for 50 minutes, stirring and flipping the crispies a few times to ensure even browning. Once the cereal is evenly golden brown and lightly crispy, it's ready. 6. Allow the cereal to cool completely before storing in a sealed container at room temperature. This cereal will keep for about 10 days.

Per Serving:(½ cup)

calories: 195 | fat: 14g | protein: 4g | carbs: 16g | fiber: 3g

Savory Oatmeal

Prep time: 10 minutes | Cook time: 10 minutes |

Makes 2 bowls

1 cup gluten-free old-fashioned rolled oats	2 tablespoons nutritional yeast
1 carrot, peeled and shredded	½ chopped avocado
1½ cups water	2 tablespoons roasted pumpkin seeds
1 cup stemmed and chopped kale	Smoked paprika or crushed red pepper (optional)
¼ cup salsa or marinara sauce	Salt and black pepper (optional)

1. Cook the oats and carrot: Combine the oats and carrot in a small saucepan over medium heat. Add the water (use more or less to achieve the consistency you prefer; 1½ cups water yields a fairly thick oatmeal). Heat until simmering, then cook, stirring often, until everything is tender, about 5 minutes. 2. Add the kale, salsa, and nutritional yeast: Stir in the kale, salsa, and nutritional yeast. 3. Serve with toppings: Pour into a bowl and top with the avocado and pumpkin seeds. Sprinkle with smoked paprika and crushed red pepper, if desired. Season with salt (if desired) and pepper to taste, and serve.

Per Serving:(½ bowl)

calories: 153 | fat: 7g | protein: 9g | carbs: 24g | fiber: 7g

Fluffiest Multigrain Pancakes

Prep time: 15 minutes | Cook time: 20 minutes |

Makes 9 pancakes

½ cup whole spelt flour	1 tablespoon ground chia seeds
½ cup millet flour	¼ cup fresh orange juice
½ cup oat flour	¼ cup filtered water
1 tablespoon coconut sugar or maple sugar (optional)	1 teaspoon pure vanilla extract
1½ tablespoons aluminum-free baking powder	2 tablespoons coconut oil, plus extra for cooking (optional)
½ teaspoon fine sea salt (optional)	Serve:
	Sliced fresh fruit or whole berries
1 cup unsweetened almond milk	Pure maple syrup (optional)
2 teaspoons apple cider vinegar	Coconut butter
	Other toppings of your choice

1. Preheat the oven to 275ºF (135ºC). Place a baking sheet in the oven. 2. In a large bowl, combine the spelt flour, millet flour, oat flour, coconut sugar, baking powder, and sea salt, if using. 3. In a medium bowl, vigorously whisk together the almond milk, apple cider vinegar, and ground chia seeds. The mixture should appear foamy on the top. 4. Add the almond milk mixture to the dry ingredients in the large bowl. Then, add the orange juice, water, vanilla, and coconut oil, if using. Gently mix the batter together with a fork. It should be mostly combined with lumps and dry flour bits throughout. Avoid overmixing. 5. Let the batter sit for about 10 minutes while you heat a large skillet. A touch above medium heat is ideal for these pancakes. 6. When you're ready to make the pancakes, lightly grease the skillet, and drop the batter in by the ⅓ cup. You should hear a moderate sizzle. Gently spread the pancake batter with a spatula. Cook the pancakes until dry around the edges, with bubbles popping through the surface, about 1 minute. The pancakes should be lightly browned on the underside. Flip the pancakes over and cook another 45 seconds to 1 minute. 7. Keep the pancakes warm on the baking sheet in the oven while you repeat this process with the remaining batter, using more oil to cook the pancakes if you find it necessary. 8. Serve pancakes with fruit, maple syrup, coconut butter, and other toppings of your choice.

Per Serving:(1 pancakes)

calories: 139 | fat: 4g | protein: 5g | carbs: 21g | fiber: 2gStuffed

Breakfast Sweet Potatoes

Prep time: 5 minutes | Cook time: 10 minutes |

Serves 2

2 medium sweet potatoes	2 tablespoons maple syrup (optional)
2 tablespoons almond butter	
2 tablespoons plain plant-based yogurt	½ cup store-bought granola

1. Prepare the sweet potatoes: Scrub the sweet potatoes well. Using a fork, poke holes all over each potato. 2. Cook the sweet potatoes: Put the potatoes on a microwave-safe plate and microwave on high for 2-minute intervals, turning them over after each, until the sweet potatoes are easily pierced with a fork. Alternatively, you can bake them in the oven on a sheet pan at 400ºF (205ºC) for about 40 minutes, until they can be easily pierced with a fork. 3. Let the sweet potatoes cool and prepare toppings: Let the sweet potatoes cool for a few minutes, just until you can handle them. Cut each potato lengthwise down the middle and expose the insides. Using a fork, lightly mash the insides and open the potato wider. Drizzle each with almond butter, yogurt, and maple syrup (if using) and sprinkle the granola on top. 4. Serve: Serve hot.

Per Serving:

calories: 410 | fat: 16g | protein: 9g | carbs: 62g | fiber: 8g

Five-Ingredient Peanut Butter Bites

Prep time: 5 minutes | Cook time: 20 minutes |

Makes 10 bites

1 teaspoon canola oil, for greasing (optional)	2 ripe bananas
½ cup raisins	1 cup creamy or chunky peanut butter
1 cup hot water	⅔ cup old-fashioned rolled oats

1. Preheat the oven to 350ºF (180ºC), and lightly grease a muffin tin. 2. Put the raisins in the hot water for 2 minutes to soften, then drain the water. 3. In a food processor or high-powered blender, blend the softened raisins, bananas, peanut butter, and oats for 1 minute or until smooth. 4. Spoon the batter into the muffin tin, filling each cup halfway. 5. Bake for 18 to 20 minutes or until the bites are golden.

Per Serving:(1 bite)

calories: 196 | fat: 14g | protein: 8g | carbs: 14g | fiber: 4g

Carrot Cake Oatmeal

Prep time: 10 minutes | Cook time: 15 minutes | Serves 2

¼ cup pecans
1 cup finely shredded carrot
½ cup old-fashioned oats
1¼ cups unsweetened nondairy milk
1 tablespoon pure maple syrup

(optional)
1 teaspoon ground cinnamon
1 teaspoon ground ginger
¼ teaspoon ground nutmeg
2 tablespoons chia seeds

1. Toast and chop the pecans: In a small skillet over medium-high heat, toast the pecans for 3 to 4 minutes, stirring often, until browned and fragrant (watch closely, as they can burn quickly). Pour the pecans onto a cutting board and coarsely chop them. Set aside. 2. Cook the oatmeal: In an 8-quart pot over medium-high heat, combine the carrot, oats, milk, maple syrup (if using), cinnamon, ginger, and nutmeg. Bring to a boil, then reduce the heat to medium-low. Cook, uncovered, for 10 minutes, stirring occasionally.
Add the pecans and chia seeds: Stir in the chopped pecans and chia seeds.
2.Serve: Serve the oatmeal immediately.

Per Serving:
calories: 307 | fat: 17g | protein: 7g | carbs: 35g | fiber: 11g

Fruity Granola

Prep time: 15 minutes | Cook time: 45 minutes | Makes 5 cups

2 cups rolled oats
¾ cup whole-grain flour
1 tablespoon ground cinnamon
1 teaspoon ground ginger (optional)
½ cup sunflower seeds or walnuts, chopped
½ cup almonds, chopped
½ cup pumpkin seeds

½ cup unsweetened shredded coconut
1¼ cups pure fruit juice (cranberry, apple, or something similar)
½ cup raisins or dried cranberries
½ cup goji berries (optional)

1. Preheat the oven to 350ºF (180ºC). 2. Mix together the oats, flour, cinnamon, ginger, sunflower seeds, almonds, pumpkin seeds, and coconut in a large bowl. 3. Sprinkle the juice over the mixture, and stir until it's just moistened. You might need a bit more or a bit less liquid, depending on how much your oats and flour absorb. 4. Spread the granola on a large baking sheet (the more spread out it is the better), and put it in the oven. After about 15 minutes, use a spatula to turn the granola so that the middle gets dried out. Let the granola bake until it's as crunchy as you want it, about 30 minutes more. 5. Take the granola out of the oven and stir in the raisins and goji berries (if using). 6. Store leftovers in an airtight container for up to 2 weeks.

Per Serving:(½ cup)
calories: 222 | fat: 10g | protein: 9g | carbs: 32g | fiber: 6g

Choco Berry Pudding

Prep time: 5 minutes | Cook time: 0 minutes | Serves 2

3 peeled bananas
2 scoops soy protein isolate, chocolate flavor
¼ cup flaxseeds
1 cup fresh or frozen mixed berries

3 cups water
Optional Toppings:
Mint leaves
Cocoa powder
Coconut flakes

1. Add all the ingredients to a blender and blend until smooth. Alternatively, blend the berries and 2 tablespoons of flaxseeds first and half fill two glasses, bowls or Mason jars with the berry mix. 2. Blend the remaining ingredients afterwards, and top the berry mix with the banana protein mix. 3. Serve with the optional toppings and enjoy! 4. Store the pudding in an airtight container in the fridge, and consume within 2 days. Alternatively, store in the freezer for a maximum of 60 days and thaw at room temperature.

Per Serving:
calories: 407 | fat: 7g | protein: 32g | carbs: 53g | fiber: 11g

Overnight Chocolate Chia Pudding

Prep time: 2 minutes | Cook time: 0 minutes | Serves 2

¼ cup chia seeds
1 cup unsweetened nondairy milk
2 tablespoons raw cacao

powder
1 teaspoon vanilla extract
1 teaspoon pure maple syrup (optional)

1. In a large bowl, stir together the chia seeds, milk, cacao powder, vanilla, and maple syrup (if using). Divide between 2 (½-pint) covered glass jars or containers. Refrigerate overnight. 2. Stir before serving.

Per Serving:(1 jar)
calories: 213 | fat: 10g | protein: 9g | carbs: 20g | fiber: 15g

Pan con Tomate

Prep time: 5 minutes | Cook time: 0 minutes | Makes 2 slices

2 large slices toast
1 garlic clove, halved
1 Roma tomato, halved

Salt (optional)
Nutritional yeast (optional)

1. Rub each slice of toast with a garlic clove half and half a Roma tomato. Sprinkle with salt and, if desired, nutritional yeast.

Per Serving:(1 slice)
calories: 90 | fat: 1g | protein: 3g | carbs: 17g | fiber: 2g

Sunrise Smoothie Bowl

Prep time: 10 minutes | Cook time: 0 minutes |
Serves 2

2 cups fresh spinach	1 tablespoon fresh lemon juice
½ cup water	½ cup sliced strawberries
1 orange, peeled and segmented	½ cup diced peaches
2 cups sliced peaches, preferably frozen	1 kiwifruit, diced
	¼ cup raw cashews
1 ripe banana, frozen	4 fresh mint leaves, chopped

1. In a blender, purée the spinach, water, and orange until smooth. Add the sliced peaches and the banana and pulse a few times, then purée until the mixture is thick and smooth. You will need to stop the blender occasionally to scrape down the sides. Add a little extra water if needed. The texture should be thick and creamy like frozen yogurt. 2. Divide between 2 bowls and top each with half of the strawberries, diced peaches, kiwi, cashews, and mint. Serve immediately.

Per Serving:

calories: 307 | fat: 9g | protein: 7g | carbs: 56g | fiber: 9g

Granola

Prep time: 15 minutes | Cook time: 35 minutes |
Makes 15 cups

4 cups rolled oats	seeds
2 cups raw buckwheat groats	¼ cup chia seeds
4 cups unsweetened flaked dried coconut	1 teaspoon fine sea salt (optional)
1 cup whole raw almonds	1 teaspoon ground cinnamon
1 cup raw nuts, roughly chopped	¾ cup brown rice syrup or yacon syrup (optional)
1 cup raw pumpkin seeds	½ cup melted extra-virgin coconut oil (optional)
½ cup raw sunflower seeds	
½ cup raw unhulled sesame	1 tablespoon vanilla extract

1. Preheat the oven to 300ºF (150ºC). Line two rimmed baking sheets with parchment paper and set aside. 2. Combine the oats, buckwheat, coconut, almonds, raw nuts, pumpkin seeds, sunflower seeds, sesame seeds, chia seeds, salt, if using, and cinnamon in a large bowl; stir well and set aside. If using brown rice syrup, combine it with the coconut oil in a small saucepan and gently warm over low heat, stirring until smooth. Then add the vanilla and stir again. Or, if using yacon syrup, just stir the syrup and oil together in a small bowl, then stir in the vanilla. Pour the syrup mixture over the oat-nut mixture and mix well to combine. 3. Divide the mixture between the baking sheets and spread out evenly. Bake for 15 minutes, then stir, rotate the trays, and return to the oven for another 15 minutes, or until the granola is golden and fragrant. (You may need to bake the granola for another couple of minutes, but be careful, as it can easily burn; and keep in mind that it will crisp up further as it cools.) Remove from the oven and let cool completely. Store the granola in airtight jars for up to 6 weeks.

Per Serving:(1 cup)

calories: 343 | fat: 22g | protein: 12g | carbs: 37g | fiber: 8g

Breakfast Scramble

Prep time: 20 minutes | Cook time: 20 minutes |
Serves 6

1 medium red onion, peeled and cut into ½-inch dice	Salt, to taste (optional)
1 medium red bell pepper, seeded and cut into ½-inch dice	½ teaspoon freshly ground black pepper
1 medium green bell pepper, seeded and cut into ½-inch dice	1½ teaspoons turmeric
2 cups sliced mushrooms (from about 8 ounces / 227 g whole mushrooms)	¼ teaspoon cayenne pepper, or to taste
	3 cloves garlic, peeled and minced
1 large head cauliflower, cut into florets, or 2 (19 ounces / 539 g) cans Jamaican ackee, drained and gently rinsed	1 to 2 tablespoons low-sodium soy sauce
	¼ cup nutritional yeast (optional)

1. Sauté the vegetables: Place the onion, red and green peppers, and mushrooms in a medium skillet or saucepan and sauté over medium-high heat for 7 to 8 minutes, or until the onion is translucent. Add water 1 to 2 tablespoons at a time to keep the vegetables from sticking to the pan. 2. Add the cauliflower and seasonings: Add the cauliflower to the pan and cook for 5 to 6 minutes, or until the florets are tender. Add the salt (if using), black pepper, turmeric, cayenne pepper, garlic, soy sauce, and nutritional yeast (if using) to the pan and cook for 5 minutes more, or until hot and fragrant.

Per Serving:

calories: 65 | fat: 0g | protein: 5g | carbs: 11g | fiber: 4g

Homemade Granola Clusters

Prep time: 15 minutes | Cook time: 1 minute | Makes
2 cups

1½ creamy or chunky cups peanut butter	½ cup raisins
	¾ cup raw sunflower seeds
¼ cup agave or maple syrup (optional)	Optional Toppings:
	¼ cup coconut shreds
1½ cups old-fashioned rolled oats	1 teaspoon cinnamon
¾ cup flaxseed meal	Pinch of salt (optional)

1. Add the peanut butter and maple syrup (if desired) to a medium, microwave-safe bowl. Microwave on high for 30-second intervals, stirring between intervals until the mixture is creamy and well combined. 2. Add the oats, flaxseed meal, raisins, and sunflower seeds, and stir together with a spoon until thoroughly combined. 3. Transfer the mixture to a baking sheet. 4. Place in the freezer for at least 25 minutes. Store in the refrigerator in an airtight container for up to 7 days.

Per Serving:(¼ cup)

calories: 510 | fat: 29g | protein: 31g | carbs: 34g | fiber: 11g

Buckwheat Porridge with Cherries and Almonds

Prep time: 5 minutes | Cook time: 25 minutes | Serves 2

½ cup buckwheat groats, rinsed
2 cups water
1 cup unsweetened vanilla almond milk
½ cup dried cherries, no added sugar
½ cup sliced almonds, toasted
1 tablespoon maple syrup (optional)

1. In a small pot, combine the buckwheat and water. Bring to a boil; then reduce to a simmer. Cover and simmer for 15 minutes. 2. Turn off the heat. Keep covered and steam for another 5 minutes. 3. Pour the cooked buckwheat into two serving bowls, and divide the almond milk evenly between the bowls. 4. Top with the cherries and almonds, and drizzle with the maple syrup (if using).

Per Serving:
calories: 433 | fat: 14g | protein: 11g | carbs: 68g | fiber: 9g

Fruited Barley

Prep time: 10 minutes | Cook time: 55 minutes | Serves 2

1 to 1½ cups orange juice
1 cup pearled barley
2 tablespoons dried currants
3 to 4 dried unsulfured apricots, chopped
1 small cinnamon stick
⅛ teaspoon ground cloves
Pinch salt, or to taste (optional)

1. Bring 1 cup of water and 1 cup of the orange juice to a boil in a medium saucepan over medium heat. Add the barley, currants, apricots, cinnamon stick, cloves, and salt, if using. Bring the mixture to a boil, cover, reduce the heat to medium-low, and cook for 45 minutes. If the barley is not tender after 45 minutes, add up to an additional ½ cup of orange juice and cook for another 10 minutes. 2. Remove the cinnamon stick before serving.

Per Serving:
calories: 420 | fat: 1g | protein: 10g | carbs: 93g | fiber: 16g

Cinnamon Apple Toast

Prep time: 5 minutes | Cook time: 10 to 20 minutes | Makes 2 slices

1 to 2 teaspoons coconut oil (optional)
½ teaspoon ground cinnamon
1 tablespoon maple syrup or coconut sugar (optional)
1 apple, cored and thinly sliced
2 slices whole-grain bread

1. Prepare the apples: In a large bowl, mix the coconut oil (if using), cinnamon, and maple syrup (if using) together. Add the apple slices and toss with your hands to coat them. 2. Cook the apples and bread: Place the apple slices in a medium skillet on medium-high and cook for about 5 minutes, or until slightly soft, then transfer to a plate. Cook the bread in the same skillet for 2 to 3 minutes on each side. Top the toast with the apples. 3. Alternatively, bake the toast: Use your hands to rub each slice of bread with some of the coconut oil mixture on both sides. Lay them on a small baking sheet, top with the coated apples, and put in the oven or toaster oven at 350ºF (180ºC) for 15 to 20 minutes, or until the apples have softened.

Per Serving:(1 slice)
calories: 172 | fat: 3g | protein: 4g | carbs: 33g | fiber: 3g

Fruit Salad

Prep time: 15 minutes | Cook time: 0 minutes | Serves 4

1 pint fresh strawberries, stems removed, sliced
1 pint fresh blueberries
2 cups seedless grapes
1 ripe pear, cored and diced
2 tablespoons fresh lemon juice
2 tablespoons date syrup (optional)
Pinch ground cinnamon

1. Combine all ingredients in a bowl and mix well. Chill until ready to serve.

Per Serving:
calories: 172 | fat: 0g | protein: 1g | carbs: 44g | fiber: 5g

Polenta with Seared Pears

Prep time: 10 minutes | Cook time: 50 minutes | Serves 4

5¼ cups water, divided, plus more as needed
1½ cups coarse cornmeal
3 tablespoons pure maple syrup (optional)
1 tablespoon molasses
1 teaspoon ground cinnamon
2 ripe pears, cored and diced
1 cup fresh cranberries
1 teaspoon chopped fresh rosemary leaves

1. Simmer the water: In an 8-quart pot over high heat, bring 5 cups of water to a simmer. 2. Cook the polenta: While whisking continuously to avoid clumping, slowly pour in the cornmeal. Cook, stirring often with a heavy spoon, for 30 minutes. The polenta should be thick and creamy. 3. Prepare the cranberry-pear topping: While the polenta cooks, in a saucepan over medium heat, stir together the maple syrup (if using), molasses, the remaining ¼ cup of water, and the cinnamon until combined. Bring to a simmer. Add the pears and cranberries. Cook for 10 minutes, stirring occasionally, until the pears are tender and start to brown. Remove from the heat. Stir in the rosemary and let the mixture sit for 5 minutes. If it is too thick, add another ¼ cup of water and return to the heat. 4. Serve: Top the polenta with the cranberry-pear mixture.

Per Serving:
calories: 282 | fat: 2g | protein: 4g | carbs: 65g | fiber: 12g

Banana Almond Granola

Prep time: 10 minutes | Cook time: 50 minutes |
Serves 16

8 cups rolled oats
2 cups pitted and chopped dates
2 ripe bananas, peeled and chopped
1 teaspoon almond extract

1 teaspoon salt, or to taste (optional)
1 cup slivered almonds, toasted (optional)

1. Preheat the oven to 275ºF (135ºC). 2. Add the oats to a large mixing bowl and set aside. Line two 13 × 18-inch inch baking pans with parchment paper. 3. Place the dates in a medium saucepan with 1 cup of water, bring to a boil, and cook over medium heat for 10 minutes. Add more water if needed to keep the dates from sticking to the pan. Remove from the heat and add the mixture to a blender with the bananas, almond extract, and salt (if using). Process until smooth and creamy. 4. Add the date mixture to the oats and mix well. Divide the granola between the two prepared pans and spread evenly in the pans. Bake for 40 to 50 minutes, stirring every 10 minutes, until the granola is crispy. Remove from the oven and let cool before adding the slivered almonds, if desired (the cereal will get even crispier as it cools). Store the granola in an airtight container.

Per Serving:
calories: 220 | fat: 6g | protein: 10g | carbs: 49g | fiber: 10g

Tofu Rancheros

Prep time: 10 minutes | Cook time: 20 minutes |
Serves 4

1 (15 ounces / 425 g) can black beans, drained and rinsed
½ teaspoon onion powder
½ teaspoon garlic powder
2½ cups water, divided
1 teaspoon extra-virgin olive oil (optional)
½ head cauliflower, cut into florets (about 2 cups)
1 red or yellow bell pepper, seeded and diced small
1 (16 ounces / 454 g) package extra firm-tofu, drained and diced small
½ teaspoon salt, plus more as

needed (optional)
1 teaspoon smoked paprika
2 medium tomatoes, cut into ½-inch pieces
2 teaspoons tomato paste
1 teaspoon chili powder
2 avocados, peeled and pitted
8 (6-inch) corn tortillas
3 tablespoons chopped fresh cilantro, for serving
2 scallions, white and green parts, thinly sliced, for serving
1 lime, cut into quarters, for serving

1. In a small saucepan over medium heat, combine the beans, onion powder, garlic powder, and ½ cup of water and cook until heated through, 5 to 7 minutes. Set aside. 2. In a large saucepan, heat the oil over medium heat. Add the cauliflower and bell pepper and cook, stirring occasionally, for 2 to 3 minutes. Add the tofu, salt (if using), and smoked paprika and cook, stirring often, for 5 minutes. 3. Add the tomatoes, tomato paste, and chili powder and cook, stirring often, until the tomatoes release their juices and the tomato paste turns dark red, 2 to 3 minutes. Add the remaining 2 cups

water, stir well, and bring to a boil. Cook until the sauce is thick and the flavors meld, about 4 minutes. 4. In a small bowl, combine the avocados and a pinch of salt and mash until well mixed. 5. In a large skillet, warm the tortillas over medium-high heat, about 2 minutes on each side. Put 2 tortillas on a plate, layer with the tofu mixture, scallions, cilantro, a big dollop of mashed avocado, and a squeeze of lime juice. Put a scoop of black beans on the side and serve.

Per Serving:
calories: 590 | fat: 27g | protein: 27g | carbs: 69g | fiber: 18g

Liver Flush Juice

Prep time: 15 minutes | Cook time: 0 minutes |
Serves 1

1 beet, scrubbed and trimmed
1 (1-inch) piece fresh turmeric, or 1 teaspoon ground turmeric
5 carrots, scrubbed and trimmed

1 grapefruit, peeled
1 lemon, peeled
¼ cup purified water, if using a blender

Using a Juicer:
Juice the ingredients: Put all the ingredients through your juicer. Stir and serve immediately.
Without a Juicer:
1.Cut the vegetables: Cut the vegetables into bite-sized pieces. 2.Blend the ingredients: In a blender, combine all the ingredients and blend until smooth, adding about ¼ cup of purified water. 3. Strain the juice: Place a fine-mesh strainer over a large bowl and pour the juice through. Use a wooden spoon or spatula to press the pulp down and squeeze out all the juice. Allow to sit for 2 to 3 minutes to let most of the juice drain. 4. Serve and drink: Discard the pulp and pour your juice into a serving glass. Drink immediately.

Per Serving:
calories: 261 | fat: 1g | protein: 6g | carbs: 60g | fiber: 14g

Almond and Protein Shake

Prep time: 5 minutes | Cook time: 0 minutes | Serves 2

1½ cups soy milk
3 tablespoons almonds
1 teaspoon maple syrup (optional)
1 tablespoon coconut oil (optional)

2 scoops of chocolate or vanilla flavor vegan protein powder
2 to 4 ice cubes
1 teaspoon cocoa powder (optional)

1. Add all the required ingredients, and if desired, the optional cocoa powder, to a blender. Blend for 2 minutes. Transfer the shake to a large cup or shaker. Serve and enjoy!

Per Serving:
calories: 340 | fat: 17g | protein: 32g | carbs: 15g | fiber: 2g

Vanilla Coconut Coffee Creamer

Prep time: 5 minutes | Cook time: 0 minutes | Makes 2 cups

6 Medjool dates, pitted
1 can (13½ ounces / 383 g) full-fat coconut milk
2 teaspoons pure vanilla extract

1 tablespoon coconut oil (optional)
Tiny pinch of fine sea salt (optional)

1. If your dates are very soft, proceed to the next step. If your dates are a little dry, place them in a small bowl and cover them in boiling water for 5 to 10 minutes. Thoroughly drain the dates. 2. In a blender, combine the pitted dates, coconut milk, vanilla, coconut oil, and sea salt, if using. Blend on high until you have a smooth and thick liquid with minimal chunks of date visible. 3. Over a medium bowl, strain the creamer with a fine-mesh strainer. Store the strained creamer in a jar with a tight-fitting lid. Keep the jar of creamer in the refrigerator. Shake to combine before using. The creamer will keep for roughly 1 week.

Per Serving:

calories: 297 | fat: 19g | protein: 1g | carbs: 32g | fiber: 5g

Banana-Date Shake with Oats

Prep time: 15 minutes | Cook time: 0 minutes | Serves 1

1 Medjool date
10 ounces (283 g) unsweetened vanilla almond milk
1 small banana (fresh or frozen)
2 tablespoons almond butter

¼ cup rolled oats, uncooked
3 ice cubes
Pinch ground cinnamon (optional)

1. Soften the date: Soak the date in hot water for 5 minutes to soften it. 2. Blend the ingredients: Remove the date from the hot water, place it in a blender, and add the milk, banana, almond butter, oats, ice cubes, and cinnamon (if using). Blend until smooth. 3. Serve: Enjoy the drink immediately.

Per Serving:

calories: 526 | fat: 22g | protein: 19g | carbs: 72g | fiber: 11g

Chapter 5 Beans and Grains

Green Chile Rice with Black Beans

Prep time: 20 minutes | Cook time: 1 hour | Serves 4

1 poblano chile pepper, seeded and diced small
1 (4 ounces / 113 g) can mild green chiles
1 cup coarsely chopped cilantro
½ cup spinach
4 cups vegetable stock, or low-sodium vegetable broth
1½ cups medium-grain brown rice

1 medium yellow onion, peeled and diced small
1 teaspoon ground cumin
1 jalapeño pepper, seeded and minced
2 cups cooked black beans, or 1 (15 ounces / 425 g) can, drained and rinsed
Zest of 1 lime
Salt, to taste (optional)

1. In a blender, purée poblano pepper, green chiles, cilantro, and spinach. Add some of the vegetable stock, as needed, to achieve a smooth consistency. Pour the mixture into a medium saucepan with the remaining vegetable stock. Add brown rice and bring to a boil over high heat. Reduce the heat to medium and cook, covered, until the rice is tender, 45 to 50 minutes. 2. In a large saucepan, sauté onion over medium heat for 7 to 8 minutes. Add water 1 to 2 tablespoons at a time to prevent sticking. Add cumin, jalapeño pepper, and black beans and cook for 5 minutes longer. Fold in the cooked rice and lime zest. Season with salt, if desired.

Per Serving:

calories: 403 | fat: 2g | protein: 13g | carbs: 71g | fiber: 11g

Baked Falafel

Prep time: 15 minutes | Cook time: 30 minutes | Serves 6

1 cup dried chickpeas
½ cup packed chopped fresh parsley
½ cup packed chopped fresh cilantro (or parsley if preferred)
½ cup chopped yellow onion
3 garlic cloves, peeled
1½ tablespoons chickpea flour

or wheat flour (if gluten is not a concern)
2 teaspoons ground cumin
1 teaspoon ground coriander
½ teaspoon baking powder
2 tablespoons freshly squeezed lemon juice

1. The night before making falafel, in a large bowl, combine the dried chickpeas with enough water to cover by 3 inches. Cover the bowl and soak for at least 8 hours or overnight. Drain. 2. Preheat the oven to 375ºF (190ºC). Line a baking sheet with parchment paper. 3. In a high-speed blender or food processor, combine the soaked chickpeas, parsley, cilantro, onion, garlic, flour, cumin, coriander, baking powder, and lemon juice. Pulse until all ingredients are well combined but not smooth; it should have the consistency of sand but stick together when pressed. 4. Using a cookie scoop or two spoons, divide the falafel mixture into 20 balls and place them on the prepared baking sheet. Lightly flatten each ball using the bottom of a measuring cup. This will help them cook more evenly. 5. Bake for 15 minutes. Flip. Bake for 10 to 15 minutes more, until lightly browned. 6. Refrigerate in an airtight container for up to 1 week or freeze for up to 1 month.

Per Serving:

calories: 129 | fat: 2g | protein: 7g | carbs: 22g | fiber: 6g

Double-Decker Red Quinoa Sandwich

Prep time: 20 minutes | Cook time: 35 minutes | Serves 3

½ cup red quinoa
1 cup vegetable broth
4 large portabella mushroom caps
2 tablespoons coconut oil, divided (optional)
¼ cup finely chopped onion
½ cup raw pecans
2 chopped green spring onions
2 teaspoons rice wine vinegar
1 teaspoon garlic powder

2 tablespoons nutritional yeast
2 tablespoons raw shelled hempseed
¼ cup flour
3 whole wheat burger buns
Toppings and Condiments:
lettuce
tomatoes
red onion,
mustard
dairy-free spicy mayo

1. Place the quinoa in a sieve and rinse well. Combine the quinoa and broth in a small saucepan. Bring to a boil (if desired), cover, and reduce to a simmer. Cook for 10 to 15 minutes or until the broth is absorbed. Remove from the heat and let set with the cover on for 5 minutes. 2. Remove the gills from the mushrooms and discard. Chop up the mushroom caps. 3. Heat 1 tablespoon oil (if desired) in a large skillet. Add the onion and mushrooms and sauté for 10 minutes. Add the pecans and sauté for 5 more minutes. Remove from the heat and let cool. 4. Add the mushroom mixture, green onion, and vinegar to a food processor. Process until very fine. It will not be smooth. 5. Transfer to a large bowl and add the quinoa, garlic powder, nutritional yeast, hempseed, and flour. Mix until well blended. Form into six patties the size of the burger buns. 6. Heat remaining oil in a large skillet and fry one patty at a time so that you can flip it easily. Fry until golden brown on each side. 7. Assemble the double deckers: Lay down the bottom of the bun, add mustard, lettuce, patty, red onion, lettuce, dairy-free spicy mayo, patty, dairy-free spicy mayo, tomatoes, and top of bun.

Per Serving:

calories: 498 | fat: 27g | protein: 24g | carbs: 43g | fiber: 10g

Orange Quinoa with Black Beans

Prep time: 15 minutes | Cook time: 20 minutes | Serves 4

1½ cups quinoa, rinsed and drained
1½ teaspoons cumin seeds, toasted and ground
2 cups cooked black beans, or 1 (15 ounces / 425 g) can, drained and rinsed
1½ teaspoons grated ginger
2 tablespoons balsamic vinegar
Zest and juice of 1 orange (about ¼ cup juice)
4 green onions (white and green parts), thinly sliced
Salt and freshly ground black pepper, to taste

1. In a medium pot with a tight-fitting lid, add 3 cups of water and bring to a boil over high heat. Add quinoa and return the pot to a boil over high heat. Reduce the heat to medium-low and cook the quinoa, covered, for 15 to 20 minutes, or until tender. 2. Place the cooked quinoa in a large bowl and add cumin, black beans, ginger, vinegar, orange zest and juice, and green onions. Mix well and season with salt and pepper.

Per Serving:

calories: 369 | fat: 4g | protein: 16g | carbs: 65g | fiber: 12g

Mushroom Risotto

Prep time: 10 minutes | Cook time: 55 minutes | Serves 4

1 yellow onion, chopped
3 garlic cloves, minced
½ celery stalk, minced
1 tablespoon water, plus more as needed
9 ounces (255 g) baby portabella mushrooms, coarsely chopped
4 ounces (113 g) shiitake mushrooms, coarsely chopped
1 tablespoon apple cider vinegar
1½ cups Arborio rice
6 cups no-sodium vegetable broth, divided
1 (15 ounces /425 g) can red kidney beans, drained and rinsed
Scallions, green parts only, cut into chiffonade, for serving

1. In an 8-quart pot over high heat, combine onion, garlic, and celery. Sauté for 2 to 3 minutes, adding water 1 tablespoon at a time to prevent burning. Add baby portabella and shiitake mushrooms and sauté for 3 to 4 minutes, stirring, until the liquid from the mushrooms evaporates. 2. Sprinkle vinegar over the vegetables, stir, and cook for 1 minute. Stir in rice and sauté for 1 minute more. 3. Add 3 cups of vegetable broth and bring to a simmer. Reduce the heat to low and cover the pot. Cook, undisturbed, for 20 minutes. 4. Add 1½ cups of vegetable broth, stir, cover the pot, and cook for 10 minutes more.
5. Add the remaining 1½ cups of vegetable broth. Cook, stirring continuously but lightly, for 5 to 10 minutes more, or until the liquid has been mostly absorbed. 6. Stir in red kidney beans. Serve warm, topped with scallions.

Per Serving:

calories: 382 | fat: 1g | protein: 14g | carbs: 80g | fiber: 7g

Chana Masala

Prep time: 10 minutes | Cook time: 25 minutes | Serves 2

2 cups cooked or canned chickpeas
1 cup canned or fresh tomato cubes
2 medium onions, minced
2 tablespoons curry spices
¼ cup water
Optional Toppings:
Fresh chili slices
Lime juice
Shredded coconut

1. If using dry chickpeas, soak and cook ⅔ cup of dry chickpeas. 2. Put a large pot over medium heat, then add tomato cubes, onions, and water. 3. Cook for a few minutes, stirring occasionally, until everything is cooked, then add curry spices and stir thoroughly. 4. Add chickpeas and stir thoroughly to make sure everything is well mixed. 5. Cook for a couple more minutes, stirring occasionally, then lower the heat to a simmer. 6.Let the curry simmer for about 20 minutes while stirring occasionally. 7. Turn off the heat and let the curry cool down for a minute. 8. Divide the curry between 2 bowls, garnish with optional toppings, serve and enjoy! 9. Store the curry in an airtight container in the fridge and consume within 2 days. Alternatively, store in the freezer for a maximum of 30 days and thaw at room temperature. Reheat the curry in the microwave or a saucepan.

Per Serving:

calories: 401 | fat: 6g | protein: 21g | carbs: 64g | fiber: 20g

Whole-Grain Corn Muffins

Prep time: 5 minutes | Cook time: 20 minutes | Makes 12 muffins

1½ tablespoons ground flaxseeds
1 cup unsweetened plain almond milk
½ cup unsweetened applesauce
½ cup 100% pure maple syrup (optional)
1 cup cornmeal
1 cup oat flour
1 teaspoon baking soda
1 teaspoon baking powder
½ teaspoon salt (optional)
1 cup corn kernels (from about 2 ears)

1.Preheat the oven to 375ºF (190ºC). Line a 12-cup muffin pan with paper muffin liners or have ready a 12-cup silicone muffin pan. 2. In a small bowl, combine flaxseeds with almond milk and set aside to allow it to gel for 5 minutes. 3. In a large mixing bowl, stir applesauce and maple syrup (if using) together. Add the flaxseed-almond milk mixture. Sift in cornmeal, oat flour, baking soda, baking powder, and salt (if using). Stir until well combined, but avoid overmixing. Fold in corn kernels. 4. Spoon out equal portions of batter into the muffin cups. Bake for 20 minutes or until a toothpick inserted into the center comes out clean. Serve warm.

Per Serving:

calories: 149 | fat: 1g | protein: 3g | carbs: 30g | fiber: 2g

Berbere-Spiced Red Lentils

Prep time: 5 minutes | Cook time: 25 minutes |

Serves 4

1 cup dried red lentils, rinsed
3 cups water
1 teaspoon extra-virgin olive oil (optional)
2 garlic cloves, minced
½ medium yellow onion,

chopped small
3 tomatoes, chopped
2 tablespoons Berbere spice
1 teaspoon salt (optional)
2 teaspoons tomato paste

1. In a large saucepan, combine lentils and water over high heat and bring to a boil. Lower the heat to medium-low and cook for 20 minutes, checking occasionally and adding more water if needed. 2. In a medium skillet, heat olive oil over medium heat. Add garlic and onion and cook until fragrant, 3 to 5 minutes. 3. Add tomatoes, Berbere spice, salt (if using), and tomato paste to the skillet and cook, stirring constantly, until the mixture turns a deep red and becomes paste-like, about 5 minutes. Set aside. 4. Add the spiced tomato-and-onion mixture to the lentils and simmer over medium heat until the flavors combine and the mixture is very thick, about 5 minutes. Serve immediately.

Per Serving:

calories: 216 | fat: 3g | protein: 13g | carbs: 38g | fiber: 8g

Spicy Chickpeas and Fennel

Prep time: 15 minutes | Cook time: 35 minutes |

Serves 4

1 large yellow onion, peeled and chopped
1 large fennel bulb, trimmed and thinly sliced
4 cloves garlic, peeled and minced
1 tablespoon minced oregano
1½ teaspoons ground fennel seeds

1 teaspoon crushed red pepper flakes
1 (28 ounces / 794 g) can diced tomatoes
4 cups cooked chickpeas, or 2 (15 ounces / 425 g) cans, drained and rinsed
Chopped flat-leaf Italian parsley

1. Place onion and fennel in a large saucepan and sauté over medium heat for 10 minutes or until the vegetables are tender. Add water 1 to 2 tablespoons at a time to keep the vegetables from sticking to the pan. 2. Add garlic, oregano, fennel seeds, and crushed red pepper flakes and cook for 3 minutes. Add tomatoes and chickpeas and bring the pan to a boil over high heat. Reduce the heat to medium and cook, covered, for 20 minutes. Serve garnished with parsley.

Per Serving:

calories: 343 | fat: 5g | protein: 17g | carbs: 61g | fiber: 19g

Red Peppers with Herby Breadcrumbs

Prep time: 10 minutes | Cook time: 40 minutes |

Serves 6

4 red bell peppers, cores and stems removed
3 tablespoons virgin olive oil, divided (optional)
Salt and pepper, to taste (optional)
2½ cups cubed stale bread

2 teaspoons minced fresh thyme leaves
1 clove garlic, minced
½ teaspoon fresh lemon zest
¼ teaspoon nutritional yeast
¼ cup chopped fresh flat-leaf parsley

1. Preheat the oven to 400°F (205°C) and line a baking sheet with parchment paper. 2. Cut each bell pepper into 4 segments, remove any white pith pieces from the center, and place them on the baking sheet. Toss the bell peppers with 1 tablespoon of olive oil, if using, and season with salt and pepper, if desired. Spread the peppers out into a single layer and roast until just tender, about 25 minutes. 3. Place cubed bread into a food processor and pulse the machine to make coarse crumbs. 4. Heat the remaining 2 tablespoons of olive oil in a medium sauté pan over medium heat. Add the breadcrumbs to the pan along with some salt and pepper, if desired. Cook the breadcrumbs, stirring frequently, until evenly golden brown, about 10 minutes. Add thyme, garlic, lemon zest, and nutritional yeast, and cook until fragrant, about 30 seconds. 5. Remove the breadcrumbs from the heat and stir in the chopped parsley. 6. Arrange the roasted peppers on a platter and sprinkle the warm breadcrumbs on top. Serve warm.

Per Serving:

calories: 252 | fat: 9g | protein: 7g | carbs: 36g | fiber: 3g

Thai-Inspired Rice Bowl

Prep time: 30 minutes | Cook time: 45 minutes |

Serves 4

Peanut Sauce:
3 tablespoons creamy peanut butter
2 tablespoons freshly squeezed lime juice
1 tablespoon packed lime zest
1 tablespoon coconut aminos
1 tablespoon grated peeled fresh ginger
2 garlic cloves, minced
½ teaspoon red pepper flakes
Rice Bowl:
1½ cups water

¾ cup brown rice
1 small red cabbage, shredded
1 red bell pepper, cut into slices
1 yellow bell pepper, cut into slices
1 cup shelled edamame
1 shallot, cut into slices
1 carrot, cut into matchsticks
¼ cup fresh cilantro, chopped
1 bunch chopped scallions, green parts only
Juice of 1 lime

Make the Peanut Sauce: 1. In a medium bowl, whisk together the peanut butter, lime juice and zest, coconut aminos, ginger, garlic, and red pepper flakes to combine. Set aside. Make the Rice Bowl: 2. In a medium pot over high heat, bring the water to a boil. Stir in the brown rice. Bring to a simmer, reduce the heat to medium-low, cover the pot, and cook, undisturbed, for 35 to 40 minutes. Check the rice after 35 minutes to see if the water has been absorbed. Remove from the heat. 3. In a large bowl, toss together the brown rice, red cabbage, red and yellow bell peppers, edamame, shallot, carrot, cilantro, scallions, and lime juice. Serve with a drizzle of peanut sauce.

Per Serving:

calories: 323 | fat: 9g | protein: 14g | carbs: 54g | fiber: 11g

Bulgur Chickpea Pilaf

Prep time: 15 minutes | Cook time: 35 minutes | Serves 4

1 medium yellow onion, peeled and diced small
3 cloves garlic, peeled and minced
1½ tablespoons grated ginger
1½ cups bulgur
3 cups vegetable stock, or low-sodium vegetable broth
2 cups cooked chickpeas, or 1 (15 ounces / 425 g) can, drained and rinsed
1 Roma tomato, chopped
Zest and juice of 1 lemon
Salt and freshly ground black pepper, to taste
4 green onions (white and green parts), thinly sliced

1. Place onion in a large saucepan and sauté over medium heat for 10 minutes. Add water 1 to 2 tablespoons at a time to keep the onion from sticking to the pan. Stir in garlic and ginger and cook for 30 seconds. Add bulgur and vegetable stock and bring to a boil over high heat. Reduce the heat to medium and cook, covered, until the bulgur is tender, about 15 minutes. 2. Stir in chickpeas, tomato, and lemon zest and juice and cook for another 5 minutes. Season with salt and pepper and serve garnished with green onions.

Per Serving:
calories: 344 | fat: 2g | protein: 14g | carbs: 69g | fiber: 13g

Peanut Butter Tempeh

Prep time: 10 minutes | Cook time: 30 minutes | Serves 4

2 (8 ounces / 227 g) packages tempeh
½ cup creamy or crunchy peanut butter
⅓ cup nutritional yeast
1 tablespoon fresh lemon juice or apple cider vinegar
1 tablespoon reduced-sodium, gluten-free tamari
½ teaspoon black pepper
¼ teaspoon salt (optional)
⅛ teaspoon cayenne pepper
⅓ to ½ cup warm water

1. Preheat the oven to 375ºF (190ºC) and line a baking sheet with parchment paper. 2. Slice each block of tempeh into 8 pieces. Smash each one slightly with the heel of your hand to increase the surface area. 3. combine peanut butter, nutritional yeast, lemon juice, tamari, pepper, salt in a shallow dish(if desired), and cayenne with enough water to form a thick sauce. The sauce should be lighter in color than peanut butter and be thinner than ketchup. If it's too thick, add water, 1 tablespoon at a time. If it gets too thin, whisk in another tablespoon or two of peanut butter. 4. Coat each piece of tempeh with the sauce and place on the prepared baking sheet. Spoon any remaining sauce on top of the tempeh slices. 5. Bake for 15 minutes, flip the tempeh, if desired, then bake for another 15 minutes, or until the sauce has formed a crust on the tempeh and turned medium brown. Serve.

Per Serving:
calories: 369 | fat: 24g | protein: 25g | carbs: 19g | fiber: 5g

Barley and Sweet Potato Pilaf

Prep time: 10 minutes | Cook time: 55 minutes | Serves 4

1 medium onion, peeled and chopped
2 cloves garlic, peeled and minced
3½ cups vegetable stock, or low-sodium vegetable broth
1½ cups pearled barley
1 large sweet potato (about ¾ pound / 340 g), peeled and diced small
¼ cup minced tarragon
Zest and juice of 1 lemon
Salt and freshly ground black pepper, to taste

1. Place the onion in a large saucepan and sauté over medium heat for 6 minutes. Add water 1 to 2 tablespoons at a time to keep the onion from sticking to the pan. Add the garlic and cook 3 minutes more. Add the vegetable stock and barley and bring the pot to a boil over high heat. 2. Reduce the heat to medium and cook, covered, for 30 minutes. Add the sweet potato and cook for 15 minutes longer, or until the potato and barley are tender. Remove from the heat, stir in the tarragon and lemon zest and juice, and season with salt and pepper.

Per Serving:
calories: 318 | fat: 0g | protein: 8g | carbs: 71g | fiber: 13g

Wild Rice, Cabbage and Chickpea Pilaf

Prep time: 20 minutes | Cook time: 1 hour 20 minutes | Serves 4

½ cup wild rice
1 medium onion, peeled and diced small
1 medium carrot, peeled and grated
1 small red bell pepper, seeded and diced small
3 cloves garlic, peeled and minced
1 tablespoon grated ginger
1½ cups chopped green cabbage
1 cup cooked chickpeas
1 bunch green onions (white and green parts), thinly sliced
3 tablespoons chopped cilantro
Salt and freshly ground black pepper, to taste

1. Bring 2 cups of water to a boil in a large saucepan. Add wild rice and bring the water back to a boil over high heat. Reduce the heat to medium and cook, covered, for 55 to 60 minutes. Drain off any excess water and set aside. 2. Heat a large skillet over medium heat. Add onion, carrot, and red pepper and sauté the vegetables for 10 minutes. Add water 1 to 2 tablespoons at a time to keep the vegetables from sticking to the pan. Add garlic and ginger and cook for another minute. Add cabbage and cook for 10 to 12 minutes or until the cabbage is tender. Add chickpeas, green onions, and cilantro. Season with salt and pepper and cook for another minute to heat the chickpeas. Remove from the heat, add the cooked wild rice and mix well.

Per Serving:
calories: 171 | fat: 1g | protein: 7g | carbs: 33g | fiber: 6g

Chickpea Tortilla Fajita Stack

Prep time: 20 minutes | Cook time: 0 minutes |

Serves 4

Chickpea Tortillas:
1 tablespoon ground chia seeds
1 cup chickpea flour
¼ teaspoon sea salt (optional)
½ teaspoon ground cumin
2 tablespoons extra virgin olive oil (optional)
Filling:
1 tablespoon extra virgin olive oil (optional)
½ cup diced white onion
1 yellow bell pepper, diced
8 ounces (227 g) white

mushrooms, diced
½ cup diced tomatoes
2 teaspoons fajita seasoning
½ teaspoon salt (optional)
¼ teaspoon ground black pepper
1 (15 ounces / 425 g) can pinto beans, drained and rinsed
2 tablespoons raw shelled hempseed
Salsa, for garnish
Avocado, for garnish

Make Chickpea Tortillas: 1. Mix ground chia seeds with 3 tablespoons water. Set aside. 2. Add 1 cup water, the chickpea flour, chia seed mixture, salt (if desired), and cumin to a medium bowl. 3. Mix until just combined. 4. Add 2 tablespoons oil (if desired) to an 8-inch skillet and heat to medium high. 5. Add ¼ cup chickpea batter and tilt the pan in a circular tilt to let the batter flow to cover the bottom of the pan, as you would a crepe. 6. Cook until golden brown and flip. Cook for another minute and remove to a plate. Continue until all the batter is gone and the tortillas are made. Make Filling: 7. Add the oil (if desired) to a large skillet and heat to medium high. Add the onion, bell pepper, and mushrooms and sauté 10 to 15 minutes or until the onion is translucent. Add the tomatoes, fajita seasoning, salt (if desired), and pepper and cook for 5 minutes. Add the beans and hempseed. Heat through. Assemble: 8. Layer the chickpea tortilla stack starting with one tortilla on a plate. Spoon on about ½ cup filling. Add another tortilla and ½ cup filling and continue until the filling is all gone. Top with a tortilla, salsa, and avocado. Cut into quarters in a pie shape and serve.

Per Serving:

calories: 358 | fat: 12g | protein: 17g | carbs: 48g | fiber: 11g

Red Lentil Pâté

Prep time: 10 minutes | Cook time: 20 minutes |

Serves 4

1 cup red lentils
1½ cups filtered water
1 (2-inch) piece kombu
3 large garlic cloves
3 tablespoons extra-virgin

olive oil, plus more for serving (optional)
½ teaspoon fine sea salt, or to taste (optional)

1. Put the lentils in a medium pot, cover them with tap water, swish them around with your fingers, and drain. Repeat and return the drained lentils to the pot. Add the filtered water, kombu, and garlic and bring to a boil over high heat. Cover the pot, reduce the heat to low, and simmer for 20 minutes, or until the lentils are soft and

all the water has been absorbed. Remove from the heat and remove the kombu (compost it). 2. Add the olive oil and salt, if using, and stir vigorously until the lentils and garlic are smooth and creamy. Drizzle with olive oil and serve warm or at room temperature. Store the cooled pâté in a jar or an airtight container in the fridge for up to 4 days.

Per Serving:

calories: 273 | fat: 11g | protein: 12g | carbs: 37g | fiber: 6g

White Beans and Escarole with Parsnips

Prep time: 20 minutes | Cook time: 30 minutes |

Serves 4

1 medium yellow onion, peeled and diced
2 large parsnips, peeled and diced
4 cloves garlic, peeled and minced
1 large head escarole, soaked

in cool water, rinsed well to remove any dirt, and chopped
4 cups cooked cannellini beans, or 2 (15 ounces / 425 g) cans, drained and rinsed
Salt and freshly ground black pepper, to taste

1. Place the onion in a large skillet and sauté over medium heat for 5 minutes. Add water 1 to 2 tablespoons at a time to keep the onion from sticking to the pan. 2. Add the parsnips and garlic and cook for 4 minutes. Add the escarole and cook until tender, about 15 minutes. Add the beans, season with salt and pepper, and cook for 5 minutes longer.

Per Serving:

calories: 127 | fat: 1g | protein: 4g | carbs: 28g | fiber: 9g

Barley Bowl with Cranberries and Walnuts

Prep time: 5 minutes | Cook time: 30 minutes |

Serves 4

1 cup pearl barley, uncooked
3 cups water
¼ cup poppy seeds

½ cup dried cranberries
½ cup chopped walnuts, toasted

1. In a medium pot, combine the barley and water and bring to a boil. Reduce the heat to medium and cook until the barley is tender, 25 to 30 minutes. Once done, drain off any excess water and let cool. 2. While the barley is cooking, place the poppy seeds and dried cranberries in a small bowl and soak them in hot water for 5 to 10 minutes; then drain the water and let cool. 3. In a large bowl, combine the cooked barley, cranberries, poppy seeds, and walnuts. Mix well, cover, and refrigerate for 30 minutes to 1 hour before serving cold.

Per Serving:

calories: 341 | fat: 14g | protein: 9g | carbs: 50g | fiber: 11g

Baked Brown Rice Risotto with Sunflower Seeds

Prep time: 10 minutes | Cook time: 1 hour | Serves 6

4 cups vegetable broth
1 cup short-grain brown rice
½ cup raw sunflower seeds
2 tablespoons dry sherry
1 shallot, minced

1 teaspoon dried tarragon
½ teaspoon dried dill
½ teaspoon salt (optional)
⅛ teaspoon black pepper
⅛ teaspoon ground turmeric

1. Preheat the oven to 400ºF (205ºC). Bring broth to a boil in a medium saucepan. 2. Add rice, sunflower seeds, sherry, shallot, tarragon, dill, salt (if desired), pepper, and turmeric to a medium baking dish. Pour the hot broth into the dish, cover, and carefully place in the oven. Bake for 30 minutes. The dish should still look soupy; if it begins to dry out, add 1 cup of water or broth. Continue to bake, covered, for another 30 minutes. Serve.

Per Serving:
calories: 196 | fat: 7g | protein: 5g | carbs: 29g | fiber: 2g

Quick Panfried Tempeh

Prep time: 5 minutes | Cook time: 10 minutes | Serves 2

2 tablespoons extra-virgin coconut oil, plus more as needed (optional)

½ pound (227 g) tempeh, cut into ¼-inch slices
Flaky or fine sea salt (optional)

1.Warm a large skillet over medium heat. Add coconut oil and tilt the pan to coat. Add sliced tempeh in a single layer and cook until golden, 3 to 4 minutes. Turn the tempeh over and cook the other side until golden and crisp, adding more oil if needed. Repeat with any remaining tempeh, adding more oil to the pan before adding the sliced tempeh. 2. Transfer the tempeh to a serving plate and sprinkle with salt. Serve warm.

Per Serving:
calories: 336 | fat: 25g | protein: 2g | carbs: 11g | fiber: 0g

Mushroom Barley Risotto

Prep time: 20 minutes | Cook time: 55 minutes | Serves 3 to 4

1 ounce (28 g) dried porcini mushrooms, soaked for 30 minutes in 1 cup of water that has just been boiled
3 large shallots, peeled and finely diced
8 ounces (227 g) cremini mushrooms, sliced
2 sage leaves, minced
3 cloves garlic, peeled and

minced
1½ cups pearled barley
½ cup dry white wine
3 to 4 cups vegetable stock, or low-sodium vegetable broth
¼ cup nutritional yeast (optional)
Salt and freshly ground black pepper, to taste

1. Drain the porcini mushrooms, reserving the liquid. Finely chop the mushrooms and set aside. 2. Place the shallots in a 2-quart saucepan and sauté over medium heat for 4 to 5 minutes. Add water 1 to 2 tablespoons at a time to keep the shallots from sticking to the pan. Add the cremini mushrooms and cook for another 5 minutes. Let the mushrooms brown by adding as little water as possible, while still making sure they don't stick to the pan. Add the sage, garlic, barley, and white wine and cook for 1 minute. Add 2 cups of the vegetable stock and the 1 cup of reserved porcini soaking liquid and bring the mixture to a boil over high heat. 3. Reduce the heat to medium and cook, covered, for 25 minutes. Add more broth if necessary and cook for another 15 to 20 minutes. Stir in the chopped porcini mushrooms and nutritional yeast (if using). Season with salt and pepper and serve immediately.

Per Serving:
calories: 354 | fat: 2g | protein: 15g | carbs: 74g | fiber: 16g

Cuban-Style Black Beans with Cilantro Rice

Prep time: 20 minutes | Cook time: 1 hour 30 minutes | Serves 4

Black Beans:
1 pound (454 g) black beans, soaked overnight
2 tablespoons ground cumin
1 large onion, peeled and diced
2 bay leaves
3 cloves garlic, peeled and minced
3 celery stalks, diced
3 medium carrots, peeled and diced
1 red bell pepper, seeded and diced
2 tablespoons minced oregano
1 cup finely chopped cilantro stems

2 tablespoons apple cider vinegar
½ teaspoon freshly ground white or black pepper
3 tablespoons chopped cilantro leaves
1 medium tomato, chopped (about 1 cup)
Salt, to taste (optional)
Cilantro Rice:
1 cup brown rice
1 tablespoon low-sodium light brown miso paste
2 tablespoons finely chopped cilantro leaves

Make the Black Beans: 1. In a large pot, combine the beans, cumin, onion, bay leaves, garlic, celery, carrots, red pepper, oregano, cilantro stems, and 5 cups of water and bring to a boil. Reduce the heat to a simmer and cook for 90 minutes, or until the beans are tender. Remove one-quarter of the beans, mash them in a separate bowl, and return them to the pot. Add the apple cider vinegar, pepper, cilantro leaves, and tomato and stir. Once the beans are fully cooked, season with salt (if using) and remove the bay leaves. Make the Cilantro Rice: 2. Combine the rice, 2 cups of water, and the miso paste in a large saucepan and bring to a boil. Reduce the heat to medium and simmer, covered, for 20 minutes. Reduce the heat to low and simmer for an additional 30 minutes. Fluff the rice and stir in the cilantro. 3. To serve, divide the rice among 4 individual plates and top with the beans.

Per Serving:
calories: 432 | fat: 3g | protein: 18g | carbs: 85g | fiber: 13g

Eggplant and Chickpea Rice Pilaf

Prep time: 20 minutes | Cook time: 1 hour 10 minutes | Serves 4

2 cups vegetable stock, or low-sodium vegetable broth
1 cup brown basmati rice
1 large yellow onion, peeled and diced small
6 cloves garlic, peeled and minced
2 jalapeño peppers, seeded and minced
1 tablespoon cumin seeds, toasted and ground
1 tablespoon ground coriander
1 teaspoon turmeric
1 large eggplant, stemmed and cut into ½-inch cubes
2 cups cooked chickpeas, or 1 (15 ounces / 425 g) can, drained and rinsed
¼ cup finely chopped mint
½ cup finely chopped basil
Salt, to taste (optional)
½ cup finely chopped cilantro

1. Bring the vegetable stock to a boil in a medium saucepan. Add the rice and bring the mixture back to a boil over high heat. Reduce the heat to medium and cook, covered, until the rice is tender, about 45 minutes. 2. Place the onion in a large saucepan and sauté over medium heat for 7 to 8 minutes. Add water 1 to 2 tablespoons at a time to keep the onion from sticking to the pan. Add the garlic, jalapeño peppers, cumin, coriander, turmeric, and eggplant and cook until the eggplant is tender, about 12 minutes. Add the cooked rice, chickpeas, mint, and basil. Season with salt (if using) and serve garnished with the cilantro.

Per Serving:

calories: 373 | fat: 4g | protein: 13g | carbs: 73g | fiber: 12g

Baked Tempeh Nuggets

Prep time: 15 minutes | Cook time: 30 minutes | Serves 4

1 (8 ounces / 227 g) package tempeh, lightly steamed if desired
¼ cup almond milk
¼ cup nutritional yeast
1 tablespoon Fall & Winter All-Purpose Seasoning or other seasoning blend
1 teaspoon arrowroot powder
1 teaspoon fresh lemon juice
¼ teaspoon black pepper
¼ teaspoon hot sauce
¼ teaspoon salt (optional)
1 cup whole wheat bread crumbs

1. Preheat the oven to 400ºF (205ºC) and line a baking sheet with parchment paper. 2. Slice the tempeh in half and then quarter each half to form 8 pieces. Smash each one slightly with the heel of your hand to increase surface area and make them more nugget-like. 3. Combine almond milk, nutritional yeast, seasoning blend, arrowroot powder, lemon juice, pepper, hot sauce, and salt, in a shallow dishif desired. Add the tempeh nuggets and allow to soak for 5 minutes, turning them to get each piece well coated. 4. Place bread crumbs in another shallow dish. Using one hand for the wet and one for the dry, transfer each piece of tempeh from the batter to the bread crumbs. Place on the prepared baking sheet. 5. Bake for 30 minutes, flipping halfway, until golden brown on both sides. Serve.

Per Serving:

calories: 267 | fat: 8g | protein: 19g | carbs: 32g | fiber: 3g

Mexican Quinoa Bowl

Prep time: 10 minutes | Cook time: 22 minutes | Serves 2

1 cup cooked or canned chickpeas
1 cup cooked or canned black beans
½ cup dry quinoa
2 cups vegetable stock
2 tablespoons Mexican chorizo seasoning
Optional Toppings:
lime juice
fresh cilantro
avocado slices

1. When using dry chickpeas and beans, soak and cook ⅓ cup of dry chickpeas and black beans. 2. Put a large pot over medium-high heat and add the vegetable stock to the pot along with the quinoa. 3. Bring to a boil, then turn the heat down to medium. 4. Cook the quinoa for about 15 minutes, without covering the pot, and stir occasionally. 5. Add the Mexican chorizo seasoning, black beans and chickpeas, and cook for another 7 minutes, stirring occasionally. 6. Turn the heat off and let it cool down for a minute. 7. Divide between 2 bowls, garnish with the optional toppings, serve and enjoy! 8. Store in an airtight container in the fridge, and consume within 2 days. Alternatively, store in the freezer for a maximum of 30 days and thaw at room temperature. The bowl can be served cold or reheated in a saucepan or a microwave.

Per Serving:

calories: 487 | fat: 8g | protein: 23g | carbs: 80g | fiber: 19g

Fancy Rice

Prep time: 10 minutes | Cook time: 40 minutes | Serves 4

1 cup uncooked wild and brown rice blend, rinsed
2 teaspoons virgin olive oil (optional)
1 teaspoon apple cider vinegar
½ teaspoon ground coriander
¼ teaspoon ground sumac
¼ cup unsweetened dried
cranberries
¼ cup chopped fresh flat-leaf parsley
2 green onions, thinly sliced
Salt and pepper, to taste (optional)
¼ cup almonds, chopped, for garnish

1. Place the wild and brown rice blend in a medium saucepan. Cover the rice with cold water by 1 inch. Bring to a boil, lower the heat to a simmer, and cover. Cook the rice for 40 minutes or until all the liquid is absorbed. Remove from the heat and let the rice sit for 5 minutes. Fluff the rice with a fork, and gently transfer it to a medium bowl. 2. Add the olive oil, apple cider vinegar, coriander, sumac, dried cranberries, parsley, green onions, salt, and pepper, if using, to the rice. Toss gently to combine. Garnish the rice with the chopped almonds. Serve warm.

Per Serving:

calories: 252 | fat: 7g | protein: 5g | carbs: 25g | fiber: 3g

Southwest Stuffed Peppers

Prep time: 10 minutes | Cook time: 30 minutes |

Serves 4

4 bell peppers	1 cup vegetable broth
3 cups cooked brown rice	2 tablespoons tomato paste
1 cup cooked black beans	2 tablespoons chili powder
1 cup fresh or frozen corn	1 teaspoon ground cumin

1. Preheat the oven to 375ºF (190ºC). 2. Cut the tops off the bell peppers and remove any seeds or fibers that remain inside the core or inside the tops of the peppers. 3. In a large bowl, mix rice, beans, corn, broth, tomato paste, chili powder, and cumin until the tomato paste and spices have been thoroughly incorporated. 4. Spoon one-quarter of the rice mixture into each pepper. Set the peppers upright on a baking dish and place the tops back onto the peppers. 5. Bake for 1 hour or until the peppers are easily pierced with a fork and serve.

Per Serving:

calories: 270 | fat: 3g | protein: 11g | carbs: 55g | fiber: 9g

Koshari (Lentils with Rice and Macaroni)

Prep time: 15 minutes | Cook time: 2 hours | Serves 6

1 cup green lentils, rinsed	½ teaspoon crushed red pepper flakes
Salt, to taste (optional)	
1 cup medium-grain brown rice	2 tablespoons tomato paste
1 large onion, peeled and minced	3 large tomatoes, diced small
4 cloves garlic, peeled and minced	1 cup whole-grain elbow macaroni, cooked according to package directions, drained, and kept warm
1 teaspoon ground cumin	
1 teaspoon ground coriander	1 tablespoon brown rice vinegar
½ teaspoon ground allspice	

1. Add the lentils to a medium saucepan with 3 cups of water. Bring the pot to a boil over high heat, reduce the heat to medium, and cook, covered, for 40 to 45 minutes, or until the lentils are tender but not mushy. Drain any excess water from the lentils, season with salt (if using), and set aside. 2. Add the brown rice and 2 cups of water to a separate medium saucepan. Cover the pan with a tight-fitting lid and bring it to a boil over high heat. Reduce the heat to medium and cook for 45 minutes. 3. Heat a large skillet over high heat. Place the onion in the skillet and sauté over medium heat for 15 minutes, or until it is well browned. Add water 1 to 2 tablespoons at a time to keep the onion from sticking to the pan. Add the garlic and cook for 3 to 4 minutes more. Add the cumin, coriander, allspice, crushed red pepper flakes, and tomato paste and cook for 3 minutes longer. Add the fresh tomatoes and cook over medium heat for 15 minutes, or until the tomatoes start to break down. Season with salt, if using. 4. To serve, combine the lentils, rice, tomato mixture, cooked macaroni, and brown rice vinegar in a large bowl.

Per Serving:

calories: 298 | fat: 1g | protein: 13g | carbs: 59g | fiber: 6g

Slow Cooker Black Bean and Lentil Smoky Cajun Bowl

Prep time: 20 minutes | Cook time: 25 minutes |

Serves 4

2 cups cooked or canned black beans	1 tablespoon salt-free Cajun spices
1 cup dry quick-cooking brown rice	¼ cup water (optional)
	Optional Toppings:
1 (7 ounces / 198 g) pack smoked tofu, cubed	peeled slices
	Fresh cilantro
2 cups canned or fresh tomato cubes	Avocado slices

1. When using dry beans, soak and cook ⅔ cup of dry black beans if necessary. And cook the brown rice. 2. Put a nonstick deep frying pan over medium-high heat and add the tofu cubes, tomato cubes and the optional ¼ cup of water. 3. Stir occasionally until everything is cooked, then add the black beans, cooked brown rice and Cajun spices. 4. Turn the heat off and stir occasionally for about 5 minutes until everything is heated through. 5. Divide the smoky Cajun beans and rice between 4 bowls, serve with the optional toppings and enjoy! 6. Store the smoky Cajun beans and rice in an airtight container in the fridge, and consume within 3 days. Alternatively, store in the freezer for a maximum of 30 days and thaw at room temperature. Use a microwave, toaster oven, or nonstick frying pan to reheat the smoky Cajun beans and rice.

Per Serving:

calories: 371 | fat: 5g | protein: 20g | carbs: 60g | fiber: 12g

Chickpea Pâté

Prep time: 10 minutes | Cook time: 0 minutes |

Serves 4

1 cup whole raw nuts, toasted	½ cup filtered water
2 tablespoons extra-virgin olive oil, plus more for drizzling (optional)	1 teaspoon fine sea salt, plus more to taste (optional)
	½ teaspoon grated or pressed garlic
1 (15½ ounces / 439 g) can chickpeas, drained and rinsed well	½ teaspoon raw apple cider vinegar

1. Put the nuts and oil in a food processor and blend until completely smooth, scraping down the sides as necessary. It will take a few minutes to reach a runny consistency. Add the chickpeas, water, salt, if using, garlic, and vinegar and blend until completely smooth. Add more cooking liquid or water if necessary to get the desired consistency; this will take a couple of minutes. Add more salt to taste and serve, drizzled with olive oil. Or store in an airtight container in the fridge for up to 4 days.

Per Serving:

calories: 321 | fat: 22g | protein: 11g | carbs: 23g | fiber: 7g

Super Burritos

Prep time: 15 minutes | Cook time: 8 hours | Serves 6

2 (15 ounces / 425 g) cans diced tomatoes
¼ cup salsa
2 (15 ounces / 425 g) cans black beans, drained and rinsed
1 cup brown rice
½ cup fresh, frozen, or canned corn
2 tablespoons taco seasoning
1 teaspoon ground cumin

1 teaspoon salt (optional)
2 chipotle peppers in adobo sauce, finely chopped
2½ cups vegetable broth
½ cup lentils
12 whole wheat tortillas
Additional toppings:
Salsa
Avocado or guacamole
Black olives

1. Add the tomatoes, salsa, beans, rice, corn, taco seasoning, cumin, salt (if desired), chipotles, and broth to a slow cooker. Stir and cover. Cook on low for 6 to 8 hours or on high for 3 to 4 hours. 2. Add the lentils for the last 40 minutes of cooking. Continue cooking until the lentils are tender. The rice will be tender and most of the liquid will be absorbed. This is the filling. 3. Lay out the tortillas and place about ⅓ to ½ cup (for a very large burrito) of the filling on each tortilla. Spread the filling down through the center of the tortilla. Fold each end about 1½ inches over the point edge of the beans. Then roll up the tortilla along the long edge. If you have a certain technique that you want to use on these, go right ahead. 4. Stack up and serve with more salsa, avocado or guacamole, and black olives.

Per Serving:(2 burritos)
calories: 464 | fat: 15g | protein: 21g | carbs: 56g | fiber: 16g

Almost Instant Ramen

Prep time: 15 minutes | Cook time: 15 minutes | Serves 6

6 cups vegetable broth
1 small yellow onion, diced
2 tablespoons wakame (optional)
1 teaspoon minced or grated fresh ginger, or more to taste
1 teaspoon toasted sesame seeds
¼ teaspoon crushed red pepper, or more to taste
2 cups broccoli florets
2 cups shredded red cabbage
2 carrots, finely chopped

½ cup kimchi
8 ounces (227 g) extra-firm tofu, cubed
2 (3 ounces / 85 g) packages gluten-free ramen or soba noodles
2 tablespoons gluten-free red miso, or more to taste
2 nori sheets, cut into strips (optional)
2 scallions, sliced thin
Chopped cilantro

1. Bring the broth to a boil in a large stockpot. Add the onion, wakame (if desired), ginger, sesame seeds, and crushed red pepper. 2. Reduce the heat to medium and add the broccoli, cabbage, carrots, kimchi, and tofu. Cook for 3 minutes. 3. Add the noodles, increase the heat to medium-high, and cook for 5 minutes or according to the package instructions. 4. Remove from the heat. Whisk in the miso and serve with the nori, scallions, and cilantro.

Per Serving:
calories: 135 | fat: 3g | protein: 8g | carbs: 22g | fiber: 2g

Curried Chickpeas and Rice

Prep time: 10 minutes | Cook time: 35 minutes | Serves 4

1 cup brown basmati rice
¼ cup finely chopped green scallions
¼ teaspoons cumin seeds, toasted

¼ teaspoons curry powder
½ teaspoons salt, or to taste (optional)
1½ cups cooked chickpeas
½ tablespoon fresh lime juice

1. Rinse the rice and add it to a pot with 2½ cups of water. Bring to a boil over high heat and cook, uncovered, for 20 minutes. Reduce the heat to medium and simmer the rice, covered, for 10 minutes. 2. Add the scallions to a medium saucepan with 2 tablespoons of water and cook until soft. Add the cumin seeds, curry powder, salt (if using), and chickpeas and cook for a minute. Add the cooked rice, cook for another minute, and remove the pan from the heat. Add the lime juice and serve hot.

Per Serving:
calories: 275 | fat: 3g | protein: 9g | carbs: 53g | fiber: 6g

Spinach, Mushroom and Quinoa Pilaf

Prep time: 30 minutes | Cook time: 35 minutes | Serves 4

⅓ ounce (9 g) porcini mushrooms, soaked for 30 minutes in 1 cup of water that has just been boiled, and roughly chopped
2 large leeks (white and light green parts), diced and rinsed
8 ounces (227 g) cremini mushrooms, thinly sliced
3 cloves garlic, peeled and minced

1 tablespoon thyme
2 cups vegetable stock, or low-sodium vegetable broth, plus more as needed
1½ cups quinoa
6 cups baby spinach, chopped
Salt and freshly ground black pepper, to taste
¼ cup pine nuts, toasted (optional)

1. Drain the porcini mushrooms, reserving the liquid. Finely chop the mushrooms and set aside. 2. Place the leeks and cremini mushrooms in a large saucepan and sauté over medium heat for 10 minutes. Add water 1 to 2 tablespoons at a time to keep the vegetables from sticking to the pan. Add the garlic and thyme and cook for 30 seconds. 3. Combine the porcini mushroom soaking liquid and vegetable stock. Add more vegetable stock as needed to make 3 cups. Add the liquid, quinoa, and chopped porcini mushrooms to the pan with the sautéed mushrooms and bring the pan to a boil over high heat. Reduce the heat to medium and cook the quinoa, covered, for 15 minutes, or until it is tender. Stir in the spinach and cook for another 5 minutes, or until the spinach is wilted. Season with salt and pepper and garnish with the pine nuts, if desired.

Per Serving:
calories: 358 | fat: 10g | protein: 14g | carbs: 55g | fiber: 7g

Chapter 6 Snacks and Appetizers

Garlic Hummus

Prep time: 10 minutes | Cook time: 0 minutes |
Makes 3 cups

3 garlic cloves
2 (15 ounces / 425 g) cans chickpeas, drained and rinsed
3 tablespoons extra-virgin olive oil, plus more as needed (optional)

Juice of 2 lemons
¼ cup tahini
½ teaspoon salt
½ teaspoon ground cumin
1 tablespoon sesame seeds, for garnish (optional)

1. In a blender, combine garlic, chickpeas, olive oil, lemon juice, tahini, salt, and cumin. 2. Blend until smooth and creamy, adding more oil or water for desired consistency. 3. Spoon hummus into a bowl, drizzle with olive oil, and garnish with sesame seeds.

Per Serving:

calories: 58 | fat: 4g | protein: 2g | carbs: 5g | fiber: 2g

Baked Vegetable Chips

Prep time: 20 minutes | Cook time: 35 minutes |
Serves 2

1 pound (454 g) starchy root vegetables, such as russet potato, sweet potato, rutabaga, parsnip, red or golden beet, or taro
1 pound (454 g) high-water vegetables, such as zucchini or summer squash
Kosher salt, for absorbing

moisture
1 teaspoon garlic powder
1 teaspoon paprika
½ teaspoon onion powder
½ teaspoon freshly ground black pepper
1 teaspoon avocado oil or other oil (optional)

1. Preheat the oven to 300ºF (150ºC) and line baking sheets with parchment paper. 2. Slice root vegetables, such as potatoes, beets, or carrots, into ⅛-inch-thick slices. 3. Sprinkle with kosher salt and let sit for 15 minutes to draw out moisture. 4. Dab off excess moisture and salt, then toss with garlic powder, paprika, onion powder, and pepper. 5. Place the sliced vegetables in a single layer on baking sheets, brush with oil if desired, and sprinkle with spice mix. 6. Bake for 15 minutes, switch pan positions, and bake for another 20 minutes or until crispy. 7. Transfer chips to a wire rack to cool and crisp further.

Per Serving:

calories: 250 | fat: 3g | protein: 8g | carbs: 51g | fiber: 6g

Spirulina-Golden Berry Power Bars

Prep time: 2 minutes | Cook time: 0 minutes | Makes
8 bars

1 cup mixed raw seeds (pumpkin, sunflower, sesame, hemp)
1 tablespoon chia seeds
1 cup Medjool dates (about 10 large), pitted

2 tablespoons chopped fresh mint
2 teaspoons spirulina powder
1 tablespoon fresh lime juice
½ cup golden berries

1.Using the S blade attachment, combine all ingredients in a food processor, excluding the golden berries. 2. Continue processing until a rough dough forms, which may take a few minutes. Stop the machine and check the consistency by pinching the dough between two fingers. It should stick together easily to avoid crumbly bars. If the dough is dry, add ½ teaspoon of water at a time and blend until the desired stickiness is achieved. 3. Once the dough is ready, add the golden berries and pulse a few times to coarsely chop them, providing the bars with an excellent texture. 4. Place a large piece of parchment paper on a flat surface and transfer the dough on top. Bring it together into a solid mass, then fold the parchment paper over the dough and flatten it to about ¼ inch (6 mm) thickness using a rolling pin. 5. Freeze the dough for several hours and then use a knife or cookie cutter to cut it into desired shapes. 6. Store the bars in an airtight glass container for 2 to 3 weeks or in the freezer for up to 3 months.

Per Serving:

calories: 186 | fat: 8g | protein: 6g | carbs: 26g | fiber: 3g

Cherry Chocolate Hemp Balls

Prep time: 20 minutes | Cook time: 0 minutes |
Makes 24 balls

1 cup old-fashioned oats
½ cup unsweetened shredded coconut
½ cup chopped dried cherries
½ cup chopped pistachios

⅓ cup dairy-free chocolate chips
⅓ cup peanut butter
¼ cup maple syrup (optional)
¼ cup raw shelled hempseed

1. Mix all of the ingredients to a large bowl with a sturdy wooden spoon. 2. Roll into 24 balls. 3. Store in the refrigerator for up to 5 days or freeze for up to 6 months.

Per Serving:(2 balls)

calories: 1117 | fat: 6g | protein: 10g | carbs: 16g | fiber: 3g

Strawberry Shortcake Rice Bites

Prep time: 20 minutes | Cook time: 25 minutes |
Makes 8 balls

3 cups water
3 cups white sushi rice
½ cup coconut sugar (optional)
3 tablespoons fresh lemon juice
½ teaspoon vanilla extract

2 cups strawberries, hulled and quartered
3 tablespoons chia seeds
Salt (optional)

1. In a large saucepan, bring water to a boil and then reduce heat to medium-low. Stir in the rice and cook for about 15 to 20 minutes, stirring occasionally, until it's soft and moist, yet sticky and tender.
2. Transfer the cooked rice to a large bowl and add in the sugar, lemon juice, and vanilla. Mix well and allow it to cool slightly.
3. Prepare a sushi mat or silicone liner by covering it with plastic wrap. Spread 1 cup of rice on top of the plastic and use wet hands to press it into a ½-inch thick layer. 4. Place a row of strawberries, end to end, about 1 inch from the bottom edge of the rice. Sprinkle 1 teaspoon of chia seeds on top. Roll the rice tightly into a cylinder, starting with the edge closest to you and using the plastic wrap and mat to assist. Pull the plastic and mat away from the rice as you roll. Repeat with the remaining ingredients.
5. If desired, sprinkle salt on the outside of the rolls. Let them sit for 5 minutes, then slice each roll into 8 to 10 pieces with a sharp knife. To eat on the go, wrap each piece tightly in parchment paper and plastic wrap. Store in the fridge for up to 2 days or freeze for up to 3 months (thaw overnight before eating if frozen).

Per Serving:
calories: 385 | fat: 2g | protein: 9g | carbs: 87g | fiber: 5g

Pineapple, Peach, and Mango Salsa

Prep time: 15 minutes | Cook time: 2 to 3 hours |
Makes about 6 cups

1 medium onion, finely diced
2 garlic cloves, minced
1 medium orange, red, or yellow bell pepper, finely diced
1 (20 ounces / 567 g) can crushed pineapple in juice
1 (15 ounces / 425 g) can no-sugar-added mango in juice, drained and finely diced

1 (15 ounces / 425 g) can no-sugar-added sliced peaches in juice, drained and finely diced
½ teaspoon ground cumin
1 teaspoon paprika
Juice of 1 lime
3 to 4 tablespoons chopped fresh mint (about 10 to 15 leaves)

1. Place the onion, garlic, and bell pepper in the slow cooker. Add the pineapple with its juices, mango, and peaches. Sprinkle cumin and paprika into the slow cooker and pour in lime juice. Stir thoroughly to combine. 2. Cover the slow cooker and cook on Low for 2 to 3 hours until the onion and peppers are cooked through and softened. Let the salsa cool slightly, then add in the mint just before serving.

Per Serving:
calories: 36 | fat: 0g | protein: 1g | carbs: 9g | fiber: 1g

Greens and Beans Dip

Prep time: 10 minutes | Cook time: 0 minutes |
Makes about 2 cups

1 (14 ounces / 397 g) can white beans, drained and rinsed, or 1½ cups cooked
Zest and juice of 1 lemon
1 tablespoon almond butter, tahini, or other mild nut or seed butter
1 to 2 leaves kale, rinsed and

stemmed
1 tablespoon nutritional yeast (optional)
1 to 2 teaspoons curry powder
1 to 2 teaspoons ground cumin
1 teaspoon smoked paprika
¼ teaspoon sea salt (optional)

1. Take all the ingredients and add them to a food processor. Pulse the mixture until it comes together. If a food processor is unavailable, mash the beans and chop the kale, then mix them together. 2. Taste the mixture for seasoning and adjust as needed. Add more spices, lemon juice, or salt (if using) to achieve the desired taste.

Per Serving:(1 cup)
calories: 112 | fat: 5g | protein: 6g | carbs: 13g | fiber: 6g

Basic Oil-Free Hummus

Prep time: 10 minutes | Cook time: 0 minutes |
Makes 1½ cups

1 (15 ounces / 425 g) can chickpeas, drained and rinsed
1 tablespoon tahini
¼ teaspoon garlic powder

¼ teaspoon ground cumin
¼ cup lemon juice
1/16 teaspoon cayenne
¼ teaspoon za'atar

1.Using a food processor, blend together the chickpeas, tahini, garlic powder, cumin, lemon juice, cayenne, and za'atar until the mixture becomes smooth and creamy.

Per Serving:
calories: 136 | fat: 6g | protein: 3g | carbs: 21g | fiber: 3g

Peanut Butter Balls

Prep time: 0 minutes | Cook time: 30 minutes | Makes 12 balls
1 cup old-fashioned rolled oats
½ cup creamy peanut butter
¼ cup raisins

1. Combine all the ingredients in a large bowl and mix thoroughly using your hands. 2. Shape the mixture into small balls, approximately the size of a tablespoon, and place them on a baking sheet. 3. Chill the baking sheet in the freezer for 30 minutes. 4. Enjoy the balls straight from the freezer, or keep them in an airtight container or plastic bag in the refrigerator for up to 5 days.

Per Serving:(2 balls)
calories: 168 | fat: 13g | protein: 8g | carbs: 14g | fiber: 4g

Showtime Popcorn

Prep time: 5 minutes | Cook time: 1 minute | Serves 2

¼ cup popcorn kernels
1 tablespoon nutritional yeast

¼ teaspoon garlic powder
¼ teaspoon onion powder

1. Put the popcorn kernels in a paper lunch bag, folding over the top of the bag so the kernels won't spill out. 2. Microwave on high for 2 to 3 minutes, or until you hear a pause of 2 seconds in between kernels popping. 3. Remove the bag from the microwave, and add the nutritional yeast, garlic powder, and onion powder. Fold the top of the bag back over, and shake to thoroughly coat. 4. Pour into a bowl and enjoy.

Per Serving:

calories: 48 | fat: 1g | protein: 4g | carbs: 6g | fiber: 2g

Toast Points

Prep time: 5 minutes | Cook time: 20 minutes |

Serves 2 to 4

8 whole-grain bread slices
(thawed if frozen)
Balsamic vinegar, for brushing

(optional)
Garlic powder, for seasoning

1. Arrange the bread in a single layer on a baking sheet lined with parchment paper. 2. Brush a light coating of vinegar (if preferred) over the bread. 3. Sprinkle garlic powder on top. 4. Place the baking sheet in a cold oven and set the temperature to 350ºF (180ºC). 5. Once the oven reaches the desired temperature, flip the bread over and bake for an additional 5 to 15 minutes until it reaches your desired level of crispiness. Finally, remove from the oven.

Per Serving:

calories: 165 | fat: 1g | protein: 8g | carbs: 31g | fiber: 6g

Steamed Seitan Smoky Nuggets

Prep time: 10 minutes | Cook time: 40 minutes |

Serves 4

¾ cup vital wheat gluten
¼ cup plus 2 tablespoons chickpea flour
2 teaspoons garlic powder
2 teaspoons onion powder
½ cup vegetable broth

2 tablespoons tomato sauce
1 tablespoon tamari
1 teaspoon liquid smoke
½ teaspoon coconut oil
(optional)

1. In a large bowl, combine gluten, flour, garlic powder, and onion powder.
2. In a separate small bowl, mix together broth, tomato sauce, tamari, liquid smoke, and oil (if desired). Pour the liquid mixture into the dry ingredients and stir until well combined. Knead the dough for 2 minutes until it becomes elastic. As you knead, the dough will naturally form a rounder shape. Note that the dough is

firm and will not rise significantly during cooking.
3. Add 5 cups of water to a saucepan and bring it to a boil. Place a steamer basket inside and reduce the heat to a simmer. 4. Use a pastry cutter to slice the seitan into irregular pieces. You can shape them into balls or leave them chunky. Alternatively, you can steam the seitan as a single log and cut it into pieces after it has steamed and cooled. 5. Steam the seitan for 40 minutes.
6. Once cooked, remove the seitan from the steamer and let it cool. Store it in the refrigerator for up to 5 days or freeze it for up to 4 months.

Per Serving:(½ cup)

calories: 234 | fat: 2g | protein: 31g | carbs:12 g | fiber: 2g

Rainbow Veggie Protein Pinwheels

Prep time: 20 minutes | Cook time: 0 minutes |

Serves 6

¼ cup hummus
¼ cup tempeh, crumbled in a food processor
2 large spinach tortillas
¼ cup thinly sliced red bell pepper

¼ cup thinly sliced yellow bell pepper
1 thinly sliced carrot
¼ cup thinly sliced purple cabbage

1. Combine the hummus and tempeh in a bowl. 2. Lay out the tortillas and spread a thin layer of the hummus mixture over the entire surface, leaving a 1-inch border around the edges. Place a thin strip of each vegetable in a row next to each other on top of the hummus mixture. 3. Roll each tortilla tightly and cut it crosswise into pinwheels. The hummus will help the pinwheels stick together at the edges, but you can use toothpicks if needed.

Per Serving:(2 pinwheels)

calories: 66 | fat: 2g | protein: 9g | carbs: 8g | fiber: 4g

Nacho Cheese

Prep time: 5 minutes | Cook time: 10 minutes |

Makes 3 cups

2 cups peeled and diced russet potatoes
1 cup sliced carrots
½ cup water
1 tablespoon lemon juice

½ cup nutritional yeast
1 teaspoon onion powder
1 teaspoon garlic powder
½ teaspoon salt (optional)

1.Take a large pot and fill it with water. Add the potatoes and carrots and place it on medium-high heat. Bring the water to a boil and continue cooking until the vegetables are soft, which should take around 10 minutes. Once done, remove the pot from the heat and drain the water. 2. Take a blender and add the boiled potatoes, carrots, water, lemon juice, nutritional yeast, onion powder, garlic powder, and salt (if desired). Blend all the ingredients until they are completely smooth.

Per Serving:(½ cup)

calories: 88 | fat: 1g | protein: 7g | carbs: 15g | fiber: 2g

Chickpea Salad Crostini

Prep time: 15 minutes | Cook time: 5 minutes | Serves 6

1 baguette, cut into 12 slices
2 tablespoons extra virgin olive oil (optional)
1 (15 ounces / 425 g) can chickpeas, drained and rinsed
1 (15 ounces / 425 g) can black beans, drained and rinsed
1 (8 ounces / 227 g) can corn, drained and rinsed

1 (4 ounces / 113 g)can black olives, drained and sliced
1 tablespoon fresh lime juice
2 teaspoons flaxseed meal
1 teaspoon ground cumin
¼ teaspoon chili powder
¼ teaspoon onion powder
¼ teaspoon salt (optional)
Fresh thyme, for garnish

Make Crostini Toasts: 1. Lay out the bread slices on a baking sheet. Lightly brush each slice of bread with oil. (The new silicone brushes are great for this, and they wash up really easily.) Put the baking sheet under the broiler. Don't do anything else. Just stand there and keep checking the bread and don't let it burn. It only takes a couple of minutes. After the toasts are lightly browned, remove the sheet from the oven. You can make these ahead of time and keep them in the refrigerator for later use, too. Assemble: 2. In a large bowl, mix all the remaining ingredients together, except the thyme. 3. Top each toast with the chickpea mixture just before serving. Garnish with fresh thyme.

Per Serving:(2 crostini)
calories: 279 | fat: 11g | protein: 10g | carbs: 39g | fiber: 8g

Calorie Bomb Cookies

Prep time: 15 minutes | Cook time: 30 minutes | Makes 24 cookies

4 cups old-fashioned rolled oats
1½ cups whole wheat flour
1 teaspoon baking powder
½ teaspoon salt (optional)
3 ripe bananas
1 cup coconut sugar (optional)
⅓ cup coconut oil (optional)
¼ cup plus 2 tablespoons water

2 tablespoons chia seeds or ground flaxseeds
2 teaspoons vanilla extract
1 cup dark chocolate chips
1 cup raw walnut pieces
½ cup raw sunflower seeds
½ cup unsweetened shredded coconut (optional)

1. Preheat the oven to 350ºF (180ºC). Line two baking sheets with parchment paper. 2. Place 2 cups of the oats in a food processor or blender and pulse until they are finely ground. Transfer to a large bowl and add the flour, baking powder, salt (if desired), and remaining oats. 3. Combine the bananas, sugar, oil (if desired), water, chia seeds, and vanilla in the blender or food processor. Add to the oat mixture and stir with a sturdy wooden spoon until combined. Add the chocolate chips, walnuts, sunflower seeds, and coconut. 4. With wet hands, form about ¼ cup dough. Flatten them to ¾ to 1 inch thick. 5. Bake for 30 minutes, or until golden brown. Allow to cool completely before removing from the baking sheets. Store in an airtight container for up to 1 week or freeze for up to 3 months. Wrap in parchment paper for on-the-go eating.

Per Serving:(2 cookies)
calories: 491 | fat: 24g | protein: 9g | carbs: 68g | fiber: 9g

Peanut Butter Chocolate Seed Balls

Prep time: 15 minutes | Cook time: 25 minutes | Serves 16

16 ounces (454 g) dairy-free chocolate chips
½ cup creamy peanut butter
½ cup raw shelled hempseed
½ cup unsweetened shredded

coconut
1 cup sunflower seed kernels, pulsed fine in a mini food processor, divided

1. Using a double boiler, melt the chocolate and stir in the peanut butter until well blended. Remove from heat and add in the hempseed, shredded coconut, and ½ cup of sunflower seeds. Refrigerate the mixture for about 30 minutes until the dough is firm enough to use a small cookie scoop. 2. After refrigeration, remove the dough and scoop out forty-eight balls. You can roll them into smoother balls using your palms. While the balls are still warm from rolling, coat them with the remaining pulsed sunflower seeds. 3. These balls can be stored in the fridge for up to 3 weeks or in the freezer for up to 6 months.

Per Serving:(3 balls)
calories: 150 | fat: 9g | protein: 7g | carbs: 14g | fiber: 2g

Herbed Smashed Potatoes with Lemon Aioli

Prep time: 5 minutes | Cook time: 1 hour | Serves 4

Potatoes:
12 small red potatoes
2 tablespoons extra-virgin olive oil (optional)
1 teaspoon garlic powder
½ teaspoon salt (optional)
1 teaspoon Italian seasoning

2 tablespoons finely chopped fresh parsley
Lemon Aioli:
½ cup store-bought plant-based mayonnaise
Juice of 1 lemon
1 garlic clove, minced

1. Heat the oven to 400ºF (205ºC). 2. To make the Potatoes, put them in a large pot and add enough water to cover them. Place the pot over high heat and bring to a boil. Cook for 15 minutes, then drain the water well and pat the potatoes dry with a clean kitchen towel. Transfer the potatoes to a large bowl.
3. Add olive oil, garlic powder, and salt to the potatoes and gently toss them until all the potatoes are coated with the seasonings. Spread out the seasoned potatoes in a single layer on a sheet pan. 4. Bake the potatoes for 15 minutes, then use tongs to turn them and continue baking for another 15 minutes. Once done, use the back of a fork to flatten the potatoes. Sprinkle them with Italian seasoning and bake for an additional 10 minutes until crispy and golden.
5. While the potatoes finish baking, mix together mayo, lemon juice, and garlic in a small bowl to make the lemon Aioli. 6. Transfer the potatoes to a platter, sprinkle them with parsley, and serve with the lemon aioli on the side for dipping.

Per Serving:
calories: 520 | fat: 17g | protein: 12g | carbs: 84g | fiber: 9g

Cacao Crush Smoothie

Prep time: 5 minutes | Cook time: 0 minutes | Serves 1

1½ cups unsweetened almond milk
½ cup frozen cauliflower
¼ avocado, peeled

1 tablespoon cacao powder
½ teaspoon ground cinnamon
½ teaspoon pure vanilla extract

1. Using a high-powered blender, blend almond milk, cauliflower, avocado, cacao powder, cinnamon, and vanilla until the mixture becomes smooth and creamy. 2. Pour the mixture over a glass of ice and serve immediately.

Per Serving:

calories: 254 | fat: 7g | protein: 15g | carbs: 32g | fiber: 6g

Tomatillo Salsa

Prep time: 10 minutes | Cook time: 7 minutes |

Makes 2½ cups

8 small tomatillos
½ white onion, cut in half
1½ teaspoons minced garlic
1 jalapeño, halved and seeded

⅓ cup packed chopped cilantro
1 (4 ounces / 113 g) can chopped mild green chili peppers

1. Begin by preheating the broiler and covering a spacious baking sheet with aluminum foil. 2. Take care of the tomatillos by peeling off their husks, washing them thoroughly, and halving them. 3. Place the tomatillos and onion halves face down on the prepared baking sheet, alongside the garlic and jalapeño. 4. Broil for 5 to 7 minutes or until everything is charred evenly.
5. Using a blender or food processor, blend the charred ingredients, cilantro, and chili peppers until the salsa achieves a smooth consistency.

Per Serving:(½ cup)

calories: 33 | fat: 1g | protein: 1g | carbs: 7g | fiber: 2g

Savory Granola

Prep time: 5 minutes | Cook time: 15 to 20 minutes |

Serves 8

3 cups gluten-free rolled oats
½ cup sliced raw almonds
½ cup raw sunflower seeds
½ cup raw pepitas
¼ cup almond meal
6 tablespoons avocado oil (optional)
2 tablespoons pure maple syrup (optional)

2 teaspoons dried rosemary
1 teaspoon dried thyme
½ teaspoon dry mustard powder
½ teaspoon sea salt (optional)
½ teaspoon onion powder
¼ teaspoon garlic powder
¼ teaspoon ground black pepper

1. Preheat the oven to 350°F (180°C). 2. In a large bowl, combine all the ingredients and stir well. Spread evenly on a rimmed baking sheet. Bake for 15 to 20 minutes, or until toasted. Remove and let cool completely, then transfer to an airtight container.

Per Serving:

calories: 324 | fat: 24g | protein: 11g | carbs: 30g | fiber: 7g

Carrot Cake Two-Bite Balls

Prep time: 20 minutes | Cook time: 0 minutes |

Makes 16 balls

1 cup old-fashioned oats
½ cup almond meal
½ cup pecans
⅓ cup plus 2 tablespoons unsweetened shredded coconut, divided
3 grated medium carrots

15 dates, pitted
2 tablespoons unsweetened cocoa powder
2 tablespoons almond butter
1 teaspoon ground cinnamon
½ teaspoon ground nutmeg
½ teaspoon ground ginger

1. Using a food processor, combine oats, almond meal, pecans, ⅓ cup of coconut, carrots, dates, and cocoa powder. Mix on high until all ingredients are well processed. It may be necessary to scrape the edges a few times to ensure that the dates don't clump. Add almond butter, cinnamon, nutmeg, and ginger, and mix again until thoroughly blended. If needed, scrape the edges again. 2. Transfer the mixture to a flat surface and thoroughly blend. Use your hands if necessary. Pinch off portions of the dough and roll them into sixteen balls. For added flavor, roll the balls in additional shredded coconut.

Per Serving:(2 balls)

calories: 194 | fat: 12g | protein: 8g | carbs: 24g | fiber: 6g

Mango Plantain Nice Cream

Prep time: 10 minutes | Cook time: 0 minutes |

Serves 4

2 plantains, peeled, cut into slices, and frozen
1 cup frozen mango pieces
½ cup unsweetened nondairy milk, plus more as needed

2 pitted dates or 1 tablespoon pure maple syrup
1 teaspoon vanilla extract
Juice of 1 lime

1. Using a high-speed blender or food processor, mix frozen plantains, mango, milk, dates, vanilla, and lime juice for 30 seconds. If the mixture doesn't look smooth, scrape down the sides and blend again until it reaches a smooth texture. If necessary, add more milk, 1 tablespoon at a time. 2. For a smoothie-like consistency, store any leftovers in an airtight container in the refrigerator. If you prefer a firmer ice cream texture, freeze the mixture and then thaw it slightly before serving.

Per Serving:(1 cup)

calories: 208 | fat: 1g | protein: 2g | carbs: 52g | fiber: 3g

Skillet Cauliflower Bites

Prep time: 5 minutes | Cook time: 15 minutes |

Serves 4 to 6

1 head cauliflower, cut into 1½- to 2-inch florets

1. In a nonstick skillet, cook the cauliflower over medium heat, stirring every 3 to 5 minutes, for about 15 minutes, or until browned and crisp-tender. Remove from the heat.

Per Serving:

calories: 36 | fat: 0g | protein: 3g | carbs: 8g | fiber: 4g

Carrot Cake Date Balls

Prep time: 10 minutes | Cook time: 0 minutes |

Makes 24 balls

1 cup shredded carrots	½ teaspoon ground cinnamon
1 cup pitted dates	¼ teaspoon ground ginger
½ cup walnut pieces	⅛ teaspoon ground cloves
¼ cup rolled oats	⅛ teaspoon ground nutmeg
1 tablespoon coconut flakes	

1. Line a plate with parchment paper. 2. In a food processor, combine the carrots, dates, walnuts, oats, coconut flakes, ginger, cloves, and nutmeg. Process until a paste forms. 3. Using a 1-tablespoon scoop, form the paste into balls. 4. Place the balls in a single layer on the prepared plate. Serve immediately, or refrigerate in an airtight container for up to 5 days.

Per Serving:

calories: 43 | fat: 2g | protein: 1g | carbs: 7g | fiber: 1g

Slow-Cooker Applesauce

Prep time: 10 minutes | Cook time: 4 to 5 hours |

Makes about 4½ cups

5 pounds (2.3 kg) apples, peeled, cored, and roughly chopped	3 tablespoons fresh lemon juice (from 1 lemon)
1 cup water	2 cinnamon sticks
	Pure maple syrup (optional)

1. In a slow cooker, combine the apples, water, lemon juice, and cinnamon sticks. Cook on low heat for 8 to 10 hours or on high for 4 to 5 hours, until the apples are cooked through. 2. Remove and discard the cinnamon sticks. Using an immersion blender, purée the applesauce to the desired consistency. Alternatively, mash the apples by hand. 3. Taste the applesauce. If it's not sweet enough, add maple syrup to taste.

Per Serving:

calories: 132 | fat: 0g | protein: 0g | carbs: 35g | fiber: 6g

Eggplant Caponata Bruschetta

Prep time: 20 minutes | Cook time: 2 to 3 hours |

Serves 4 to 8

1 medium eggplant, unpeeled and chopped	1 tablespoon maple syrup (optional)
1 medium onion, diced	1 teaspoon dried basil
2 small zucchini, diced	1 teaspoon dried oregano
3 celery stalks, diced	Ground black pepper
4 garlic cloves, minced	Salt (optional)
1 cup sliced pitted green olives	1 long thin loaf crusty whole-grain bread
2 (14½ ounces / 411 g) cans diced tomatoes	3 tablespoons chopped fresh flat-leaf parsley
2 tablespoons capers, drained	
¼ cup red wine vinegar	

1. Put eggplant, onion, zucchini, celery, garlic, olives, tomatoes, capers, vinegar, maple syrup, basil, oregano, pepper, and salt in a slow cooker.
2. Stir well to combine and cook on high for 2 to 3 hours or low for 5 to 6 hours. 3. Preheat the oven to 375ºF (190ºC) and toast slices of bread to make crostini. 4. Stir parsley into the caponata and spoon about 2 tablespoons onto each crostini.

Per Serving:

calories: 405 | fat: 8g | protein: 14g | carbs: 72g | fiber: 11g

Protein Power Grilled Veggie and Fruit Skewers

Prep time: 15 minutes | Cook time: 25 minutes |

Serves 4

8 ounces (227 g) extra-firm tofu, drained, pressed, and cut into 1-inch cubes	4 ounces (113 g) cremini mushrooms
2 tablespoons tamari	1 pineapple, chopped into chunks
1 tablespoon rice vinegar	1 red bell pepper, chopped into large pieces
1 tablespoon maple syrup (optional)	1 yellow bell pepper, chopped into large pieces
¼ teaspoon chili powder	Extra virgin olive oil, for grilling (optional)
1 large sweet potato, peeled and chopped into bite-size chunks	

1. Cut off the stem end of the peppers, slice lengthwise, and remove any seeds.
2. In a food processor, pulse chickpeas, olive oil, garlic, lemon juice, salt, and pepper until chunky. 3. Stir the mixture well and stuff each pepper half with about 2 tablespoons of the chickpea mixture.

Per Serving:(2 skewers)

calories: 236 | fat: 4g | protein: 16g | carbs: 45g | fiber: 6g

Seeded Bars

Prep time: 10 minutes | Cook time: 25 minutes |

Makes 20 bars

1 cup raw sunflower seeds
1 cup raw pumpkin seeds
1 cup raw unhulled sesame seeds
2 cups unsweetened flaked dried coconut

½ teaspoon fine sea salt, plus more to taste (optional)
⅓ cup brown rice syrup or yacon syrup (optional)
1 teaspoon vanilla extract

1. Preheat the oven to 300ºF (150ºC)). Choose your pan and line the bottom and sides with parchment paper. 2. Put the sunflower, pumpkin, and sesame seeds in a large strainer and rinse well under cold running water, then drain and set over a bowl to drain thoroughly while the oven heats. 3. Line a rimmed baking sheet with parchment paper and spread out the seeds. Toast for 15 minutes. Remove the pan from the oven and sprinkle the coconut over top. Return to the oven for another 8 minutes, or until the coconut is browning and the seeds are toasted. Transfer the mixture to a bowl, add the salt, if using, and mix well. Transfer 2 cups of the mixture to a food processor and process, scraping the sides as necessary, until the mixture is smooth and liquid; set aside. 4. If using rice syrup, bring it to a simmer in a small saucepan over medium heat. Stir in the vanilla and remove from the heat. If using yacon syrup, just combine it with the vanilla in a medium bowl. Add the ground seed mixture to the syrup mixture and stir until smooth. Pour into the bowl with the remaining toasted seeds and coconut and stir until thoroughly combined; you may need to use your hands to do this. Using clean, damp hands, press the mixture firmly and evenly into the parchment-lined pan. 5. Put the bars in the fridge for 1 hour or in the freezer for 30 minutes, or until thoroughly chilled and set. Cut into wedges, slices, or squares, depending on the pan, and store in an airtight container at cool room temperature for up to 4 weeks; in warmer weather, store in the fridge. The bars can be frozen for up to 3 months.

Per Serving:(1 bar)

calories: 166 | fat: 13g | protein: 5g | carbs: 9g | fiber: 2g

Watermelon with Coconut-Lime Yogurt

Prep time: 10 minutes | Cook time: 0 minutes |

Serves 1

¾ cup unsweetened coconut milk yogurt, plain or vanilla
1 teaspoon maple syrup (optional)

Zest and juice of 1 lime, plus 1 lime cut into wedges for garnish
1¼ cups cubed seedless watermelon

1. Place the yogurt in a small bowl and add the maple syrup, if using. 2. Zest 1 lime on top of the yogurt; then halve the lime and squeeze the juice into the yogurt. Mix well. 3. Serve the watermelon cubes with the coconut-lime yogurt. 4. Garnish with the lime wedges.

Per Serving:

calories: 209 | fat: 3g | protein: 6g | carbs: 43g | fiber: 2g

Chocolate Sunflower Protein Cookies

Prep time: 15 minutes | Cook time: 10 minutes |

Serves 12

1 cup dairy-free butter
¾ cup plus 2 tablespoons coconut sugar (optional)
2 tablespoons ground chia seeds
2¼ cups whole wheat pastry flour
¼ cup protein powder

1 teaspoon baking soda
½ teaspoon baking powder
¼ teaspoon salt (optional)
1 teaspoon vanilla extract
1 cup dairy-free chocolate chips
¼ cup sunflower seed kernels

1. Preheat the oven to 375ºF (190ºC). Cut parchment paper to fit on a baking sheet. Set aside. 2. Add the butter and sugar (if desired) to the bowl of stand mixer and mix together on medium-low speed for 5 minutes. 3. Meanwhile, mix ground chia seeds with 6 tablespoons water and set aside. 4. Mix together the flour, protein powder, baking soda, baking powder, and salt (if desired) in a medium bowl. 5. Add the vanilla and chia mixture to the butter mixture. Mix until well blended. Mix in the flour mixture a little at a time. On low speed, mix in the chocolate chips and sunflower seeds. 6. Form into round balls and set on the prepared baking sheet about 2 inches apart. Flatten to about ½ inch thick. Bake for 8 to 9 minutes. 7. Cool on a wire rack.

Per Serving:(2 cookies)

calories: 281 | fat: g | protein: 7g | carbs: 16g | fiber: 3g

Creamy Roasted Red Pepper Hummus

Prep time: 20 minutes | Cook time: 0 minutes |

Serves 8

1 (15 ounces /425 g) can chickpeas, 3 tablespoons aquafaba (chickpea liquid from the can) reserved, remaining liquid drained, rinsed
¼ cup tahini
1 tablespoon freshly squeezed lemon juice

1 teaspoon Hungarian paprika
½ teaspoon ground cumin
¼ teaspoon freshly ground black pepper
2 garlic cloves, peeled and stemmed
2 roasted red peppers

1. Pour the chickpeas into a bowl and fill the bowl with water. Gently rub the chickpeas between your hands until you feel the skins coming off. Add more water to the bowl and let the skins float to the surface. Using your hand, scoop out the skins. Drain some of the water and repeat this step once more to remove as many of the chickpea skins as possible. Drain to remove all the water. Set the chickpeas aside. 2. In a food processor or high-speed blender, combine the reserved aquafaba, tahini, and lemon juice. Process for 2 minutes. 3. Add the paprika, cumin, black pepper, garlic, and red peppers. Purée until the red peppers are incorporated. 4. Add the chickpeas and blend for 2 to 3 minutes, or until the hummus is smooth. 5. Refrigerate leftovers in an airtight container for up to 1 week.

Per Serving:

calories: 99 | fat: 5g | protein: 4g | carbs: 11g | fiber: 3g

Choco Almond Bars

Prep time: 10 minutes | Cook time: 15 minutes |

Makes 4 bars

1 cup raw and unsalted almonds
5 pitted dates
1 scoop soy protein isolate, chocolate flavor

Optional Toppings:
Shredded coconut
Cocoa powder

1. Preheat the oven to 257ºF (125ºC) and line a baking sheet with parchment paper. 2. Put the almonds on the baking sheet and roast them for about 10 to 15 minutes or until they're fragrant. 3. Meanwhile, cover the dates with water in a small bowl and let them sit for about 10 minutes. Drain the dates after soaking and make sure no water is left. 4. Take the almonds out of the oven and let them cool down for about 5 minutes. 5. Add all the ingredients to a food processor and blend into a chunky mixture. 6. Alternatively, add all ingredients to a medium bowl, cover it, and process using a handheld blender. 7. Line a loaf pan with parchment paper. Add the almond mixture to the loaf pan, spread it out and press it down firmly until it is 1 inch (2.5 cm) thick all over. 8. Divide into 4 bars, serve cold with the optional toppings and enjoy! 9. Store the bars in an airtight container in the fridge and consume within 4 days. Alternatively, store in the freezer for a maximum of 90 days and thaw at room temperature.

Per Serving:
calories: 254 | fat: 18g | protein: 16g | carbs: 8g | fiber: 4g

Pepita and Almond Squares

Prep time: 20 minutes | Cook time: 15 minutes |

Makes 16 squares

1 cup almonds, coarsely chopped
1 cup old-fashioned oats
⅔ cup pepitas
⅔ cup dried cranberries
½ cup unsweetened shredded

coconut
¼ cup raw shelled hempseed
⅓ cup peanut butter
⅔ cup brown rice syrup
¼ cup maple syrup (optional)
2 teaspoons vanilla extract

1. Line an 8-inch square baking dish with parchment paper and come up about 3 inches on opposite sides. This will act as a handle to remove the squares from the dish. 2. In a large mixing bowl, add the almonds, oats, pepitas, cranberries, coconut, and hempseed. Mix well. Stir in the peanut butter and try to get it evenly combined. You can use your fingers when most of it is worked in. 3. Add the brown rice syrup, maple syrup (if desired), and vanilla to a small saucepan. Bring to a boil and continue boiling until it reaches the hard ball stage, 260ºF (127ºC), on a candy thermometer. When this temperature is reached, quickly pour over the almond mixture and stir well. It will start to harden up quickly. Pour into the prepared dish and press down firmly into the dish and as evenly as possible. Refrigerate for at least 30 minutes. 4. Grab the "handles" of the parchment paper and lift out of the dish. Place on a cutting sheet and slice into sixteen squares.

Per Serving:(2 squares)
calories: 198 | fat: 11g | protein: 12g | carbs: 22g | fiber: 4g

Pita Chips

Prep time: 5 minutes | Cook time: 20 minutes |

Serves 2 to 4

4 to 6 whole-grain pita breads, cut into triangles

1. Spread the pita triangles out in a single layer on a parchment-lined baking sheet. 2. Transfer the baking sheet to a cold oven, and heat to 350ºF (180ºC). 3. When the oven reaches temperature, flip the pitas over. Bake for another 10 to 15 minutes, or until crispy.

Per Serving:
calories: 150 | fat: 1g | protein: 11g | carbs: 32g | fiber: 6g

Peanut Butter Granola Bars

Prep time: 10 minutes | Cook time: 0 minutes |

Makes 12 bars

1 cup packed pitted dates
¼ cup pure maple syrup (optional)
¼ cup creamy natural peanut

butter or almond butter
1 cup coarsely chopped roasted unsalted almonds
1½ cups old-fashioned oats

1. In a food processor, combine the dates, maple syrup (if using), and peanut butter. Process for 1 to 2 minutes, or until the mixture starts to come together and feels slightly sticky. Stop right before or as it starts to turn into a ball of loose dough. 2. Add the almonds and oats and process for 1 minute. Press the dough into an 8-by-8-inch baking dish and cover with plastic wrap. Refrigerate for 20 minutes. 3. Remove the dough and cut into 12 pieces. Refrigerate in a sealable bag or airtight container for 1 to 2 weeks, or freeze for up to 6 months.

Per Serving:(1 bar)
calories: 181 | fat: 9g | protein: 5g | carbs: 24g | fiber: 4g

Vanilla-Cinnamon Fruit Cocktail

Prep time: 10 minutes | Cook time: 0 minutes |

Serves 4 to 6

1 pint blueberries
2 cups diced Granny Smith apples
1 cup halved mandarin orange slices

1 cup sliced strawberries
2 tablespoons lemon juice
2 tablespoons chia seeds
½ teaspoon vanilla extract
¼ teaspoon ground cinnamon

1. In a large bowl, using a wooden spoon or rubber spatula, mix together the blueberries, apples, orange slices, strawberries, lemon juice, chia seeds, vanilla, and cinnamon. Serve immediately, or refrigerate until serving.

Per Serving:
calories: 114 | fat: 2g | protein: 2g | carbs: 25g | fiber: 6g

Sweet Potato Fries with Maple, Mint, and Tahini Dipping Sauce

Prep time: 5 minutes | Cook time: 30 minutes | Serves 2

Fries:
3 sweet potatoes, cut into wedges
2 teaspoons extra-virgin olive oil (optional)
½ teaspoon salt (optional)
½ teaspoon garlic powder
Sauce:

⅓ cup tahini
1 tablespoon maple syrup
½ teaspoon salt (optional)
Juice of 1 lemon
4 mint leaves
1 garlic clove
Pinch red pepper flakes (optional)

1. Preheat the oven to 400°F (205°C). 2. Make the Fries: In a large bowl, combine the potatoes, olive oil, salt, and garlic powder and toss until the potatoes are well coated with the seasonings. 3. Spread out the sweet potatoes in a single layer on a sheet pan and bake for 15 minutes. Using a spatula, turn the potatoes, then continue to bake for another 15 minutes. 4. Make the Sauce: While the fries are in the oven, in a blender, combine the tahini, maple syrup, salt (if using), lemon juice, mint, and garlic and blend until smooth. Transfer to a small bowl, add the red pepper flakes (if using), and stir well. Cover and refrigerate until ready to use.

Per Serving:

calories: 479 | fat: 26g | protein: 10g | carbs: 57g | fiber: 10g

Orange Cranberry Power Cookies

Prep time: 10 minutes | Cook time: 10 minutes | Serves 12

1 cup dairy-free butter, softened
1 cup coconut sugar (optional)
⅓ cup orange juice
2 teaspoons organic vanilla extract
1½ cups whole wheat flour
2 tablespoons protein powder

1 teaspoon baking powder
¼ teaspoon baking soda
1 cup old-fashioned oats
1 cup dairy-free chocolate chips
1 cup chopped walnuts
1 cup dried cranberries

1. Preheat the oven to 375°F (190°C). 2. Beat the butter and sugar (if desired) together in the bowl of a stand mixer. Add the orange juice and vanilla extract. Mix well. 3. Add flour, protein powder, baking powder, and baking soda to a medium bowl. Mix and add to the wet mixture. Mix on medium speed until well blended. Add the oats, chocolate chips, walnuts, and cranberries. Mix on low. 4. Drop heaping tablespoons about 2 inches apart on an ungreased baking sheet. These are big cookies. They spread out to 3 to 4 inches in diameter. Bake for 10 to 11 minutes. 5. Cool a minute and then transfer to a wire rack to cool completely.

Per Serving:(2 cookies)

calories: 294 | fat: 21g | protein: 6g | carbs: 25g | fiber: 4g

Slow Cooker Spiced Peanuts

Prep time: 10 minutes | Cook time: 1 hour | Serves 6

3 cups peanuts
2 teaspoons extra virgin olive oil (optional)
½ teaspoon ground cumin

½ teaspoon powdered garlic
½ teaspoon cayenne powder
½ teaspoon smoked paprika
½ teaspoon salt (optional)

1. Put the peanuts in a slow cooker. Add the oil (if desired) and stir so that there is a little bit of oil on all the peanuts. It will be enough. Add the spices and stir. Cook on low for 45 minutes. Uncover and then cook 15 more minutes.

Per Serving:(½ cup)

calories: 429 | fat: 37g | protein: 19g | carbs: 12g | fiber: 6g

Tortilla Chips

Prep time: 5 minutes | Cook time: 20 minutes | Serves 2 to 4

4 to 6 oil-free corn tortillas, cut into triangles

1. Spread the tortilla triangles out in a single layer on a parchment-lined baking sheet. 2. Transfer the baking sheet to a cold oven, and heat to 350°F (180°C). 3. When the oven reaches temperature, flip the tortillas over. Bake for another 10 to 15 minutes, or until crispy.

Per Serving:

calories: 180 | fat: 3g | protein: 5g | carbs: 35g | fiber: 5g

Nori Snack Rolls

Prep time: 5 minutes | Cook time: 8 to 10 minutes | Makes 4 rolls

2 tablespoons almond, cashew, peanut, or other nut butter
2 tablespoons tamari or soy sauce

4 standard nori sheets
1 mushroom, sliced
1 tablespoon pickled ginger
½ cup grated carrots

1. Preheat the oven to 350°F (180°C). 2. Mix the nut butter and tamari until smooth and very thick. 3. Lay out a nori sheet, rough side up, the long way. 4. Spread a thin line of the tamari mixture on the far end of the nori sheet, from side to side. 5. Lay the mushroom slices, ginger, and carrots in a line at the other end (the end closest to you). 6. Fold the vegetables inside the nori, rolling toward the tahini mixture, which will seal the roll. 7. Repeat to make 4 rolls. 8. Put on a baking sheet and bake for 8 to 10 minutes, or until the rolls are slightly browned and crispy at the ends. 9. Let the rolls cool for a few minutes, then slice each roll into 3 smaller pieces.

Per Serving:(1 roll)

calories: 62 | fat: 4g | protein: 2g | carbs: 3g | fiber: 1g

Chocolate-Coconut-Pecan Chewy Bars

Prep time: 15 minutes | Cook time: 10 minutes |

Makes 8 bars

1 cup pitted dates, soaked in hot water for 10 minutes and drained

¼ cup brown rice syrup

⅓ cup plus ¼ cup chopped pecans

1½ cups old-fashioned rolled oats

⅓ cup mini chocolate chips

⅓ cup unsweetened shredded coconut

1. Preheat the oven to 300ºF (150ºC). Line a 9-inch square baking dish with parchment paper. 2. Pulse, then process the dates in a food processor until smooth. Transfer to a large bowl, then stir in the brown rice syrup. 3. Process ¼ cup of the pecans and ½ cup of the oats in the now-empty food processor until finely ground. Add to the bowl with the dates, then fold in the remaining pecans, remaining oats, the chocolate chips, and coconut. (The dates and syrup make this thick so you'll need to use some muscle to fold the ingredients.) 4. Transfer to the dish. Bake for 10 minutes, or until fragrant and golden brown. Allow to cool completely, then slice into 8 bars using a sharp knife and serve. 5. Store in an airtight container for up to 1 week. Individual bars can be wrapped in parchment and taken on the go.

Per Serving:(1 bar)

calories: 293 | fat: g | protein: 3g | carbs: 51g | fiber: 4g

Miso Nori Chips

Prep time: 10 minutes | Cook time: 15 minutes |

Makes 48 chips

6 tablespoons almond or cashew butter

¼ cup unpasteurized chickpea miso or sweet white miso

4 teaspoons mirin

1 tablespoon melted extra-

virgin coconut oil (optional)

1 tablespoon filtered water

8 sheets nori

½ cup raw unhulled sesame seeds, toasted

1. Preheat your oven to 300ºF (150ºC) and line a rimmed baking sheet with parchment paper. Set aside. 2. In a small bowl, mix together the nut butter, miso, mirin, oil, and water until smooth. Place one sheet of nori on a cutting board and spread 3 tablespoons of the miso mixture evenly over it, all the way to the edges. Sprinkle 2 tablespoons of sesame seeds on top, place another nori sheet on top, and press down to seal. Cut the stacked nori lengthwise in half, then crosswise into 6 strips to get 12 pieces. Arrange them on the prepared baking sheet and repeat with the remaining nori and miso mixture.

3. Bake for 10 to 15 minutes until the nori is crinkled. The chips will become crisp as they cool. Remove from the oven and allow to cool. Store the chips in an airtight container for up to 2 weeks.

Per Serving:(2 chips)

calories: 50 | fat: 4g | protein: 1g | carbs: 3g | fiber: 1g

Pump Up the Power Energy Balls

Prep time: 20 minutes | Cook time: 0 minutes |

Makes 32 balls

1 cup old-fashioned oats

¾ cup almond meal

⅓ cup wheat germ

¼ cup flaxseed meal

¼ cup pepitas

2 tablespoons raw shelled hempseed

1 teaspoon ground cinnamon

¼ teaspoon ground nutmeg

½ cup dried currants

½ cup peanut butter

⅓ cup maple syrup (optional)

1 teaspoon vanilla extract

¼ teaspoon salt (optional)

1. Mix the oats, almond meal, wheat germ, flaxseed meal, pepitas, hempseed, cinnamon, nutmeg, and currants together in a medium bowl. 2. Add the peanut butter, maple syrup, vanilla, and salt (if desired) to the bowl of a stand mixer. Mix on medium speed until well combined. Pour the dry ingredients into the wet mixture. Mix on low until well combined. 3. Roll into thirty-two balls.

Per Serving:(3 balls)

calories: 168 | fat: 8g | protein: 10g | carbs: 22g | fiber: 4g

Quick and Easy Falafel Pitas

Prep time: 5 minutes | Cook time: 20 minutes |

Makes 4 wraps

Olive oil cooking spray

1 (15 ounces / 425 g) can chickpeas, drained and rinsed

1 garlic clove, minced

2 tablespoons minced fresh parsley, or 2 teaspoons dried parsley

½ teaspoon salt (optional)

½ teaspoon ground cumin

3 tablespoons whole-wheat

flour

½ teaspoon baking soda

4 (6-inch) whole-wheat pita breads

8 tablespoons store-bought hummus

3 ounces (85 g) spring mix or arugula (3 to 4 cups)

2 tomatoes, cut into slices

1. Preheat the oven to 400ºF (205ºC). Spray a sheet pan with cooking spray. 2. In a large bowl, mash the chickpeas with a fork or potato masher. Add the garlic, parsley, salt (if using), cumin, flour, and baking soda and mix well to form a crumbly and sticky mixture. 3. Using your hands, form the mixture into 8 balls, using about 2 tablespoons for each one, and put them on the prepared baking sheet. Bake for 10 minutes. Using tongs, carefully turn the balls and continue to bake for another 10 minutes. 4. To warm the pita breads, place them directly on a rack in the oven and bake for 2 minutes, until they are more pliable. 5. To assemble, spread 2 tablespoons of hummus in the middle of each pita and top with spring mix, sliced tomatoes, and 2 falafel balls. Fold the pita around the fillings.

Per Serving:

calories: 341 | fat: 6g | protein: 14g | carbs: 62g | fiber: 11g

Crispy Baked Chickpeas

Prep time: 5 minutes | Cook time: 25 minutes |
Makes 1½ cups

1 (15 ounces / 425 g) can
chickpeas, drained and rinsed
1 tablespoon extra-virgin olive
oil (optional)

½ teaspoon smoked paprika
½ teaspoon salt
¼ teaspoon garlic powder

1. Preheat the oven to 425°F (220°C). 2. In a medium bowl, combine chickpeas, olive oil, smoked paprika, salt, and garlic powder. 3. Toss until well coated. 4. Spread seasoned chickpeas on a sheet pan and bake for 15 minutes.
5. Turn the chickpeas using a spatula and bake for another 10 minutes or until crispy.

Per Serving:

calories: 147 | fat: 6g | protein: 5g | carbs: 18g | fiber: 5g

Overnight Cookie Dough Oats

Prep time: 10 minutes | Cook time: 0 minutes |
Serves 2

1 cup almond milk
½ cup quick or rolled oats
2 scoops vanilla flavor vegan
protein powder
1 tablespoon flaxseeds

1 tablespoon peanut butter
1 tablespoon maple syrup
(optional)
1 tablespoon carob chips
(optional)

1. In a lidded bowl or jar, combine oats, flaxseed, protein powder, and almond milk. 2. Stir until well combined and the mixture is runny. 3. Add peanut butter and mix well. 4. Close the lid and refrigerate overnight or for at least five hours. 5. Serve the oats, optionally topped with carob chips and a drizzle of maple syrup.

Per Serving:

calories: 316 | fat: 11g | protein: 31g | carbs: 23g | fiber: 4g

Green Energy Bites

Prep time: 15 minutes | Cook time: 0 minutes |
Makes 36 bites

1½ cups pitted dates, soaked
in hot water for 5 minutes and
drained
½ cup raw sunflower seeds
½ cup roasted, unsalted
cashews

¼ cup carob or chocolate chips
2 tablespoons spirulina powder
or another greens powder
2 tablespoons unsweetened
shredded coconut
Pinch of salt (optional)

1. Place the dates in a food processor and pulse until they become a paste. Next, add the cashews and sunflower seeds and pulse until they are roughly chopped. Include the spirulina and carob and pulse a few times before processing until everything is well combined. 2.

Line a rectangular glass dish with parchment paper and transfer the mixture into it. Use a small piece of parchment paper to press the mixture down, preventing your fingers from sticking to the bars. If desired, sprinkle with coconut and salt. 3. Pull the parchment paper out of the container and slice the mixture into 36 pieces. Store the bars in an airtight container for a maximum of one week or freeze for up to three months.

Per Serving:(4 bites)

calories: 192 | fat: 9g | protein: 4g | carbs: 26g | fiber: 2g

Mexikale Crisps

Prep time: 10 minutes | Cook time: 15 minutes |
Serves 2

8 cups large kale leaves,
chopped
2 tablespoons avocado oil
(optional)
2 tablespoons nutritional yeast
1 teaspoon garlic powder

1 teaspoon ground cumin
½ teaspoon chili powder
1 teaspoon dried oregano
1 teaspoon dried cilantro
Salt and pepper to taste
(optional)

To start, preheat your oven to 350°F (180°C) and line a baking tray with parchment paper. Set it aside. 2. Ensure that any excess water is removed from the chopped kale leaves by using paper towels. Place the leaves in a large bowl and mix in the avocado oil, yeast, and seasonings. Shake everything well before adding more yeast and seasonings if desired. Mix all the ingredients again. 3. Spread the kale chips out on the baking tray and bake them in the oven for 10 to 15 minutes. Check on them every minute after the 10-minute mark until they reach your preferred level of crispiness. Once done, remove the tray from the oven and set it aside to cool. 4. You can now serve and enjoy your kale chips, or store them in a container for later!

Per Serving:

calories: 313 | fat: 14g | protein: 12g | carbs: 33g | fiber: 7g

Kale Chips

Prep time: 5 minutes | Cook time: 20 minutes |
Serves 4

¼ cup vegetable broth
1 tablespoon nutritional yeast
½ teaspoon garlic powder

½ teaspoon onion powder
6 ounces (170 g) kale, stemmed
and cut into 2- to 3-inch pieces

1. Preheat the oven to 300°F (150°C). Line a baking sheet with parchment paper. 2. In a small bowl, mix together the broth, nutritional yeast, garlic powder, and onion powder. 3. Put the kale in a large bowl. Pour the broth and seasonings over the kale, and toss well to thoroughly coat. 4. Place the kale pieces on the baking sheet in an even layer. Bake for 20 minutes, or until crispy, turning the kale halfway through.

Per Serving:

calories: 41 | fat: 0g | protein: 4g | carbs: 7g | fiber: 2g

Peanut Butter Snack Squares

Prep time: 10 minutes | Cook time: 20 minutes |
Serves 8

½ cup coconut sugar (optional)
1 cup creamy peanut butter
1 teaspoon vanilla extract
¾ cup whole wheat flour
¼ cup garbanzo flour
1 teaspoon baking soda

½ teaspoon baking powder
1 cup old-fashioned oats
½ cup dairy-free milk
½ cup peanuts
½ cup dates, pitted and chopped small

1.Preheat the oven to 350°F (180°C) and grease an 8-inch square baking dish.
2. Mix sugar (optional), peanut butter, vanilla, flours, baking soda, baking powder, and oats until well combined. 3. Fold in peanuts and dates. 4. Press the dough into the prepared dish and bake for 15 to 20 minutes until golden brown. 5. Cool on a wire rack, cut into squares, and store in the refrigerator.

Per Serving:(2 squares)
calories: 366 | fat: 17g | protein: 14g | carbs: 44g | fiber: 7g

Pressure Cooker Thai Nuggets

Prep time: 10 minutes | Cook time: 5 minutes | Serves 4

¾ cup plus 3 tablespoons vital wheat gluten
¼ cup chickpea flour
½ teaspoon ground ginger
½ teaspoon salt (optional)
¼ teaspoon garlic powder
¼ teaspoon paprika

¾ cup vegetable broth
2 teaspoons tamari, divided
4 teaspoons red curry paste, divided
1½ cups vegetable broth, divided

1. Add the gluten, flour, ginger, salt (if desired), garlic powder, and paprika to a large bowl. 2. Mix ¾ cup vegetable broth, 1 teaspoon tamari, and 2 teaspoons red curry paste in a small bowl. Pour the wet mixture into the dry ingredients. 3. Mix and then knead for about 2 to 3 minutes or until elastic. It's a very wet dough but you will see it is still elastic. It should be mildly stretchy and pull back but still pliable. Pinch off pieces of seitan dough into very small balls, about 1 to 1½ inches in diameter. They will fatten up when cooking. 4. Place in an electric pressure cooker. 5. Add 1½ cups vegetable broth, 1½ cups water, and 2 teaspoons red curry paste to a bowl and stir well. Pour over the nuggets in the pressure cooker. Close the lid, make sure the top knob is turned to sealing. Press Manual on the front of the pot. Push button to 4 (meaning 4 minutes). The pressure cooker will make a click and start to build pressure. It will take about 15 minutes to build pressure and cook. Leave the nuggets in the pot to set. They will cook more as the pressure is naturally releasing. Don't vent. 6. After about an hour, go ahead and vent. It may already have cooled completely, but vent to make sure the pressure has released and then open the lid. 7. Remove the nuggets from the liquid and set aside to cool. You can eat them right away, add to a recipe, or keep in the fridge overnight. They are great the next day. You can also freeze them.

Per Serving:
calories: 155 | fat: 2g | protein: 26g | carbs: 11g | fiber: 2g

White Bean Tzatziki Dip

Prep time: 10 minutes | Cook time: 1 to 2 hours |
Makes about 8 cups

4 (14½ ounces / 411 g) cans white beans, drained and rinsed
8 garlic cloves, minced
1 medium onion, coarsely chopped
¼ cup store-bought low-sodium vegetable broth, plus more as

needed
Juice from one lemon, divided
2 teaspoons dried dill, divided
Salt (optional)
1 cucumber, peeled and finely diced

1. Place the beans, garlic, onion, broth, and half the lemon juice in a blender. Blend until creamy, about 1 minute, adding up to ¼ cup of additional broth as needed to make the mixture creamy. 2. Transfer the mixture to the slow cooker, stir in 1 teaspoon of dill, and season with salt (if using). Cover and cook on Low for 1 to 2 hours until heated through. 3. Meanwhile, in a medium bowl, mix the cucumber with the remaining 1 teaspoon of dill and the remaining half of the lemon juice. Toss to coat. Season with salt (if using). 4. Spoon the dip from the slow cooker into a serving bowl and top with the cucumber mixture before serving.

Per Serving:
calories: 59 | fat: 0g | protein: 3g | carbs: 11g | fiber: 4g

Packed Peanut Oatmeal Cookies

Prep time: 15 minutes | Cook time: 11 minutes |
Serves 12

1 tablespoon chia seeds or ground chia seeds
1 cups whole wheat flour
1 teaspoon baking powder
1½ cups old-fashioned oats
2 tablespoons vanilla protein powder

½ cup dairy-free butter
1 cup coconut sugar (optional)
½ cup softened dairy-free cream cheese
1 teaspoon vanilla extract
1 banana
1 cup chopped peanuts

1. Preheat the oven to 400°F (205°C). Cut parchment paper to fit on a baking sheet. Set aside. 2. Mix the chia seeds with 3 tablespoons water and set aside. 3. Add the flour, baking powder, oats, and protein powder to a large bowl. Set aside. 4. Add the butter and sugar (if desired) to the bowl of a stand mixer. Cream on medium-low speed for 5 minutes. Add the cream cheese and mix well. Turn off the beater and add the prepared chia seed mixture, vanilla, and banana. Mix well on medium speed. Add the dry ingredients and peanuts and keep mixing until just combined. 5. Spoon dollops on a cookie sheet 2 inches apart and flatten with the bottom of a glass to about ½-inch thick. Bake for 11 minutes. 6. Cool on a wire rack.

Per Serving:(2 squares)
cacalories: 233 | fat: 14g | protein: 9g | carbs: 22g | fiber: 6g

Tempeh Chickpea Stuffed Mini Peppers

Prep time: 20 minutes | Cook time: 0 minutes |
Serves 6

12 ounces (340 g) multi-colored sweet mini peppers
2 (15 ounces / 425 g) cans chickpeas, drained and rinsed
¾ cup tempeh, chopped
½ cup dairy-free mayonnaise

¼ cup cider vinegar
1 teaspoon ground mustard
3 scallions, thinly sliced
1 teaspoon salt (optional)
¼ teaspoon cayenne pepper

1. Cut off the stem end of the peppers. Slice lengthwise. Remove any seeds that are inside. Set aside. 2. Place all the remaining ingredients in a food processor. Pulse four or five times. The chickpeas should be chunky. Remove the blade and stir to make sure the mixture is blended well. 3. Stuff each pepper half full with about 2 tablespoons of the chickpea mixture. Set on a plate to serve.

Per Serving:(2 mini peppers)
calories: 231 | fat: 11g | protein: 10g | carbs: 25g | fiber: 6g

Avomame Spread

Prep time: 10 minutes | Cook time: 0 minutes |
Makes 1½ cups

1 cup frozen shelled edamame beans, thawed
1 tablespoon apple cider vinegar, or lemon juice, or lime juice
1 tablespoon tamari or soy

sauce
1 teaspoon grated fresh ginger
1 avocado, coarsely chopped
¼ cup fresh cilantro, basil, mint, or parsley, chopped
½ cup alfalfa sprouts (optional)

1. f you have a food processor, pulse the beans with some water and apple cider vinegar until they are roughly chopped. In case you don't have a food processor, thaw the beans and chop them finely. 2. Next, add tamari, ginger, and avocado to the mixture and blend everything until it becomes a smooth purée. Then, include the cilantro and sprouts (if preferred) and blend again until everything is smooth. If you don't have a food processor, mash the avocado and finely chop the remaining ingredients to mix them together.

Per Serving:
calories: 265 | fat: 18g | protein: 11g | carbs: 17g | fiber: 11g

Emerald Green Gem

Prep time: 15 minutes | Cook time: 0 minutes |
Serves 1

1 cup fresh spinach
½ cup water
1 orange, peeled

½ banana, peeled
¼ avocado, peeled
½ cup frozen peaches

1. In a high-powered blender, mix the spinach, water, and orange

until smooth and juice-like. Add the banana, avocado, and peaches, and mix again. 2. Serve over ice, if desired.

Per Serving:
calories: 235 | fat: 8g | protein: 4g | carbs: 42g | fiber: 10g

Oatmeal Granola Bar Bites

Prep time: 5 minutes | Cook time: 25 minutes |
Serves 12

1½ cups rolled oats
⅓ cup unsweetened applesauce
¼ cup unsweetened natural peanut butter
2 tablespoons pure maple syrup
2 tablespoons ground flaxseed
1 tablespoon finely chopped

pecans
1 tablespoon sliced almonds
1 tablespoon unsweetened raisins
1 tablespoon mini vegan chocolate chips

1. Preheat the oven to 350ºF (180ºC). Line an 8-by-8-inch baking dish and a baking sheet with parchment paper. 2. In a large bowl, using a wooden spoon or rubber spatula, mix together the oats, applesauce, peanut butter, maple syrup, flaxseed, pecans, almonds, raisins, and chocolate chips. 3. Using the back of a measuring cup, firmly press the mixture into the prepared baking dish. 4. Lift the pressed mixture out, and cut into 12 equal pieces. 5. Place the cut pieces in single layer on the prepared baking sheet. 6. Transfer the baking sheet to the oven, and bake for 20 to 25 minutes, flipping halfway through, or until the bars are golden brown. Remove from the oven.

Per Serving:
calories: 98 | fat: 5g | protein: 3g | carbs: 12g | fiber: 2g

Guacamole

Prep time: 10 minutes | Cook time: 0 minutes |
Makes 2 cups

3 to 4 small avocados or 2 large avocados, diced
½ tablespoon lemon or lime juice
¼ cup finely diced red, white, or yellow onion

1 teaspoon minced garlic
¾ teaspoon ground cumin
2 tablespoons chopped cilantro
½ medium tomato, chopped
Pinch of salt (optional)
Freshly ground pepper, to taste

1. In a medium bowl, mash the avocados with a fork to the desired consistency. 2. Add the lemon (or lime) juice, onion, garlic, cumin, cilantro, tomato, salt (if desired), and pepper, and mix well.

Per Serving:
calories: 249 | fat: 22g | protein: 4g | carbs: 15g | fiber: 10g

Chapter 7 Vegetables and Sides

Creamy Curried Potatoes and Peas

Prep time: 15 minutes | Cook time: 30 minutes |
Serves 4

1 tablespoon extra-virgin olive oil (optional)
8 small red potatoes (about 1 pound / 454 g), diced small
3 garlic cloves, minced
1 (2-inch) piece fresh ginger, peeled and minced
1 small yellow onion, cut into ¼-inch pieces
3 teaspoons curry powder
2 cups water
1 cup frozen peas
3 tablespoons tomato paste
1 teaspoon salt, plus more as needed (optional)
Black pepper
Red pepper flakes (optional)
¼ cup chopped fresh cilantro, for garnish

1. Heat oil in a large saucepan or wok over medium heat. Add the potatoes and cook while stirring often until they start to brown, which should take around 10 minutes. Push the potatoes to one side of the pan, then add garlic, ginger, and onion. Cook while stirring occasionally until the mixture becomes very fragrant, which should take about 5 minutes. Stir the onion mixture with the potatoes until it is well combined. 2. Add curry powder and water to the pan and stir until everything is well combined. Increase the heat to high and bring the mixture to a boil. Lower the heat to medium and cook while stirring occasionally until the potatoes become fork-tender, which should take around 10 to 15 minutes. 3. Stir in peas, tomato paste, and salt (if using) and cook while stirring occasionally until the liquid reduces to a creamy sauce, which should take around 4 to 5 minutes. 4. Taste the curry and season it with salt (if using) and black pepper as desired. Sprinkle red pepper flakes (if using) and cilantro on top before serving.

Per Serving:
calories: 323 | fat: 4g | protein: 9g | carbs: 65g | fiber: 9g

Crispy Maple Mustard Cabbage

Prep time: 5 minutes | Cook time: 40 minutes |
Serves 6

2 tablespoons virgin olive oil (optional)
1 tablespoon grainy mustard
1½ teaspoons pure maple syrup (optional)
½ head large cabbage or 1 small whole cabbage
Salt and pepper, to taste (optional)

1. Preheat your oven to 400ºF (205ºC). 2. In a small bowl, whisk together olive oil, grainy mustard, and maple syrup (if using). 3. Cut the cabbage into 1-inch wedges. Remove most of the core,

leaving a thin strip intact so that the wedge holds together through the roasting process. 4. Place the cabbage wedges on a large baking sheet. Brush the side facing up with the olive oil mixture. Season with salt and pepper (if desired). Roast in the preheated oven for 20 minutes. 5. Carefully flip the cabbage wedges over with a spatula. Brush them with the remaining olive oil mixture. Return the baking sheet to the oven and roast for another 20 minutes or until the cabbage wedges are quite browned and have crispy edges. 6. Serve the roasted cabbage warm and enjoy!

Per Serving:
calories: 75 | fat: 5g | protein: 2g | carbs: 8g | fiber: 2g

Spring Steamed Vegetables with Savory Goji Berry Cream

Prep time: 15 minutes | Cook time: 10 minutes |
Serves 6

Savory Goji Berry Cream:
¼ cup dried goji berries
1 tablespoon apple cider vinegar
1 tablespoon mellow or light miso
1 tablespoon fresh lemon juice
1 (1-inch) piece of fresh ginger, peeled and chopped
1 teaspoon pure maple syrup (optional)
3 tablespoons virgin olive oil
(optional)
Salt and pepper, to taste (optional)
Vegetables:
1½ pounds (680 g) trimmed spring vegetables
Salt and pepper, to taste (optional)
Garnishes:
Scant ¼ cup walnut halves, toasted and chopped
1 green onion, thinly sliced

1. Place the goji berries in a small bowl and pouring boiling water over them. Allow the berries to sit for about 5 minutes until they become plump and soft. 2. Transfer the goji berries to a blender, making sure to reserve the soaking water. Add apple cider vinegar, miso, lemon juice, ginger, maple syrup, olive oil, salt, and pepper (if desired) to the blender along with 3 tablespoons of the goji soaking water. Blend the mixture on high until it becomes creamy and smooth. Set aside. 3.Trim them as needed and place a large pot with about an inch of water on the stove. Bring the water to a simmer and arrange the vegetables in a steamer basket before setting it into the pot. Cover and steam the vegetables until they are just tender, which should take around 8 minutes.
4. arrange the steamed vegetables on a serving platter and top them with the Savory Goji Berry Cream. Garnish with chopped walnuts and sliced green onions.

Per Serving:
calories: 136 | fat: 9g | protein: 5g | carbs: 17g | fiber: 5g

Glowing, Fermented Vegetable Tangle

Prep time: 15 minutes | Cook time: 0 minutes
|Makes 2 quarts

1 fennel bulb, cored
1 head green cabbage, quartered cored and save the flexible outer leaves
6 medium carrots, shredded
2 medium beets, shredded
2 apples, peeled, cored and shredded
1 (2-inch) piece of fresh ginger,

peeled and finely grated
1 (2-inch) piece of fresh turmeric root, peeled and finely grated or 2 teaspoons turmeric powder
2 teaspoons cumin seeds
2 teaspoons chili flakes
Sea salt, to taste (optional)

1. Using a mandoline, slice the fennel and cabbage thinly into a large bowl. Next, add in the carrots, beets, apples, ginger, turmeric, cumin seeds, and chili flakes. Sprinkle sea salt generously over the mixture and use your hands to massage the vegetables for at least 5 minutes until liquid pools at the bottom of the bowl. Wear gloves to prevent turmeric stains on your hands. 2. Transfer the vegetable mixture into jars with tight-fitting lids, pressing down firmly with a spatula or your hands to ensure that the liquid covers the surface. Leave about an inch of space at the top of each jar. Cover the top of each jar with a flexible cabbage leaf and press down again before securing the lid. 3. To avoid any staining from the liquid, place the jars in plastic bags and tie knots at the top. Store the jars somewhere out of the way, such as a basement, and mark your calendar to check on them in 3 weeks. The vegetables should have a lightly sour and tangy taste with some texture when bitten. 4. Once the vegetables are ready, remove the cabbage leaf toppers and store the jars in the refrigerator.

Per Serving:(½ quart)

calories: 187 | fat: 1g | protein: 6g | carbs: 44g | fiber: 14g

Lemony Roasted Cauliflower with Coriander

Prep time: 15 minutes | Cook time: 50 minutes |
Serves 6

1 medium cauliflower, cut into 1-inch florets
¼ cup raw cashew butter
2 tablespoons filtered water
Grated zest of 1 lemon
2 tablespoons freshly squeezed lemon juice
2 tablespoons melted extra-

virgin coconut oil (optional)
2 teaspoons ground coriander
1 teaspoon fine sea salt (optional)
1 large garlic clove, grated or pressed
¼ teaspoon ground turmeric

1. Preheat your oven to 400°F (205°C). Line a rimmed baking sheet with parchment paper and set it aside. 2. Set up a steamer and fill the pot with about 1 inch of filtered water. Bring it to a boil over high heat and place the steamer basket in position. Arrange the cauliflower evenly in the basket and steam for 5 minutes or until a knife slides easily into a floret. Transfer the cauliflower to a bowl and set it aside. 3. In a small bowl, combine cashew butter, water, lemon zest, and lemon juice. Stir everything together until smooth. Add coconut oil, coriander, salt (if desired), garlic, and turmeric. Mix everything well to combine. Pour the mixture over the cauliflower and use your hands to gently and thoroughly mix, ensuring that every floret is thoroughly coated. 4. Spread the cauliflower out on the parchment-lined baking sheet and roast for 20 to 25 minutes until it is browned on the bottom. Remove it from the oven and turn each piece over. Roast for another 10 to 15 minutes until it is golden brown. 5. Serve the roasted cauliflower warm. It is best served right away, but any leftovers can be stored in an airtight container in the fridge for 2 to 3 days.

Per Serving:

calories: 130 | fat: 10g | protein: 4g | carbs: 9g | fiber: 2g

Braised Red Cabbage with Beans

Prep time: 25 minutes | Cook time: 38 minutes |
Serves 4

1 large yellow onion, peeled and diced
2 large carrots, peeled and diced
2 celery stalks, diced
2 teaspoons thyme
1½ cups red wine
2 tablespoons Dijon mustard
1 large head red cabbage, cored

and shredded
4 cups cooked navy beans, or 2 (15 ounces / 425 g) cans, drained and rinsed
2 tart apples (such as Granny Smith), peeled, cored, and diced
Salt and freshly ground black pepper, to taste

1. In a large saucepan, sauté the onion, carrots, and celery over medium heat for 7 to 8 minutes. If needed, add water in small increments (1 to 2 tablespoons) to prevent the vegetables from sticking to the pan. Stir in the thyme, red wine, and mustard, and continue cooking until the wine is reduced by half, which should take about 10 minutes. 2. Add the cabbage, beans, and apples to the pan, and cover it while cooking until the cabbage becomes tender, approximately 20 minutes. Season with salt and pepper to taste.

Per Serving:

calories: 315 | fat: 1g | protein: 14g | carbs: 60g | fiber: 20g

Daikon Beet Pickle with Lime

Prep time: 5 minutes | Cook time: 0 minutes | Serves 6

1 medium-large daikon radish, peeled
2 small beets, peeled
¼ cup freshly squeezed lime

juice, or more to taste
1 teaspoon fine sea salt, or more to taste (optional)

1. Using a mandoline or sharp knife, thinly shave the daikon and beets. Transfer them to a medium-sized bowl. 2. Add lime juice and salt (if using) to the bowl containing the shaved daikon and beets. Mix everything well to combine. 3. If needed, add more lime juice or salt to taste. 4. You can serve the dish immediately or store it in a jar in the fridge for up to 2 weeks.

Per Serving:

calories: 15 | fat: 0g | protein: 0g | carbs: 4g | fiber: 1g

Sheet-Pan Garlicky Kale

Prep time: 5 minutes | Cook time: 15 minutes |

Serves 2

2 garlic cloves, minced
2 teaspoons extra-virgin olive oil (optional)
1 bunch kale, roughly chopped

¼ teaspoon salt (optional)
¼ teaspoon black pepper
¼ teaspoon garlic powder

1. Preheat your oven to 400°F (205°C). 2. In a large bowl, combine garlic, olive oil, kale, salt (if desired), black pepper, and garlic powder. Toss everything together until well combined. 3. Spread the kale out on a sheet pan and bake in the preheated oven for 10 minutes. 4. Use a spatula to turn the kale over and continue baking for another 5 minutes until it is wilted and bright green. 5. Remove the kale from the oven and serve immediately as a side dish or snack. Enjoy!

Per Serving:

calories: 144 | fat: 6g | protein: 9g | carbs: 19g | fiber: 7g

Beet Sushi and Avocado Poke Bowls

Prep time: 20 minutes | Cook time: 20 minutes |

Serves 2

2 red beets, trimmed and peeled
3 cups water
2 teaspoons low-sodium soy sauce or gluten-free tamari
½ teaspoon wasabi paste (optional)
1 tablespoon maple syrup (optional)
1 teaspoon sesame oil (optional)
1 teaspoon rice vinegar
1 cup frozen shelled edamame

1 cup cooked brown rice
1 cucumber, peeled and cut into matchsticks
2 carrots, cut into matchsticks
1 avocado, peeled, pitted, and sliced
1 scallion, green and white parts, chopped small, for garnish
2 tablespoons sesame seeds, for garnish (optional)

1. In a medium-sized saucepan, combine beets and water and bring to a boil over high heat. Reduce the heat to medium and cook until the beets are tender but not mushy, which should take around 15 minutes. Drain, rinse, and set them aside to cool. 2. In a small bowl, mix together soy sauce, wasabi (if using), maple syrup, sesame oil, and rice vinegar to make the dressing. Set it aside. 3. Once the beets have cooled, slide off their skins and cut them into very thin slices with a sharp knife to resemble tuna sashimi. Place the beet slices in a small bowl and top them with 1 teaspoon of the dressing. Set them aside to marinate. 4. Put the edamame in a microwave-safe bowl, add enough water to cover them, and cook them in the microwave for 1 minute. Drain and set them aside. 5. To assemble the bowls, divide the rice between two bowls. Top each bowl with sliced beets, cucumbers, carrots, edamame, and avocado. Drizzle the remaining dressing on top of each bowl. Garnish with scallions and sesame seeds (if desired). Enjoy your delicious and healthy beet sashimi bowl!

Per Serving:

calories: 488 | fat: 22g | protein: 16g | carbs: 63g | fiber: 18g

Grilled Cauliflower "Steaks" with Spicy Lentil Sauce

Prep time: 20 minutes | Cook time: 1 hour 14 minutes | Serves 4

2 medium heads cauliflower
2 medium shallots, peeled and minced
1 clove garlic, peeled and minced
½ teaspoon minced sage
½ teaspoon ground fennel
½ teaspoon crushed red pepper

flakes
½ cup green lentils, rinsed
2 cups vegetable stock, or low-sodium vegetable broth
Salt and freshly ground black pepper, to taste
Chopped parsley

1. Cut each cauliflower head in half through the stem of the vegetable, which holds the "steak" together. Trim each half so that you have a 1-inch-thick cutlet and place them on a baking sheet. Save any extra cauliflower florets for other uses. 2. In a medium saucepan, sauté the shallots over medium heat for 10 minutes. Add water 1 to 2 tablespoons at a time to prevent sticking. Add garlic, sage, fennel, crushed red pepper flakes, and lentils and cook for 3 minutes. Pour in the vegetable stock and bring the mixture to a boil over high heat. Reduce the heat to medium and cook, covered, for 45 to 50 minutes or until the lentils are very tender. Add water as needed to keep the mixture from drying out. 3. Using an immersion blender or a blender with a tight-fitting lid covered with a towel, purée the lentil mixture. Return the purée to the pan if necessary and season with salt and pepper. Keep warm. 4. Prepare the grill. 5. Place the cauliflower "steaks" on the grill and cook each side for about 7 minutes. 6. To serve, place the grilled "steaks" on a plate and spoon the sauce over them. Garnish with chopped parsley.

Per Serving:

calories: 132 | fat: 0g | protein: 8g | carbs: 25g | fiber: 5g

Sautéed Collard Greens

Prep time: 10 minutes | Cook time: 25 minutes |

Serves 4

1½ pounds (680 g) collard greens
1 cup vegetable broth
½ teaspoon garlic powder

½ teaspoon onion powder
⅛ teaspoon freshly ground black pepper

1. Remove the hard middle stems from the greens, then roughly chop the leaves into 2-inch pieces. 2. In a large saucepan, combine vegetable broth, garlic powder, onion powder, and pepper. Bring the mixture to a boil over medium-high heat, then add the chopped greens. Reduce the heat to low and cover. 3. Cook the greens for 20 minutes, stirring well every 4 to 5 minutes. If you notice that the liquid has completely evaporated and the greens are beginning to stick to the bottom of the pan, stir in a few extra tablespoons of vegetable broth or water. Once done, serve.

Per Serving:

calories: 28 | fat: 1g | protein: 3g | carbs: 4g | fiber: 2g

Sweet Potato Biscuits

Prep time: 5 minutes | Cook time: 10 minutes |
Makes 12 biscuits

1 medium sweet potato
3 tablespoons melted coconut oil, divided (optional)
1 tablespoon maple syrup

(optional)
1 cup whole-grain flour
2 teaspoons baking powder
Pinch sea salt (optional)

1. Bake the sweet potato at 350ºF (180ºC) for about 45 minutes, until tender. Allow it to cool, then remove the flesh and mash. 2. Turn the oven up to 375ºF (190ºC) and line a baking sheet with parchment paper or lightly grease it. 3. Measure out 1 cup potato flesh. In a medium bowl, combine the mashed sweet potato with 1½ tablespoons of the coconut oil and the maple syrup, if using. 4. Mix together the flour and baking powder in a separate medium bowl, then add the flour mixture to the potato mixture and blend well with a fork. 5. On a floured board, pat the mixture out into a ½-inch-thick circle and cut out 1-inch rounds, or simply drop spoonfuls of dough and pat them into rounds. Put the rounds onto the prepared baking sheet. Brush the top of each with some of the remaining 1½ tablespoons melted coconut oil. 6. Bake 10 minutes, or until lightly golden on top. Serve hot.

Per Serving:(1 biscuit)
calories: 77 | fat: 3g | protein: 1g | carbs: 10g | fiber: 1g

Fluffy Mashed Potatoes with Gravy

Prep time: 10 minutes | Cook time: 15 minutes |
Serves 6

Mashed Potatoes:
8 red or Yukon Gold potatoes, cut into 1-inch cubes
½ cup plant-based milk (here or here)
1 teaspoon garlic powder
1 teaspoon onion powder
Gravy:
2 cups vegetable broth, divided

¼ cup gluten-free or whole-wheat flour
½ teaspoon garlic powder
½ teaspoon onion powder
¼ teaspoon freshly ground black pepper
¼ teaspoon dried thyme
¼ teaspoon dried sage

Make Mashed Potatoes: 1. Bring a large stockpot of water to a boil over high heat, then gently and carefully immerse the potatoes. Cover, reduce the heat to medium, and boil for 15 minutes, or until the potatoes are easily pierced with a fork. 2. Drain the liquid, and return the potatoes to the pot. Using a potato masher or large mixing spoon, mash the potatoes until smooth. 3. Stir in the milk, garlic powder, and onion powder. Make Gravy: 1. Meanwhile, in a medium saucepan, whisk together ½ cup of broth and the flour. Once no dry flour is left, whisk in the remaining 1½ cups of broth. 2. Stir in the garlic powder, onion powder, pepper, thyme, and sage. Bring the gravy to a boil over medium-high heat, then reduce the heat to low. 3. Simmer for 10 minutes, stirring every other minute, and serve with the mashed potatoes.

Per Serving:
calories: 260 | fat: 1g | protein: 8g | carbs: 56g | fiber: 4g

Teriyaki Mushrooms

Prep time: 15 minutes | Cook time: 2 hours | Serves
4 to 6

2 (8 ounces / 227 g) packages whole cremini mushrooms
½ cup low-sodium soy sauce, tamari, or coconut aminos
¼ cup maple syrup (optional)
2 tablespoons rice vinegar
2 garlic cloves, minced

1 piece (1-inch) fresh ginger, peeled and minced, or 1 teaspoon ground ginger
2 tablespoons sesame seeds, divided
2 scallions, green and white parts, chopped, for serving

1. Put the mushrooms in the slow cooker. 2. In a measuring cup or medium bowl, combine the soy sauce, maple syrup (if using), rice vinegar, garlic, and ginger. Pour the sauce over the mushrooms and sprinkle with 1 tablespoon of sesame seeds. Cover and cook on High for 2 hours or on Low for 4 hours. 3. Serve the mushrooms garnished with the scallions and the remaining 1 tablespoon of sesame seeds.

Per Serving:
calories: 129 | fat: 3g | protein: 7g | carbs: 21g | fiber: 2g

Fennel and Cherry Tomato Gratin

Prep time: 15 minutes | Cook time: 55 minutes |
Serves 6

2 fennel bulbs, long fronds and top stalks trimmed off
1 cup whole cherry tomatoes
⅓ cup vegetable stock
2 tablespoons dry white wine
1 tablespoon virgin olive oil (optional)
2 teaspoons minced fresh thyme leaves
Salt and pepper, to taste

(optional)
Topping:
½ cup raw pine nuts
½ cup raw walnut halves
1 tablespoon virgin olive oil
1 tablespoon nutritional yeast
½ teaspoon garlic powder
2 teaspoons minced fresh thyme leaves

1. Preheat the oven to 375ºF (190ºC). 2.Cut the fennel bulbs into 2-inch wedges, removing pieces of the core as you go. Arrange the fennel wedges facing up in a 13- × 9-inch glass or metal baking dish. 3. Place the tomatoes in the crevices between the fennel wedges in the pan. Carefully pour the vegetable stock and white wine into the pan so that they distribute evenly. Drizzle the olive oil over the fennel wedges. Season the fennel with minced thyme and salt and pepper (if desired). Cover the dish tightly with foil and bake in the oven for 35 minutes. 4. While the gratin is baking, make the topping. In the bowl of a food processor, combine pine nuts, walnut halves, olive oil, nutritional yeast, garlic powder, and minced thyme. Pulse until you have a crumbly topping that holds together in small chunks. 5. After baking for 35 minutes, remove the fennel from the oven. Remove the foil and sprinkle the topping all over the surface. Slide the gratin back into the oven and bake, uncovered, for another 20 minutes or until the topping is golden brown and the fennel is fork-tender. Serve the gratin hot.

Per Serving:
calories: 196 | fat: 16g | protein: 5g | carbs: 10g | fiber: 4g

Chickpea of the Sea Salad

Prep time: 15 minutes | Cook time: 4 hours | Serves 3 to 4

1 (1-pound / 454-g) bag dried chickpeas, rinsed and sorted to remove small stones and debris
7 cups water
¼ teaspoon baking soda
5 tablespoons plant-based mayonnaise
1 tablespoon yellow mustard
¼ cup diced dill pickles
¼ cup finely diced onions
1 celery stalk, diced
2 tablespoons rice vinegar
½ teaspoon kelp powder
Ground black pepper
Salt (optional)

1. Put the chickpeas, water, and baking soda in the slow cooker. Cover and cook on High for 4 hours or on Low for 8 to 9 hours. Strain and discard the liquid. 2. Transfer 2 cups of the cooked chickpeas to a food processor and pulse 5 to 10 times to break them up but not turn them to mush. Transfer the pulsed chickpeas to a medium bowl. Save the remaining chickpeas for another recipe. 3. Add the mayonnaise, mustard, pickles, onions, celery, vinegar, kelp powder, pepper, and salt (if using). Stir well to form a salad and chill until serving.

Per Serving:
calories: 313 | fat: 21g | protein: 8g | carbs: 25g | fiber: 7g

Mustard-Roasted Beets and Shallots with Thyme

Prep time: 10 minutes | Cook time: 45 minutes | Serves 4

8 medium mixed-color beets
8 large shallots
3 large garlic cloves, finely chopped
2 tablespoons coarsely chopped fresh thyme
3 tablespoons melted extra-
virgin coconut oil (optional)
3 tablespoons Dijon mustard
1 tablespoon black mustard seeds
1 tablespoon balsamic vinegar
1½ teaspoons fine sea salt (optional)

1. Preheat the oven to 400ºF (205ºC) and line a rimmed baking sheet with parchment paper. 2. Peel the beets and cut them into ½-inch wedges. Transfer the beet wedges onto the lined pan. Cut the shallots into 6 wedges each (or quarter any smaller ones) and add them to the pan along with the garlic and thyme. In a small bowl, stir together the oil, mustard, mustard seeds, balsamic vinegar, and salt (if desired), then drizzle the mixture over the vegetables. Use your hands to toss the vegetables until they are thoroughly coated, then spread them out in a single layer on the pan. 3. Roast the vegetables for 20 to 25 minutes, then stir them around and roast for an additional 20 minutes or until they are tender and have brown spots. Serve the roasted vegetables warm or at room temperature. Any leftovers can be stored in an airtight container in the refrigerator for up to 4 days.

Per Serving:
calories: 189 | fat: 11g | protein: 4g | carbs: 20g | fiber: 6g

Cumin-Citrus Roasted Carrots

Prep time: 10 minutes | Cook time: 30 minutes | Serves 6

8 large carrots, sliced into ½-inch rounds
¼ cup orange juice
¼ cup vegetable broth
1 teaspoon ground cumin
¼ teaspoon ground turmeric
Salt and black pepper (optional)
1 tablespoon fresh lime juice
Chopped flat-leaf parsley (optional)

1. Preheat the oven to 400ºF (205ºC). 2. Place the carrots in a large baking dish, then add the orange juice, broth, cumin, and turmeric. Season with salt and pepper, if desired. 3. Bake, uncovered, until the carrots are lightly browned and the juices have reduced slightly, about 30 minutes, stirring halfway through. Drizzle with the lime juice and parsley, if desired, and serve.

Per Serving:
calories: 47 | fat: 0g | protein: 1g | carbs: 11g | fiber: 3g

Savory Slow Cooker Stuffing

Prep time: 20 minutes | Cook time: 4 hours 45 minutes | Serves 5 to 7

Nonstick cooking spray (optional)
2 (12 ounces / 340 g) packages stuffing cubes (about 12 cups)
2 tablespoons ground flaxseed
5 tablespoons water
2 small or 1 large onion, diced (about 2 cups)
6 large celery stalks, diced (about 2 cups)
1 (8 ounces / 227 g) package
white button mushrooms, diced
2 teaspoons dried sage
1 teaspoon poultry seasoning
1 teaspoon marjoram
1 teaspoon crushed or ground fennel seed
⅓ cup chopped fresh parsley
Ground black pepper
Salt (optional)
3½ to 5 cups store-bought low-sodium vegetable broth, divided

1. Coat the inside of the slow cooker with cooking spray (if using) or line it with a slow cooker liner. Place the dry stuffing cubes in the slow cooker. In a small bowl, stir together the flaxseed and water to make 2 flax eggs. Set aside. 2. In a cast-iron or nonstick skillet over medium-high heat, dry sauté the onions, celery, and mushrooms for 5 to 7 minutes, or until the onions are translucent, adding a splash of water or broth to avoid sticking. Stir in the sage, poultry seasoning, marjoram, fennel seed, parsley, pepper, and salt (if using) and cook for another minute or so. Transfer the mixture to the slow cooker and add 3½ cups of broth, stirring to combine. Add more broth, ½ cup at a time, to achieve your desired consistency. 3. Cover and cook on High for 45 minutes, then turn the heat to Low and cook for 3 to 4 hours, until the stuffing reaches the consistency you prefer. Add more broth as needed during the cooking time for a moister stuffing.

Per Serving:
calories: 523 | fat: 7g | protein: 20g | carbs: 77g | fiber: 10g

Ultimate Veggie Wrap with Kale Pesto

Prep time: 20 minutes | Cook time: 10 minutes |

Serves 2

Kale Pesto:
¼ cup raw cashews, soaked at least 2 hours
1 cup kale, de-stemmed and coarsely chopped
1 clove garlic
½ teaspoon salt (optional)
2 tablespoons nutritional yeast
3 tablespoons extra virgin olive oil (optional)
Wrap:

½ cup broccoli florets
2 spinach tortillas
¼ cup grated carrots
¼ cup diced red onion
½ yellow bell pepper, diced
6 ounces (170 g) spinach
2 tablespoons raw shelled hempseed
2 tablespoons sunflower seed kernels

Make Kale Pesto: 1. Place the cashews, kale, garlic, and salt (if desired) in a small food processor. Process for about 30 seconds. Add the nutritional yeast and oil and process a few more seconds until well blended. Set aside. Assemble: 2. Add water to a medium saucepan with a steamer insert and bring to a boil. Add the broccoli to the insert and steam over boiling water for 10 minutes. Remove from steamer and set aside. 3. Lay out the spinach tortillas. Divide the kale pesto between the two tortillas and spread evenly, leaving about 1 inch around all edges. Divide the remaining ingredients in half and lay out each half next to each other and down the length of each tortilla. 4. Start to roll up snugly, without tearing the tortilla. Cut each tortilla in half and serve.

Per Serving:
calories: 554 | fat: 36g | protein: 24g | carbs: 34g | fiber: 8g

Fennel and Green Cabbage Kraut

Prep time: 10 minutes | Cook time: 0 minutes |

Makes 8 cups

1 medium green cabbage, cored and thinly sliced with 1 leaf reserved
1 large fennel bulb, trimmed, cored, and shaved on a

mandoline or thinly sliced
5 teaspoons fine sea salt (optional)
2 teaspoons fennel seeds

1. Combine the cabbage, shaved or sliced fennel, salt, if using, and fennel seeds in a large bowl and use clean hands to mix the vegetables together, squeezing and softening them until they are juicy and wilted. Transfer a handful of the mixture to a large widemouthed jar or a fermentation crock and press it down with your fist. Repeat with the remaining mixture, a handful at a time, and then add any liquid left in the bowl. The liquid should completely cover the mixture; if it does not, keep pressing the mixture down until it does. You should have at least 3 inches of headspace above the vegetables. Clean the edges of the jar or crock of any stray pieces of vegetable. 2. Place the reserved cabbage leaf on top of the vegetables. Add a weight, such as a small glass jar filled with water, a flat glass plate or lid, or a fermentation weight, to keep the vegetables submerged, then seal the jar or crock. Label and date it and put it in a cool, dark place for 10 days. 3. After

10 days, carefully remove the lid, as it might pop off because of the gases that have built up, then remove the weight and cabbage leaf and use a clean fork to remove a little of the kraut to taste. If the level of tanginess and complexity of flavor are to your liking, transfer the jar or crock to the fridge, or transfer the kraut to smaller jars and refrigerate. If not, replace the leaf and the weight, tighten the lid, set aside for a few more days, and taste again. Usually 2 to 3 weeks of fermentation results in a good flavor. The kraut will keep in the fridge for months. The flavor will continue to develop, but at a much slower rate.

Per Serving:(1 cup)
calories: 39 | fat: 0g | protein: 2g | carbs: 9g | fiber: 4g

Garlicky Winter Vegetable and White Bean Mash

Prep time: 20 minutes | Cook time: 25 minutes |

Serves 4

Vegetable and Bean Mash:
2 cups peeled and diced celery root
2 cups chopped cauliflower
1 cup chopped parsnips
5 cloves garlic, peeled
1 cup cooked and drained white beans, such as navy or cannellini
¾ cup unsweetened almond milk
1 teaspoon virgin olive oil (optional)
Salt and pepper, to taste (optional)
Mushroom Miso Gravy:

1 tablespoon virgin olive oil (optional)
5 cups sliced mushrooms
2 teaspoons chopped fresh thyme leaves
4 cloves garlic, minced
Salt and pepper, to taste (optional)
2 teaspoons balsamic vinegar
1¼ cups vegetable stock
1 tablespoon mellow or light miso
2 teaspoons arrowroot powder
Freshly ground black pepper, for serving (optional)

1. Make the Vegetable And Bean Mash: Place the diced celery root, cauliflower, parsnips, and garlic cloves in a medium saucepan. Cover the vegetables with cold water and then place the pot over medium heat. Bring to a boil and then simmer until the vegetables are tender, about 15 minutes. 2. Drain the vegetables and place them in the bowl of a food processor along with the white beans. Pulse the vegetables and beans a couple of times to lightly chop them. Add the almond milk, olive oil, salt, and pepper, if using. Run the motor on high speed until you have a creamy and smooth mixture. Keep it warm. 3. Make the Mushrom Miso Gravy: Heat the olive oil in a large sauté pan over medium heat. Add the mushrooms, and let them sit for 2 full minutes. Stir them up and let them sear for another full minute. Add the thyme and garlic, and stir. After the mushrooms start to glisten slightly, season them with salt and pepper, if using. Add the balsamic vinegar and stir. 4. In a small bowl, whisk together the vegetable stock, miso, and arrowroot powder until no lumps of miso remain. Pour this mixture into the pan with the mushrooms, and stir. 5. Bring the gravy to a light simmer, and cook until the gravy has thickened slightly. 6. Serve the Mushroom Miso Gravy piping hot on top of the vegetable mash. Sprinkle with freshly ground black pepper if you like.

Per Serving:
calories: 225 | fat: 6g | protein: 10g | carbs: 36g | fiber: 8g

Grilled Vegetable Kabobs

Prep time: 25 minutes | Cook time: 15 minutes |

Serves 6

½ cup balsamic vinegar
3 cloves garlic, peeled and minced
1½ tablespoons minced rosemary
1½ tablespoons minced thyme
Salt and freshly ground black pepper, to taste
1 green bell pepper, seeded and cut into 1-inch pieces

1 red bell pepper, seeded and cut into 1-inch pieces
1 pint cherry tomatoes
1 medium zucchini, cut into 1-inch rounds
1 medium yellow squash, cut into 1-inch rounds
1 medium red onion, peeled and cut into large chunks

1. Prepare the grill. 2. Soak 12 bamboo skewers in water for 30 minutes. 3. Combine the balsamic vinegar, garlic, rosemary, thyme, and salt and pepper in a small bowl. 4. Skewer the vegetables, alternating between different-colored vegetables for a nice presentation. Place the skewers on the grill and cook, brushing the vegetables with the vinegar mixture and turning every 4 to 5 minutes, until the vegetables are tender and starting to char, 12 to 15 minutes.

Per Serving:

calories: 50 | fat: 0g | protein: 1g | carbs: 10g | fiber: 2g

Roasted Cauliflower Bowls

Prep time: 10 minutes | Cook time: 20 minutes |

Serves 2

Cauliflower:
½ head cauliflower, cut into florets (about 2 cups)
1 tablespoon extra-virgin olive oil (optional)
¼ teaspoon black pepper
Juice of ½ lemon
½ teaspoon smoked paprika
1 tablespoon nutritional yeast
Garlic-Tahini Sauce:
1 jalapeño pepper, seeded
3 tablespoons tahini
2 garlic cloves

Juice of 1 lemon
½ teaspoon salt (optional)
3 tablespoons chopped cilantro
½ cup water
Serve:
2 cups arugula leaves (about 2 ounces / 57 g)
1 red bell pepper, seeded and thinly sliced
10 Kalamata olives, chopped
1 Persian cucumber, sliced
2 tablespoons sesame seeds
1 cup cooked brown rice

1. Preheat the oven to 425ºF (220ºC). 2. In a large bowl, mix together the cauliflower florets, olive oil, black pepper, lemon juice, smoked paprika, nutritional yeast, and salt (if desired) until they are evenly coated. Spread the cauliflower out in a single layer on a sheet pan and bake for 10 minutes. Using a spatula, turn the cauliflower over and continue baking for another 10 minutes. 3. While the cauliflower is roasting, make the Garlic-Tahini Sauce. Combine the jalapeño, tahini, garlic, lemon juice, salt (if desired), cilantro, and water in a blender, and blend until smooth and creamy. Transfer the sauce to a small bowl, cover, and refrigerate until needed. 4. When ready to serve, divide the arugula between two plates. Top each plate evenly with bell pepper, olives, and cucumbers. Add

the roasted cauliflower on top and serve with ½ cup of brown rice on the side. Sprinkle sesame seeds over everything and drizzle the sauce on top.

Per Serving:

calories: 439 | fat: 27g | protein: 11g | carbs: 43g | fiber: 9g

Indian Spiced Eggplant

Prep time: 20 minutes | Cook time: 25 minutes |

Serves 4

2 medium onions, peeled and diced
1 large red bell pepper, seeded and diced
2 medium eggplants, stemmed, peeled, and cut into ½-inch dice
2 large tomatoes, finely chopped
3 tablespoons grated ginger
2 teaspoons cumin seeds,

toasted and ground
1 teaspoon coriander seeds, toasted and ground
½ teaspoon crushed red pepper flakes
Pinch cloves
Salt, to taste (optional)
½ bunch cilantro, leaves and tender stems, finely chopped

1. Place the onions and red pepper in a large saucepan and sauté over medium heat for 10 minutes. Add water 1 to 2 tablespoons at a time to keep the vegetables from sticking to the pan. 2. Add the eggplant, tomatoes, ginger, cumin, coriander, crushed red pepper flakes, and cloves and cook until the eggplant is tender, about 15 minutes. Season with salt (if using) and serve garnished with the cilantro.

Per Serving:

calories: 111 | fat: 1g | protein: 4g | carbs: 25g | fiber: 9g

Blackened Sprouts

Prep time: 10 minutes | Cook time: 20 minutes |

Serves 4

1 pound (454 g) fresh Brussels sprouts, trimmed and halved
2 tablespoons avocado oil (optional)
Sea salt and ground black

pepper, to taste
1 cup walnut halves
1 tablespoon pure maple syrup (optional)

1. Preheat the oven to 425ºF (220ºC). Line a baking sheet with parchment paper or grease it well. 2. In a medium bowl, toss the sprouts with oil (if desired) and season with salt and pepper to taste. Arrange the sprouts in a single layer on the prepared baking sheet. 3. Roast the sprouts for approximately 20 minutes or until the edges start to blacken. 4. While the sprouts are roasting, place the walnuts in a separate bowl and drizzle them with maple syrup (if desired). Toss until the walnuts are well coated. During the last 3 minutes of roasting time for the sprouts, add the coated walnuts to the same baking sheet to toast and caramelize. 5. Once done, let the sprouts and walnuts cool slightly before serving.

Per Serving:

calories: 254 | fat: 20g | protein: 6g | carbs: 16g | fiber: 5g

Ratatouille

Prep time: 30 minutes | Cook time: 25 minutes | Serves 4

1 medium red onion, peeled and diced
1 medium red bell pepper, seeded and diced
1 medium eggplant, about 1 pound / 454 g, stemmed and diced

1 small zucchini, diced
4 cloves garlic, peeled and minced
½ cup chopped basil
1 large tomato, diced
Salt and freshly ground black pepper, to taste

1. Place the onion in a medium saucepan and sauté over medium heat for 10 minutes. Add water 1 to 2 tablespoons at a time to keep the onions from sticking to the pan. Add the red pepper, eggplant, zucchini, and garlic. Cook, covered, for 15 minutes, stirring occasionally. 2. Stir in the basil and tomatoes, and season with salt and pepper.

Per Serving:

calories: 34 | fat: 0g | protein: 1g | carbs: 7g | fiber: 2g

Vegetable Korma Curry

Prep time: 10 minutes | Cook time: 20 minutes | Serves 4

1 tablespoon extra-virgin olive oil (optional)
2 garlic cloves, minced
2 tablespoons minced fresh ginger
½ small yellow onion, diced small
1 medium sweet potato, peeled and cut into small cubes
½ head cauliflower, cut into small florets (about 2 cups)
3 medium tomatoes, diced small
Pinch of salt (optional)

2 cups water, divided
1 cup softened cashews
1 tablespoon curry powder
2 tablespoons tomato paste
½ cup frozen green beans
½ cup frozen peas
1 (15 ounces / 425 g) can light unsweetened coconut milk
2 cups cooked brown rice or quinoa, for serving
Chopped fresh cilantro, for garnish
Black pepper

1. In a large sauté pan, heat the oil over medium heat. Add the garlic, ginger, and onion and cook until browned and fragrant, about 5 minutes. Add the sweet potato, cauliflower, tomatoes, and salt (if using) and cook until the tomatoes begin to break down, about 5 minutes. Add 1 cup of water, stir until combined, and bring the mixture to a boil. Cook until the sweet potatoes are soft, about 10 minutes. 2. In a blender or food processor, combine the cashews with the remaining 1 cup water and blend until you have a smooth paste. 3. Add the blended cashews, curry powder, tomato paste, green beans, peas, and coconut milk to the pan and stir well to combine. Lower the heat to medium-low and simmer for 5 minutes. Taste and adjust the seasoning as desired. 4. Put ½ cup of rice into each serving bowl and top with the curry. Sprinkle with fresh cilantro and black pepper.

Per Serving:

calories: 535 | fat: 29g | protein: 14g | carbs: 55g | fiber: 8g

Shaved Fennel and Lemon Pickle

Prep time: 5 minutes | Cook time: 0 minutes | Serves 6

1 large fennel
3 tablespoons freshly squeezed lemon juice, or more to taste
¾ teaspoon fine sea salt, or more to taste (optional)

1. Begin by trimming off the stalks from the fennel bulbs. Quarter each bulb and remove any tough outer layers and cores. You can either use a mandoline to shave the fennel or slice it thinly with a sharp knife. Place the sliced fennel into a medium-sized bowl, add lemon juice and salt (if desired), and mix well to combine. Taste and adjust seasoning as needed with additional salt or lemon juice. 2. Serve immediately or store in a jar in the refrigerator for up to 1 week.

Per Serving:

calories: 14 | fat: 0g | protein: 1g | carbs: 3g | fiber: 1g

Roasted Carrots with Ginger Maple Cream

Prep time: 10 minutes | Cook time: 25 minutes | Serves 6

Carrots:
1 pound (454 g) medium carrots, cut into ½-inch batons
1 teaspoon minced fresh thyme leaves
2 teaspoons virgin olive oil (optional)
Salt and pepper, to taste (optional)
Ginger Maple Cream:

2 tablespoons raw cashew butter
1½ tablespoons filtered water
1 tablespoon pure maple syrup (optional)
1½ teaspoons fresh lemon juice
1 piece of fresh ginger, peeled and finely grated
Salt, to taste (optional)

1. Begin by preheating the oven to 400ºF (205ºC) and lining a baking sheet with parchment paper. 2. For the carrots, place them onto the prepared baking sheet and toss them with thyme, olive oil, salt, and pepper (if desired). Arrange the carrots in a single layer and slide the baking sheet into the oven. Roast the carrots until they are just tender, which should take about 25 minutes. Flip and toss the carrots at the halfway mark to ensure even cooking.
3. To make the Ginger Maple Cream, start by stirring the cashew butter and water together in a medium bowl until there are no large chunks of cashew butter left. Press the cashew butter against the side of the bowl and slowly work it into the water. Whisk in the maple syrup, lemon juice, and grated ginger. Season the cream with salt (if desired). 4. Once the carrots are done roasting, arrange them on a serving platter. Drizzle the Ginger Maple Cream over the carrots and serve warm.

Per Serving:

calories: 85 | fat: 4g | protein: 2g | carbs: 11g | fiber: 2g

Garlic Toast

Prep time: 5 minutes | Cook time: 5 minutes | Makes 1 slice

1 teaspoon coconut oil or olive oil (optional)
Pinch sea salt (optional)
1 to 2 teaspoons nutritional

yeast
1 small garlic clove, pressed, or
¼ teaspoon garlic powder
1 slice whole-grain bread

1. In a small bowl, mix together the oil, salt (if using), nutritional yeast, and garlic. 2. You can either toast the bread and then spread it with the seasoned oil, or brush the oil on the bread and put it in a toaster oven to bake for 5 minutes. If you're using fresh garlic, it's best to spread it onto the bread and then bake it.

Per Serving:

calories: 134 | fat: 5g | protein: 4g | carbs: 16g | fiber: 2g

Yellow Bell Pepper Boats

Prep time: 30 minutes | Cook time: 50 minutes | Serves 6

Bell Pepper Boats:
2 medium potatoes, halved
1 ear corn, kernels removed (about ½ cup)
½ small onion, peeled and finely chopped
1 small green bell pepper, seeded and finely chopped (about ¼ cup)
¼ teaspoon grated ginger
½ clove garlic, peeled and minced
½ teaspoon minced serrano chile, or to taste (for less heat, remove the seeds)

½ teaspoon salt, or to taste (optional)
1 teaspoon fresh lime juice
2 yellow bell peppers
¼ cup sunflower seeds, toasted
Hot Sauce:
1 large tomato, chopped (about 2 cups)
½ teaspoon cayenne pepper
½ teaspoon salt, or to taste (optional)
½ clove garlic, peeled and mashed to a paste
½ tablespoon finely chopped cilantro

Make the Bell Pepper Boats: 1. Preheat the oven to 350ºF (180ºC). 2. Boil the potatoes in a saucepan of water for 15 minutes over medium heat, until tender. Remove from the heat, drain, and let cool. Mash the potatoes in a mixing bowl. 3. Place the corn and 1 cup of water in a small pan. Cook on medium heat until the corn is tender, 5 to 7 minutes. Drain and add to the potatoes along with the onion, green pepper, ginger, garlic, serrano chile, salt (if using), and lime juice. Mix well. 4. Cut the yellow peppers into 3 long slices each, making boat shapes, and remove the seeds. Divide the potato mixture among the slices and, sprinkle with sunflower seeds. Bake, covered, for 30 to 35 minutes, until the yellow peppers are soft when poked with a fork. Make the Hot Sauce: 5. Purée the tomato in a blender. Add the purée to a saucepan with the cayenne pepper, salt (if using), and garlic, bring to a boil, and cook for 5 minutes. Reduce the heat to low and simmer for 5 more minutes. 6. To serve, spread the hot sauce on top of the baked bell peppers. Garnish with cilantro.

Per Serving:

calories: 138 | fat: 3g | protein: 4g | carbs: 25g | fiber: 4g

Vegetable Spring Rolls with Spicy Peanut Dipping Sauce

Prep time: 15 minutes | Cook time: 10 minutes | Serves 2

Spicy Peanut Dipping Sauce:
2 tablespoons defatted peanut powder
1 tablespoon maple syrup (optional)
1 tablespoon rice vinegar
½ teaspoon onion powder
½ teaspoon garlic powder
½ teaspoon red pepper flakes

Spring Rolls:
6 rice paper wraps
6 large lettuce leaves
1½ cups cooked brown rice
1 cup shredded carrots
1 bunch fresh cilantro
1 bunch fresh mint
1 bunch fresh basil

Make Spicy Peanut Dipping Sauce: 1. In a small saucepan over medium heat, combine the peanut powder, maple syrup (if desired), rice vinegar, onion powder, garlic powder, and red pepper flakes. Cook for 10 minutes, stirring occasionally. Remove the sauce from the heat, and set aside to cool. Make Spring Rolls: 1. Fill a shallow bowl or pan with warm water, and dip a rice paper wrap in the water for 10 to 15 seconds. Remove and place on a cutting board or other clean, smooth surface. 2. Lay a lettuce leaf down flat on a rice paper wrap, then add ¼ cup of brown rice, 2 to 3 tablespoons of shredded carrots, and a few leaves each of cilantro, mint, and basil. 3. Wrap the sides of the rice paper halfway into the center, then roll the wrap from the bottom to the top to form a tight roll. 4. Repeat for the remaining spring rolls. Serve with the sauce in a dipping bowl on the side.

Per Serving:

calories: 263 | fat: 3g | protein: 11g | carbs: 46g | fiber: 5g

Mango-Tempeh Wraps

Prep time: 15 minutes | Cook time: 10 minutes | Serves 6

2 (8 ounces / 227 g) blocks tempeh, drained and crumbled
1 tablespoon coconut oil (optional)
6 large lettuce leaves
2 medium ripe mangoes, peeled

and diced
¼ cup sweet chili sauce
1 tablespoon hoisin sauce
1 tablespoon garlic powder
¼ teaspoon lime juice
¼ teaspoon salt (optional)

1. Heat the coconut oil in a large skillet over medium heat. Cook the tempeh crumbles until browned, stirring constantly, for about 4 minutes and turn the heat down to low. Add the hoisin, garlic, salt (if desired), and lime juice; heat for an additional 2 minutes and set aside. 2. Cut the mangoes into ¼-inch cubes. Pour the sweet chili sauce into a small bowl and mix it with the mango cubes. 3. Scoop the cooked tempeh and divide it evenly between the lettuce leaves, using the leaves as wraps. Top the wraps with the chunks of mango and a bit of lime juice, and close the wraps. 4. Serve, share, or store!

Per Serving:

calories: 259 | fat: 8g | protein: 16g | carbs: 1g | fiber: 10g

Sautéed Root Vegetables with Parsley, Poppy Seeds, and Lemon

Prep time: 10 minutes | Cook time: 10 minutes |

Serves 4

2 tablespoons extra-virgin coconut oil (optional)
2 large garlic cloves, finely chopped
1 pound (454 g) root vegetables, grated
1 teaspoon fine sea salt, plus

more to taste (optional)
1 tablespoon poppy seeds
Grated zest of 1 small lemon
1 tablespoon freshly squeezed lemon juice
1½ cups fresh flat-leaf parsley leaves, coarsely chopped

1. Warm the oil in a large skillet over medium heat. Add the garlic and sauté for 1 minute, or until golden. Stir in the grated vegetables and salt, if using, and cook for 8 minutes, or until the vegetables are softened. Remove from the heat and stir in the poppy seeds, lemon zest, lemon juice, and parsley. Season to taste with more salt and serve warm or at room temperature. Any leftovers can be stored in an airtight container in the fridge for up to 3 days.

Per Serving:

calories: 130 | fat: 8g | protein: 2g | carbs: 14g | fiber: 4g

Fermented Carrots with Turmeric and Ginger

Prep time: 15 minutes | Cook time: 0 minutes |

Makes 8 cups

10 medium-large carrots, grated
½ medium cabbage, cored and thinly sliced with 1 leaf reserved
1 (3-inch) piece fresh turmeric, peeled and finely grated

1 (2-inch) piece fresh ginger, peeled and finely grated
1 small shallot, finely chopped
5 teaspoons fine sea salt (optional)

1. In a large bowl, combine the carrots, cabbage, turmeric, ginger, shallot, and salt (if desired). Use clean hands to mix the vegetables together, squeezing and softening them until they become juicy and wilted. Transfer a handful of the mixture at a time into a large widemouthed jar or fermentation crock, pressing down each layer well with your fist. Continue adding more of the carrot mixture until all of it is in the jar or crock. Ensure that the liquid completely covers the vegetables; if not, press down on the mixture until it does. If there isn't enough liquid, add cooled brine to cover. Leave at least 3 inches of headspace above the vegetables and clean any stray pieces of vegetable from the edges of the jar or crock. Place a reserved cabbage leaf on top of the vegetables, followed by a weight such as a small glass jar filled with water, a flat glass plate or lid, or a fermentation weight to keep the vegetables submerged. Seal the jar or crock, label it with the date, and place it in a cool, dark area for 10 days. 2. After 10 days, carefully remove the lid, as gases may have built up and could cause it to pop off. Remove the weight and cabbage leaf and use a clean fork to taste a little of the carrots. If the level of tanginess and complexity of flavor are to your liking, transfer the jar or crock to the refrigerator, or transfer the mixture to smaller jars and refrigerate. If not, replace the leaf and weight, tighten the lid, set aside for a few more days, and taste again. Typically, fermenting for 2 to 3 weeks results in a good flavor. The fermented carrots will keep in the fridge for months, and their flavor will continue to develop, albeit at a much slower rate.

Per Serving:(1 cup)

calories: 37 | fat: 0g | protein: 1g | carbs: 9g | fiber: 3g

Oven-Roasted Dijon Veggies

Prep time: 5 minutes | Cook time: 20 minutes |

Serves 4

½ large head cauliflower, cut into florets (about 2 cups)
½ large head broccoli, cut into florets (about 2 cups)
1 red or yellow bell pepper, seeded and cut into 2-inch-thick slices

2 carrots, peeled and cut into 1-inch rounds
1 teaspoon extra-virgin olive oil (optional)
1 teaspoon Dijon mustard
½ teaspoon salt (optional)

1. Preheat oven to 425ºF (220ºC). 2. In a large bowl, combine the cauliflower, broccoli, bell pepper, carrots, olive oil, Dijon mustard, and salt (if using) and toss until the veggies are well coated with seasonings. 3. Transfer the vegetables to a sheet pan and bake for 10 minutes. Using a spatula, turn the veggies and continue to bake for another 10 minutes, or until they are browned and slightly crispy outside and tender inside. Oven temperatures vary, so if your veggies are not done yet, continue to bake in increments of 5 minutes until cooked to your desired doneness.

Per Serving:

calories: 64 | fat: 1g | protein: 3g | carbs: 13g | fiber: 4g

Ugly Veggie Mash

Prep time: 10 minutes | Cook time: 25 minutes |

Serves 8

1 pound (454 g) parsnips, peeled, trimmed, and cut into 1-inch pieces
1 large rutabaga, peeled and chopped into 1-inch cubes

1 large celeriac, peeled using a paring knife and chopped into 1-inch cubes
2 cups vegetable broth
Salt and black pepper (optional)

1. Place the parsnips, rutabaga, and celeriac in a large pot with a tight-fitting lid. Add the broth, cover, and bring to a boil over high heat. Reduce the heat to low and cook until the vegetables are fork-tender and most of the liquid has evaporated, 20 to 25 minutes. 2. Mash with a potato masher or serving fork, season with salt and pepper, if desired and serve.

Per Serving:

calories: 82 | fat: 0g | protein: 2g | carbs: 19g | fiber: 5g

Grilled Eggplant "Steaks"

Prep time: 10 minutes | Cook time: 10 minutes | Serves 4

3 tablespoons balsamic vinegar
Juice of 1 lemon
2 tablespoons low-sodium soy sauce

Freshly ground black pepper, to taste
1 large eggplant, stemmed and cut into ¾-inch slices

1. Start by preparing the grill. 2. In a small bowl, combine balsamic vinegar, lemon juice, soy sauce, and pepper. 3. Brush both sides of the eggplant slices with the marinade. 4. Once the grill is hot, place the eggplant on it and cook for 4 to 5 minutes on each side, brushing periodically with additional marinade.

Per Serving:

calories: 51 | fat: 0g | protein: 2g | carbs: 11g | fiber: 4g

Spicy Miso-Roasted Tomatoes and Eggplant

Prep time: 25 minutes | Cook time: 50 minutes | Serves 6

1 medium eggplant, cut into 1 x 3-inch wedges
4 medium tomatoes, cut into 6 wedges each
1 medium yellow onion, cut into ¼-inch slices
3 tablespoons melted extra-virgin coconut oil or olive oil (optional)
2 tablespoons unpasteurized sweet white miso
2 tablespoons mirin, or 1 teaspoon maple syrup (optional)
1 tablespoon freshly squeezed lemon juice

1 large garlic clove, grated or pressed
1 teaspoon ground coriander
1 teaspoon red chili pepper flakes
½ teaspoon ground turmeric
½ teaspoon fine sea salt, plus more to taste (optional)
¾ cup cooked chickpeas, well drained
Chopped fresh flat-leaf parsley or cilantro leaves for garnish

1. Preheat your oven to 400ºF (205ºC). 2.Line a large baking sheet with parchment paper and place the eggplant, tomatoes, and onion on it. In a small bowl, combine oil, miso, mirin, lemon juice, garlic, coriander, red chili pepper flakes, turmeric, and salt (if desired). Stir until smooth and pour over the vegetables. Toss everything together until the vegetables are evenly coated. Spread them out on the pan, ensuring that they are almost in a single layer with just a few overlapping. 3. Roast the vegetables for 20 to 25 minutes or until they are browned on the bottom. Remove them from the oven and turn them over as best you can. If they are too juicy, you may end up just stirring them. Roast them for another 15 to 20 minutes until they are completely soft and browned in spots. Scatter chickpeas over the vegetables, sprinkle with a little more salt (if desired), and return to the oven for 5 more minutes to warm the chickpeas through. 4. Transfer the vegetables to a serving platter and top them with herbs. Serve the dish warm or at room temperature. Any leftovers can be stored in an airtight container in the fridge for up to 3 days.

Per Serving:

calories: 152 | fat: 8g | protein: 4g | carbs: 18g | fiber: 6g

Chapter 8 Stews and Soups

Cauliflower, Chickpea, Quinoa, and Coconut Curry

Prep time: 15 minutes | Cook time: 3 to 4 hours |
Serves 5 to 7

1 head cauliflower, cut into bite-size pieces (about 4 cups)
1 medium onion, diced
3 garlic cloves, minced
1 medium sweet potato (about ⅓ pound / 136 g), peeled and diced
1 (14½ ounces / 411 g) can chickpeas, drained and rinsed
1 (28 ounces / 794 g) can no-salt-added diced tomatoes
¼ cup store-bought low-sodium vegetable broth
¼ cup quinoa, rinsed
2 (15 ounces / 425 g) cans full-fat coconut milk
1 (1-inch) piece fresh ginger, peeled and minced
2 teaspoons ground turmeric
2 teaspoons garam masala
1 teaspoon ground cumin
1 teaspoon curry powder
Ground black pepper
Salt (optional)
½ bunch cilantro, coarsely chopped (optional)

1. Begin by placing cauliflower, onion, garlic, sweet potato, chickpeas, tomatoes, broth, quinoa, coconut milk, ginger, turmeric, garam masala, cumin, curry powder, pepper, and salt (if desired) in the slow cooker. 2. Cover the slow cooker and cook on High for 3 to 4 hours or on Low for 7 to 8 hours. Once done, stir in cilantro (if desired), reserving a couple of tablespoons to garnish each dish.

Per Serving:
calories: 503 | fat: 32g | protein: 11g | carbs: 48g | fiber: 12g

Black Bean Soup

Prep time: 15 minutes | Cook time: 15 minutes |
Serves 4

3 cups cooked or canned black beans
1 cup canned or fresh tomato cubes
4 cups vegetable stock
1 cup cooked or canned sweet corn
4 carrots, sliced
Optional Toppings:
Jalapeño slices
Fresh cilantro
Lemon slices

1. If using dry beans, start by soaking and cooking 1 cup of black beans. 2. Place a large pot over medium-high heat and add vegetable stock and black beans. 3. Bring the stock to a boil, then reduce the heat to a simmer for about 10 minutes. 4. Add tomato cubes, corn, and carrot slices to the pot, stirring well, and let it simmer for another 5 minutes. 5. Turn off the heat and allow the

soup to cool for 5 minutes. 6. Divide the soup between two bowls, serve with optional toppings, and enjoy!7. Store any leftover soup in an airtight container in the fridge and consume within 2 days. Alternatively, store in the freezer for a maximum of 60 days and thaw at room temperature. The soup can be reheated in a pot or microwave.

Per Serving:
calories: 233 | fat: 1g | protein: 14g | carbs: 41g | fiber: 14g

Tofu Noodle Soup with Coconut Lemongrass Broth

Prep time: 15 minutes | Cook time: 10 minutes |
Serves 6

4 cups vegetable stock
2 stalks fresh lemongrass, chopped
1 cup full-fat coconut milk
1 cup tightly packed fresh cilantro leaves
Salt and pepper, to taste
1 tablespoon virgin coconut oil (optional)
1 medium shallot, small diced
1 small green chili pepper, seeded and minced
1 (2-inch) piece fresh ginger,
peeled and minced
1 cup snow peas
1½ cups small broccoli florets
1 block (14 ounces / 397 g) extra-firm tofu, drained and cut into ½-inch cubes
1 teaspoon gluten-free tamari soy sauce
2 tablespoons fresh lime juice
Serve:
Cooked rice or rice noodles
Lime wedges

1. Start by bringing vegetable stock and chopped lemongrass to a boil in a large pot. Remove from heat and allow the lemongrass to steep for 10 minutes. Strain the broth and discard the lemongrass. 2. Transfer the broth to a blender and add coconut milk, cilantro, salt, and pepper (if desired). Blend on high until completely smooth. Set aside. 3. In the same large pot, heat coconut oil over medium heat. Add shallots, chili, and ginger. Stir and sauté until onions are translucent and slightly soft, about 2 minutes. 4. Add snow peas and broccoli florets, stirring well. Season vegetables with salt and pepper (if desired). Add tofu and stir. Pour coconut lemongrass broth and tamari into the pot, stirring to combine. Taste the broth for seasoning and adjust if necessary. 5. Bring the soup to a boil, then lower the heat to a simmer and cook uncovered until broccoli is tender, about 4 minutes. Stir in lime juice.
6. Serve the hot soup with cooked rice or rice noodles and lime wedges on the side.

Per Serving:
calories: 204 | fat: 16g | protein: 10g | carbs: 9g | fiber: 2g

Roasted Red Pepper and Butternut Squash Soup

Prep time: 10 minutes | Cook time: 40 to 50 minutes | Makes 6 bowls

1 small butternut squash
1 tablespoon olive oil (optional)
1 teaspoon sea salt (optional)
2 red bell peppers
1 yellow onion
1 head garlic
2 cups water or vegetable broth
Zest and juice of 1 lime
1 to 2 tablespoons tahini
Pinch cayenne pepper
½ teaspoon ground coriander
½ teaspoon ground cumin
Toasted squash seeds (optional)

1.Set the oven to 350ºF (180ºC) to preheat. 2. To prepare the squash for roasting, cut it in half lengthwise and scoop out the seeds. Poke some holes in the flesh with a fork and reserve the seeds if desired. Rub a small amount of oil over the flesh and skin, then sprinkle with sea salt. Place the halves skin-side down in a large baking dish and put them in the oven while you prepare the rest of the vegetables. 3. Prepare the peppers in the same way as the squash, but they do not need to be poked. Slice the onion in half and rub oil on the exposed faces. Slice the top off the head of garlic and rub oil on the exposed flesh. 4. After the squash has cooked for 20 minutes, add the peppers, onion, and garlic to the baking dish and roast for another 20 minutes. If desired, toast the squash seeds by putting them in a separate baking dish in the oven 10 to 15 minutes before the vegetables are finished. Keep a close eye on them.
5. Once the vegetables are cooked, remove them from the oven and allow them to cool before handling. The squash should be very soft when poked with a fork. 6. Scoop the flesh out of the squash skin into a large pot (if using an immersion blender) or into a blender. Roughly chop the pepper, remove the onion skin and chop the onion, and squeeze the garlic cloves out of the head, all into the pot or blender. Add water, lime zest and juice, and tahini. Purée the soup, adding more water if needed, until it reaches your desired consistency. 7. Season the soup with salt (if using), cayenne, coriander, and cumin. Serve garnished with toasted squash seeds (if desired).

Per Serving:(1 bowl)

calories: 58 | fat: 3g | protein: 1g | carbs: 5g | fiber: 0g

Quick Creamy Herbed Tomato Soup

Prep time: 5 minutes | Cook time: 15 minutes | Serves 4

2 teaspoons extra-virgin olive oil (optional)
4 garlic cloves, roughly chopped
2 (15 ounces / 425 g) cans crushed tomatoes
½ teaspoon maple syrup (optional)
2 cups plain unsweetened plant-based milk
1 teaspoon Italian seasoning
2 tablespoons roughly chopped fresh mint
½ teaspoon salt (optional)
Black pepper

1. Heat the oil in a medium saucepan over medium heat. Add garlic

and cook until it becomes fragrant and starts to turn golden, around 2 minutes. Remove from heat and let it cool. 2. Combine tomatoes, maple syrup, plant-based milk, Italian seasoning, mint, salt (if using), and cooled garlic in a blender or food processor. Blend until smooth. 3. Pour the mixture back into the saucepan and bring it to a boil over high heat. Reduce heat to medium-low and simmer for 5 minutes, stirring occasionally. Serve by ladling into bowls, sprinkling with black pepper.

Per Serving:

calories: 126 | fat: 5g | protein: 6g | carbs: 17g | fiber: 5g

Curried Zucchini Soup

Prep time: 10 minutes | Cook time: 3 to 4 hours | Serves 4 to 6

1 medium onion, chopped
3 garlic cloves, minced
3 medium zucchini (about 1½ pounds / 680 g), chopped into 1-inch pieces
2 yellow potatoes (about ⅔ pound / 272 g), unpeeled and
chopped
5 cups store-bought low-sodium vegetable broth
1 tablespoon curry powder
Ground black pepper
Salt (optional)

1. Combine onion, garlic, zucchini, potatoes, broth, curry powder, pepper, and salt (if using) in a slow cooker. Cover and cook on High for 3 to 4 hours or on Low for 6 to 7 hours. 2. Before serving, use an immersion blender to blend until smooth or transfer the contents to a blender in batches. Carefully blend, starting on low and gradually increasing speed to prevent hot soup from splattering.

Per Serving:

calories: 119 | fat: 1g | protein: 5g | carbs: 25g | fiber: 5g

Cream of Broccoli Soup

Prep time: 10 minutes | Cook time: 20 minutes | Serves 6

3 large leeks (white parts only), sliced and rinsed
1 teaspoon thyme leaves
4 cups broccoli florets (from about 2 large heads)
4½ cups vegetable stock, or
low-sodium vegetable broth, plus more as needed
3 tablespoons nutritional yeast (optional)
Salt and freshly ground black pepper, to taste

1. Sauté leeks in a large saucepan over medium heat for 10 minutes. Add water 1 to 2 tablespoons at a time to prevent sticking. Add thyme and cook for another minute. Then, add broccoli, vegetable stock, and nutritional yeast (if using). Bring to a boil over high heat, reduce to medium, and cover. Cook until the broccoli is tender, approximately 10 minutes. 2. Use an immersion blender or a blender with a tight-fitting lid covered with a towel to purée the soup in batches. Return the soup to the pot and season with salt and pepper.

Per Serving:

calories: 61 | fat: 0g | protein: 3g | carbs: 11g | fiber: 3g

Minty Beet and Sweet Potato Soup

Prep time: 10 minutes | Cook time: 40 minutes |
Makes 6 bowls

5 cups water, or salt-free vegetable broth (if salted, omit the sea salt below)
1 to 2 teaspoons olive oil or vegetable broth
1 cup chopped onion
3 garlic cloves, minced
1 tablespoon thyme, fresh or dried
1 to 2 teaspoons paprika
2 cups peeled and chopped beets

2 cups peeled and chopped sweet potato
2 cups peeled and chopped parsnips
½ teaspoon sea salt (optional)
1 cup fresh mint, chopped
½ avocado, or 2 tablespoons nut or seed butter (optional)
2 tablespoons balsamic vinegar (optional)
2 tablespoons pumpkin seeds

1. Bring water to a boil in a large pot. 2. In another large pot, sauté onion and garlic in olive oil (if using) until softened for about 5 minutes. 3. Add thyme, paprika, beets, sweet potato, parsnips, boiling water, and salt (if using). Cover and let it gently boil for approximately 30 minutes or until the vegetables are soft. 4. Reserve some mint for garnish and add the rest along with avocado (if using). Stir well. 5. Use an immersion blender or transfer the soup to a blender to purée. Add balsamic vinegar (if using). 6. Serve topped with fresh mint, pumpkin seeds, and avocado chunks (if used).

Per Serving:(1 bowl)

calories: 157 | fat: 5g | protein: 3g | carbs: 26g | fiber: 6g

Lentil Chickpea stew

Prep time: 15 minutes | Cook time: 25 minutes |
Serves 4

⅔ cup dried green lentils
1 cup cooked or canned chickpeas
4 carrots, sliced
2 stalks celery, sliced

4 cups vegetable stock
Optional Toppings:
Fresh or dried parsley
Black pepper

1. If using dry chickpeas, start by soaking and cooking ⅓ cup of chickpeas if necessary. 2. Place a large pot over medium-high heat and add vegetable stock along with green lentils. 3. Bring the stock to a boil and then reduce the heat to medium. 4. Cook the lentils for about 15 minutes without covering the pot. Remove any foam produced by the lentils and stir occasionally. 5. Add carrots and celery, bring the heat down to a simmer, cover the pot with a lid, and let it simmer for another 10 minutes. 6. Turn off the heat and allow the soup to cool for 5 minutes. 7. Divide the soup between two bowls, serve with optional toppings, and enjoy! 8. Store any leftover soup in an airtight container in the fridge and consume within 2 days. Alternatively, store in the freezer for a maximum of 60 days and thaw at room temperature. The soup can be reheated in a pot or microwave.

Per Serving:

calories: 234 | fat: 1g | protein: 14g | carbs: 14g | fiber: 11g

Vegetable Goulash

Prep time: 5 minutes | Cook time: 25 minutes |
Serves 4 to 6

4 cups vegetable broth
4 cups diced (½-inch) yellow potatoes
2 cups frozen carrots
2 tablespoons tomato paste
½ cup chopped water-packed roasted red pepper
¼ cup sweet paprika
1 teaspoon whole caraway

seeds
3 strips dried porcini mushrooms, chopped (about 2 tablespoons)
1 tablespoon onion powder
½ teaspoon garlic powder
2 teaspoons dried parsley
½ teaspoon smoked paprika
1 bay leaf

1. Combine broth, potatoes, carrots, tomato paste, roasted red pepper, sweet paprika, caraway, mushrooms, onion powder, garlic powder, parsley, smoked paprika, and bay leaf in a large Dutch oven or saucepan. Bring to a boil over high heat. 2. Reduce the heat to low, cover, and simmer for 15 to 20 minutes or until the potatoes are tender and a knife can easily slide through them.
3. Remove the bay leaf and serve.

Per Serving:

calories: 295 | fat: 2g | protein: 14g | carbs: 55g | fiber: 10g

Lentil Chili

Prep time: 30 minutes | Cook time: 55 minutes |
Serves 6 to 8

3 medium yellow onions, peeled and chopped (about 1½ cups)
1½ cups chopped celery
2 medium carrots, peeled and sliced (about 1 cup)
2 medium bell peppers, seeded and chopped (about 1 cup)
1 to 2 cloves garlic, peeled and minced
6 cups vegetable stock, or low-sodium vegetable broth
1½ tablespoons chili powder
1 teaspoon ground cumin

1 teaspoon paprika
½ teaspoon chipotle powder or smoked paprika
½ teaspoon cayenne pepper
2 cups red lentils, rinsed
1 (28 ounces / 794 g) can crushed tomatoes
1 (15 ounces / 425 g) can kidney beans, drained and rinsed
Zest and juice of 1 lime
Salt and freshly ground black pepper, to taste

1. In a large pot over medium-high heat, combine onion, celery, carrots, bell peppers, garlic, and 1 cup of vegetable stock. Cook for 5 to 7 minutes, stirring occasionally, until the vegetables soften. Stir in chili powder, cumin, paprika, chipotle powder, and cayenne pepper and cook for an additional minute.
2. Add lentils, tomatoes, kidney beans, and remaining vegetable stock to the pot. Cover and bring to a boil over high heat. Reduce heat to medium-low and simmer, stirring occasionally, for about 45 minutes or until lentils are soft. Finally, add lime zest and juice and season with salt and pepper.

Per Serving:

calories: 279 | fat: 1g | protein: 16g | carbs: 52g | fiber: 11g

Chickpea, Kale, and Lentil Stew

Prep time: 15 minutes | Cook time: 3 to 4 hours |
Serves 4 to 6

1 medium onion, diced
2 celery stalks, diced
5 garlic cloves, minced
4 ounces (113 g) kale (about 5
or 6 large leaves), chopped
½ cup chopped fresh parsley,
divided
1 (1-inch) piece fresh ginger,
peeled and minced, or 2
teaspoons ground ginger
1 (14½ ounces / 411 g) can
chickpeas, drained and rinsed
1 cup dried brown or green

lentils, rinsed and sorted
1 (28 ounces / 794 g) can no-
salt-added crushed tomatoes
7 cups store-bought low-sodium
vegetable broth
2 teaspoons paprika
1 teaspoon ground coriander
1 teaspoon ground cumin
½ teaspoon ground cinnamon
¼ teaspoon red pepper flakes
Ground black pepper
Salt (optional)
Juice from ½ lemon

1. Put the onion, celery, garlic, kale, ¼ cup of parsley, the ginger, chickpeas, lentils, tomatoes, broth, paprika, coriander, cumin, cinnamon, red pepper flakes, black pepper, and salt (if using) in the slow cooker. Cover and cook on High for 3 to 4 hours or on Low for 6 to 8 hours. 2. Just before serving, stir in the remaining ¼ cup of parsley and the lemon juice.

Per Serving:
calories: 398 | fat: 3g | protein: 22g | carbs: 69g | fiber: 31g

Fiesta Soup

Prep time: 15 minutes | Cook time: 30 minutes |
Serves 6

1 tablespoon avocado oil
(optional)
1 yellow onion, diced
1 red bell pepper, diced
1 zucchini, diced
3 garlic cloves, minced
2 tablespoons taco seasoning
4 cups vegetable stock
1 (15 ounces / 425 g) can black
beans, drained and rinsed
1 (15 ounces / 425 g) can pinto
beans, drained and rinsed
1 (15 ounces / 425 g) can
organic diced tomatoes,
undrained

1 (7 ounces / 198 g) can diced
green chiles
1 cup organic frozen corn
2 tablespoons fresh lime juice
(from 1 lime)
¼ cup fresh cilantro, chopped
Sea salt and ground black
pepper, to taste
For Serving:
½ cup organic corn tortilla
strips
3 ripe avocados, diced
½ cup fresh cilantro, roughly
chopped
1 lime, cut into wedges

1. Heat a large pot over medium-high heat. If using oil, add and warm for 30 seconds. Add onion and bell pepper. Cook while stirring frequently for 5 minutes or until the bell peppers start to brown and onions become translucent. Add zucchini and garlic and cook for 1 minute until fragrant. Add taco seasoning and continue cooking while stirring constantly to toast the spices. 2. Add stock, beans, tomatoes, and chiles. Stir well. Bring it to a boil then reduce heat to low and simmer for 20 minutes or until veggies are tender and flavors blend. Stir in corn, lime juice, and cilantro. Season with

salt and black pepper. Remove from heat. Ladle into bowls and top with tortilla strips, avocado, and cilantro. Serve with a lime wedge.

Per Serving:
calories: 330 | fat: 18g | protein: 8g | carbs: 38g | fiber: 14g

Potato, Carrot, and Mushroom Stew

Prep time: 5 minutes | Cook time: 25 minutes |
Serves 4 to 6

4 cups vegetable broth
1½ pounds (680 g) yellow
potatoes, cut into ½-inch dice
(about 4 cups)
1 cup frozen carrots
1 cup frozen pearl onions
2 tablespoons tomato paste
3 strips dried porcini
mushrooms, chopped (about 2

tablespoons)
1 tablespoon onion powder
½ teaspoon dried thyme
¼ teaspoon garlic powder
1 bay leaf
½ cup frozen peas
2 tablespoons red miso paste
1 tablespoon balsamic vinegar

1. Combine broth, potatoes, carrots, onions, tomato paste, mushrooms, onion powder, thyme, garlic powder, and bay leaf in a large Dutch oven or saucepan. Bring to a boil over high heat. 2. Reduce the heat to low, cover, and simmer for 15 minutes or until the potatoes are tender and a knife can easily slide through them. Remove from heat. 3. Add peas, miso, and vinegar. Stir until the miso has dissolved. 4. Remove the bay leaf and serve immediately.

Per Serving:
calories: 183 | fat: 1g | protein: 8g | carbs: 36g | fiber: 5g

Chickpea Noodle Soup

Prep time: 15 minutes | Cook time: 2 to 3 hours |
Serves 6 to 8

1 medium onion, diced
3 carrots, diced
3 celery stalks, diced
4 garlic cloves, minced
2 (14½ ounces / 411 g) cans
chickpeas, drained and rinsed
8 cups store-bought low-sodium
vegetable broth
1 teaspoon dried parsley

1 bay leaf
Ground black pepper
Salt (optional)
10 ounces (283 g) whole-wheat
pasta spirals
Juice of ½ lemon
3 tablespoons chopped fresh
parsley

1. Put the onion, carrots, celery, garlic, chickpeas, broth, dried parsley, bay leaf, pepper, and salt (if using) in the slow cooker. Cover and cook on High for 2 to 3 hours or on Low for 5 to 6 hours. 2. In the final 30 minutes of cooking, remove and discard the bay leaf. Add the pasta, stirring well. After 30 minutes, check the pasta for your preferred level of doneness. Remove and discard the bay leaf. Stir in the lemon juice and fresh parsley before serving.

Per Serving:
calories: 332 | fat: 4g | protein: 14g | carbs: 64g | fiber: 13g

Creamy Winter Vegetable Stew with Mustard and Lemon

Prep time: 15 minutes | Cook time: 30 minutes | Serves 4

1 tablespoon virgin olive oil (optional)
1 large cooking onion, small diced
1 leek, small diced
4 cloves garlic, minced
2 teaspoons minced fresh thyme leaves
1 medium parsnip, peeled and chopped
½ large or 1 small celery root, peeled and chopped into 1-inch pieces
2 cups cauliflower florets
1½ tablespoons grainy mustard
Salt and pepper, to taste (optional)
2 teaspoons nutritional yeast
1 teaspoon Old Bay seasoning
¼ cup fresh lemon juice
3½ cups vegetable stock, plus extra if needed

1. Heat the olive oil in a large, heavy-bottomed pot over medium heat. Add the diced onions and sauté until soft and translucent, about 4 minutes. Add the leeks and continue to sauté until the leeks are soft, about 4 minutes more. Add the minced garlic and thyme, and cook until fragrant, about 30 seconds, stirring constantly. 2. Add the chopped parsnips, celery root, and cauliflower florets and stir to coat in the oil. Add the grainy mustard, salt and pepper, if using, nutritional yeast, and Old Bay seasoning. Stir to coat the vegetables in the spices. Add the lemon juice and stir. 3. Add the vegetable stock, stir again, cover, and bring to a boil. Once boiling, remove the lid and reduce the heat to a simmer. Let the chowder cook and bubble until the parsnips and celery root pieces are tender, about 15 to 18 minutes. 4. Ladle half of the stew into a blender, and carefully purée until smooth. Pour the puréed portion of stew back into the soup pot. If the stew is too thick, add enough vegetable stock to loosen it up to your liking. Bring the stew back to a boil and serve hot.

Per Serving:

calories: 263 | fat: 10g | protein: 16g | carbs: 29g | fiber: 7g

White Bean and Mushroom Stew

Prep time: 20 minutes | Cook time: 30 minutes | Serves 4

1 medium onion, peeled and diced
1 pound (454 g) cremini mushrooms, halved
6 cloves garlic, peeled and chopped
1 (14 ounces / 397 g) can diced tomatoes
¼ cup minced basil
1 tablespoon minced thyme
2 teaspoons minced rosemary
1 bay leaf
4 cups cooked navy beans, or 2 (15 ounces / 425 g) cans, drained and rinsed
Salt and freshly ground black pepper, to taste

1. Place the onion and mushrooms in a large saucepan and sauté over medium heat for 10 minutes. Add water 1 to 2 tablespoons at a time to keep the vegetables from sticking to the pan. 2. Add the garlic and cook for 1 minute. Stir in the tomatoes, basil, thyme, rosemary, bay leaf, and beans and bring the pot to a boil over high heat. Reduce the heat to medium and cook, covered, for 15 minutes. Season with salt and pepper.

Per Serving:

calories: 316 | fat: 1g | protein: 19g | carbs: 59g | fiber: 23g

White Bean Gazpacho

Prep time: 20 minutes | Cook time: 0 minutes | Serves 4

6 large ripe tomatoes (about 4 pounds / 1.8 kg)
2 large cucumbers, peeled, halved, seeded, and diced
1 large red bell pepper, seeded and diced small
1 medium Vidalia onion, peeled and diced small
¼ cup red wine vinegar
Zest of 1 lemon
½ cup chopped basil
Salt and freshly ground black pepper, to taste
2 cups cooked cannellini beans, or 1 (15 ounces / 425 g) can, drained and rinsed

1. Start by coarsely chopping 2 of the tomatoes and puréeing them in a blender. Transfer the purée to a large bowl. 2. Chop the remaining 4 tomatoes and add them to the bowl along with cucumbers, red pepper, onion, red wine vinegar, lemon zest, basil, salt, pepper, and beans. Mix well. 3. Chill the mixture for 1 hour before serving.

Per Serving:

calories: 100 | fat: 1g | protein: 4g | carbs: 20g | fiber: 6g

Fall Harvest Vegetable Chowder

Prep time: 30 minutes | Cook time: 55 minutes | Serves 6

1 medium yellow onion, peeled and diced (about 1 cup)
3 celery stalks, diced (about 1 cup)
2 medium carrots, peeled and diced (about 1 cup)
6 cups vegetable stock, or low-sodium vegetable broth
2 small zucchini, diced
2 small yams, peeled and diced
4 bay leaves
2 tablespoons thyme
3 to 4 ears corn, kernels removed (about 2 cups)
4 cups packed spinach leaves

1. Place the onion, celery, carrots, and ½ cup of vegetable stock in a large soup pot and sauté over medium-high heat for 6 to 8 minutes, or until the onion is translucent. 2. Add the zucchini, yams, bay leaves, thyme, and the remaining broth and bring to a boil over high heat. Reduce the heat to medium-low and simmer for 20 to 30 minutes, or until the vegetables are tender. 3. Add half the corn and cook for 10 to 15 more minutes. Remove the bay leaves. 4. Purée the soup using an immersion blender or in batches in a blender with a tight-fitting lid, covered with a towel. Return the soup to the pot and add the remaining corn and spinach leaves. Cook for 5 more minutes, or until the spinach is wilted. Stir well and serve hot.

Per Serving:

calories: 150 | fat: 1g | protein: 3g | carbs: 32g | fiber: 5g

Lentil Rice Soup

Prep time: 10 minutes | Cook time: 30 minutes | Serves 4

⅓ cup dry quick-cooking brown rice
⅔ cup dried green lentils
1 cup canned or fresh tomato cubes
3 cups vegetable stock

¼ cup tahini
Optional Toppings:
Fresh chili slices
Fresh cilantro
Green peppercorns

1. Put a large pot over medium-high heat and add the vegetable stock along with the green lentils. 2. Bring the stock to a boil and turn the heat down to medium. 3. Cook the lentils for about 15 minutes, without covering the pot. From time to time, remove any foam produced by the lentils and give the pot a stir. 4. Add the brown rice and bring the heat down to a simmer, then cover the pot with a lid and let it simmer for another 10 minutes. 5. Add the tomato cubes and tahini, stir well and let it simmer for another 5 minutes. 6. Turn the heat off and let the soup cool down for 5 minutes. 7. Divide between two bowls, serve with the optional toppings and enjoy! 8. Store the soup in an airtight container in the fridge, and consume within 2 days. Alternatively, store in the freezer for a maximum of 60 days and thaw at room temperature. The soup can be reheated in a pot or the microwave.

Per Serving:
calories: 284 | fat: 10g | protein: 15g | carbs: 33g | fiber: 12g

Hot and Sour Soup

Prep time: 15 minutes | Cook time: 3 to 4 hours | Serves 6 to 8

6 ounces (170 g) shiitake mushrooms, sliced
1 (8 ounces / 227 g) can sliced bamboo shoots
4 garlic cloves, minced
1 (2-inch) piece fresh ginger, peeled and minced
1 (16 ounces / 454-g) package extra-firm tofu, drained and cut into bite-size cubes
8 cups store-bought low-sodium vegetable broth
¼ cup low-sodium soy sauce,

tamari, or coconut aminos
¼ cup rice vinegar
½ teaspoon ground white pepper
½ teaspoon red pepper flakes
3 baby bok choy, chopped into bite-size pieces
2 tablespoons cornstarch
¼ cup water
4 scallions, green and white parts, chopped, for serving
½ bunch cilantro, chopped, for serving

1. Combine mushrooms, bamboo shoots, garlic, ginger, tofu, broth, soy sauce, vinegar, white pepper, and red pepper flakes in a slow cooker. Cover and cook on High for 3 to 4 hours or on Low for 7 to 8 hours. 2. In the last 30 minutes of cooking, add bok choy. Whisk cornstarch and water together in a small bowl. Add the slurry to the slow cooker and stir well to mix. To serve, ladle soup into bowls and top with scallions and cilantro.

Per Serving:
calories: 138 | fat: 5g | protein: 11g | carbs: 14g | fiber: 4g

Broccoli and "Cheddar" Soup

Prep time: 10 minutes | Cook time: 30 minutes | Serves 4

4 cups peeled and diced butternut squash
2 sweet potatoes, peeled and diced (about 2 cups)
1 small yellow onion, peeled and halved
2 garlic cloves, peeled
4 cups water

2 teaspoons salt (optional)
1 (13 ounces / 369-g) can light unsweetened coconut milk
1 tablespoon red miso paste
3 tablespoons nutritional yeast
1 tablespoon tapioca flour
3 cups frozen broccoli

1. Combine butternut squash, sweet potatoes, onion, garlic, and water in a large pot. Bring to a boil over high heat. Reduce heat to medium-low and cook until fork-tender, about 20 minutes. 2. Use a blender to purée the mixture (including the liquid) until smooth. You may need to do this in batches.
3. Return the soup to the pot and add salt (if using), coconut milk, red miso, nutritional yeast, tapioca flour, and broccoli. Cook over medium heat, stirring often, until heated through, about 10 minutes.

Per Serving:
calories: 353 | fat: 20g | protein: 8g | carbs: 42g | fiber: 9g

Anti-Inflammatory Miso Soup

Prep time: 15 minutes | Cook time: 25 minutes | Serves 6

2¼ cup vegetable broth
4 carrots, sliced into rounds
1 large yellow onion, chopped
1 ounce (28 g) dried shiitake mushrooms, broken or chopped into bite-size pieces
4 garlic cloves, minced
2 teaspoons ground turmeric
3 cups water
½ cup quinoa, rinsed and

drained
¼ teaspoon black pepper
1 bunch bok choy, chopped
1 cup finely chopped red cabbage
¼ cup gluten-free red miso
1 red or yellow bell pepper, chopped fine
3 scallions, sliced thin

1. Place a large Dutch oven or heavy-bottomed pot over medium heat. Add ½ cup broth, then add the carrots and onion to the hot broth. Sauté, stirring often, until the vegetables are tender, about 5 minutes. 2. Add the mushrooms, garlic, and turmeric and stir to combine. 3. Add the water, 2 cups broth, quinoa, and pepper, increase the heat to medium-high, cover, and allow to simmer for 15 minutes. 4. Add the bok choy and cabbage to the pot, reduce the heat to medium, and cover. Cook until the vegetables are slightly tender, about 3 minutes. 5. Remove the lid and whisk in the miso. Remove from the heat, add the bell pepper and scallions, and serve.

Per Serving:
calories: 139 | fat: 2g | protein: 7g | carbs: 26g | fiber: 5g

Split Pea Soup

Prep time: 15 minutes | Cook time: 1 hour | Serves 4

2 cups dried split peas
1 (7 ounces / 198 g) pack
smoked tofu, cubed
5 cups vegetable stock
2 small onions, minced

4 carrots, sliced
Optional Toppings:
Parsley
Black pepper
Nigella seeds

1. Heat a large pot over medium-high heat and add vegetable stock and split peas. 2. Bring the stock to a boil and reduce the heat to medium. 3. Cook the split peas uncovered for approximately 40 minutes. 4. Remove any foam that forms on top of the peas and stir occasionally. 5. Add smoked tofu cubes, carrots, and onions to the pot. Reduce the heat to a simmer, cover with a lid, and let it cook for another 20 minutes. Stir occasionally. 6. Turn off the heat and allow the soup to cool down for 5 minutes. 7. Divide the soup into two bowls, add optional toppings, and serve. 8. Store the soup in an airtight container in the refrigerator for up to 2 days or in the freezer for up to 60 days. Thaw at room temperature before reheating in a pot or microwave.

Per Serving:

calories: 176 | fat: 4g | protein: 21g | carbs: 14g | fiber: 17g

Spinach, Barley and Carrot Soup

Prep time: 10 minutes | Cook time: 25 minutes | Serves 4

6 multicolored carrots, cut into
1-inch pieces
½ cup barley
1 (15 ounces /425 g) can diced
tomatoes
2 garlic cloves, minced
4 cups no-sodium vegetable
broth
2 cups water
4 cups fresh spinach

¼ cup chopped fresh basil
leaves, plus more for garnish
2 tablespoons chopped fresh
chives, plus more for garnish
1 (15 ounces /425 g) can
cannellini beans, rinsed and
drained
1 tablespoon balsamic vinegar
Freshly ground black pepper, to
taste

1. Combine carrots, barley, tomatoes with their juices, garlic, vegetable broth, and water in a large pot over medium heat. Bring to a simmer and cover the pot. Cook for 10 minutes or until the barley is chewy but not hard. 2. Place spinach, basil, and chives on top of the water without stirring. Cover the pot, reduce heat to low, and cook for 3 minutes to soften the leaves. 3. Add cannellini beans and vinegar to the pot, stir, and remove from heat. Let it sit covered for 5 minutes. Serve by garnishing with chives, basil, and a pinch of pepper.

Per Serving:

calories: 261 | fat: 2g | protein: 12g | carbs: 50g | fiber: 14g

Corn Chowder

Prep time: 25 minutes | Cook time: 40 minutes | Serves 6

2 medium yellow onions,
peeled and diced small
2 red bell peppers, seeded and
finely chopped
3 ears corn, kernels removed
(about 2 cups)
3 cloves garlic, peeled and
minced
2 large russet potatoes, peeled

and diced
1½ pounds (680 g) tomatoes (4
to 5 medium), diced
6 cups vegetable stock, or low-
sodium vegetable broth
¾ cup finely chopped basil
Salt and freshly ground black
pepper, to taste

1. Sauté onions and peppers in a large saucepan over medium heat for 10 minutes. Add water 1 to 2 tablespoons at a time to prevent sticking. Add corn and garlic, and sauté for another 5 minutes. Then, add potatoes, tomatoes, peppers, and vegetable stock. Bring the mixture to a boil over high heat. Reduce to medium and cook uncovered for 25 minutes or until the potatoes are tender. 2. Use a blender with a tight-fitting lid covered with a towel to purée half of the soup in batches. Return the puréed soup to the pot. Add basil and season with salt and pepper.

Per Serving:

calories: 209 | fat: 0g | protein: 6g | carbs: 48g | fiber: 5g

Navy Bean Soup with Lemon and Rosemary

Prep time: 25 minutes | Cook time: 35 minutes | Serves 6

2 large leeks (white and light
green parts), chopped and
rinsed
1 celery stalk, chopped
3 cloves garlic, peeled and
minced
2 teaspoons minced rosemary
1 pound (454 g) Yukon Gold
potatoes (about 3 medium),

peeled and cubed
2 cups cooked navy beans, or 1
(15 ounces / 425 g) can, drained
and rinsed
6 cups vegetable stock, or low-
sodium vegetable broth
Zest of 2 lemons
Salt and freshly ground black
pepper, to taste

1. Sauté leeks and celery in a large pot over medium heat for 10 minutes. Add water 1 to 2 tablespoons at a time to prevent sticking. 2. Add garlic and rosemary and cook for another minute. Then, add potatoes, beans, and vegetable stock. Bring to a boil over high heat, reduce to medium, and cover. Cook for 20 minutes or until the potatoes are tender. 3. Add lemon zest, season with salt and pepper, and cook for another 5 minutes.

Per Serving:

calories: 180 | fat: 0g | protein: 7g | carbs: 37g | fiber: 8g

Beet Bourguignon (Beet and Lentil Stew)

Prep time: 20 minutes | Cook time: 45 minutes |

Serves 6

¼ cup vegetable broth
1 yellow onion, chopped
1 (10 ounces / 283 g) package fresh white button mushrooms, trimmed and sliced
2 celery ribs, chopped
3 garlic cloves, chopped
1 sprig rosemary
1 teaspoon dried thyme
½ teaspoon black pepper, plus more to taste
¼ cup tomato paste
1 cup dry red wine

4 waxy potatoes, peeled and chopped
3 beets, chopped
3 carrots, chopped
3 cups water
1 cup mixed lentils, soaked overnight, drained, and rinsed
1 ounce (28 g) dried mushrooms, broken into pieces
2 bay leaves
2 tablespoons gluten-free red miso
Salt (optional)

1. Heat the vegetable broth in a large stockpot over medium heat. Add the onion and cook until it starts to soften and become fragrant, about 3 minutes. Add the mushrooms, celery, garlic, rosemary, thyme, and ½ teaspoon pepper. Cook until the mushrooms are dark and the vegetables are soft, about 5 minutes. 2. Add the tomato paste and cook, stirring constantly, until it darkens in color, about 2 minutes. Add the red wine and scrape the bottom of the pan to remove any cooked-on bits. Add the potatoes, beets, carrots, water, lentils, dried mushrooms, and bay leaves. 3. Increase the heat to medium-high and bring to a boil; as soon as it starts to boil, cover and reduce the heat to low. Cook until the vegetables are as tender as you desire and the lentils are cooked, about 30 minutes. Discard the bay leaves. Whisk in the miso and season with salt (if desired) and more pepper to taste. Serve.

Per Serving:

calories: 247 | fat: 1g | protein: 10g | carbs: 51g | fiber: 9g

Lentil Soup

Prep time: 5 minutes | Cook time: 25 minutes |

Serves 2 to 4

4 cups vegetable broth
1 cup dried green or brown lentils, rinsed
2 teaspoon onion powder
1 teaspoon dried parsley

½ teaspoon ground cumin
½ teaspoon smoked paprika
¼ teaspoon garlic powder
¼ teaspoon ground coriander
1 bay leaf

1. Combine broth, lentils, onion powder, parsley, cumin, paprika, garlic powder, coriander, and bay leaf in a Dutch oven or saucepan. Bring to a boil over high heat. 2. Reduce the heat to medium-low, cover, and simmer for 20 minutes or until the lentils are tender. Remove from heat. 3. Remove the bay leaf and serve immediately.

Per Serving:

calories: 100 | fat: 3g | protein: 11g | carbs: 7g | fiber: 1g

Coconut Curry Soup

Prep time: 25 minutes | Cook time: 20 minutes |

Serves 6

3 tablespoons water
¾ cup diced red, white, or yellow onion
1½ teaspoons minced garlic
1 cup diced green or red bell pepper
1 (14½ ounces / 411 g) can diced tomatoes with their juices
1 (15 ounces / 425 g) can chickpeas, drained and rinsed
4 cups vegetable broth

1½ teaspoons ground cumin
2½ teaspoons curry powder
1 (13½ ounces / 383-g) can full-fat coconut milk
½ cup cooked brown rice
Salt and pepper, to taste (optional)
Optional Toppings:
Red chili flakes
Minced cilantro

1. In a large pot, heat the water over medium heat. 2. Add the onion, garlic, and bell pepper. Cook, stirring occasionally, for 5 minutes or until the veggies are tender. 3. Add the tomatoes, chickpeas, broth, cumin, and curry powder. Bring to a boil. Reduce the heat to low and simmer gently, stirring occasionally, for 10 minutes. 4. Add the coconut milk and brown rice and cook for 5 minutes, stirring occasionally. 5. Add salt (if desired) and pepper.

Per Serving:

calories: 126 | fat: 2g | protein: 5g | carbs: 24g | fiber: 6g

Lentil Mushroom Soup

Prep time: 10 minutes | Cook time: 30 minutes |

Serves 4

⅔ cup dried green lentils
2 cups button mushrooms, sliced
1 red bell pepper
4 cups vegetable stock

¼ cup dried thyme
Optional Toppings:
Black pepper
Sun-dried tomatoes

1. Heat vegetable stock and green lentils in a large pot over medium-high heat.
2. Bring the mixture to a boil and reduce heat to medium. 3. Cook lentils for approximately 15 minutes without covering the pot, remove any foam, and stir occasionally. 4. Add mushrooms and thyme to the pot, cover with a lid, and let it simmer for another 10 minutes. 5. Dice the flesh of the bell pepper after removing stem, seeds, and placenta. 6. Add diced bell pepper to the pot, stir well, and let it simmer for another 5 minutes. 7. Turn off the heat and let the soup cool down for 5 minutes. 8. Divide the soup between two bowls, add optional toppings, and serve. 9. Store the soup in an airtight container in the fridge for up to 2 days or in the freezer for up to 60 days. Thaw at room temperature before reheating in a pot or microwave

Per Serving:

calories: 146 | fat: 1g | protein: 10g | carbs: 24g | fiber: 12g

Chilean Bean Stew

Prep time: 20 minutes | Cook time: 35 minutes |

Serves 4

1 large yellow onion, peeled and diced small
4 cloves garlic, peeled and minced
1 medium butternut squash (about 1 pound / 454 g), peeled, halved, seeded, and cut into ½-inch pieces

2 cups cooked pinto beans, or 1 (15 ounces / 425 g) can, drained and rinsed
6 ears corn, kernels removed (about 3½ cups)
Salt and freshly ground black pepper, to taste
1 cup finely chopped basil

1.Sauté onion in a large saucepan over medium heat for 10 minutes. Add water 1 to 2 tablespoons at a time to prevent sticking. 2. Add garlic, squash, beans, corn, and 2 cups of water. Cook for 25 minutes or until the squash is tender. Season with salt and pepper, then stir in the basil.

Per Serving:

calories: 305 | fat: 2g | protein: 15g | carbs: 65g | fiber: 14g

Bloody Caesar Gazpacho

Prep time: 20 minutes | Cook time: 0 minutes |

Serves 6

6 cups chopped ripe tomatoes
1 small red onion, chopped
1 English cucumber, chopped
2 stalks celery, chopped
2 cloves garlic, chopped
Fresh chili pepper, chopped, to taste (optional)
2 teaspoons celery salt (optional)
⅓ cup raw almonds, soaked for at least 6 hours
2 tablespoons red wine vinegar
⅓ cup virgin olive oil (optional)

Vegan gluten-free worcestershire sauce or gluten-free tamari soy sauce, to taste
Hot sauce, to taste
Freshly ground black pepper, to taste
Garnishes:
Thinly sliced celery
Thinly sliced red onion
Lime wedges
Pitted green olives
Additional hot sauce

1. In a large bowl, toss together the chopped tomatoes, red onions, cucumber, celery, garlic, chili, if using, and celery salt, if using. Cover the bowl with plastic wrap, and let it sit at room temperature for 1 hour. 2. Uncover the vegetables and transfer them to the bowl of a food processor. Pour all the marinating liquid from the bowl into the food processor as well. Drain the almonds and add them to the food processor. Run the motor on high until the vegetables and almonds are puréed. Reduce the speed to low, and drizzle in the red wine vinegar and olive oil, if using. Stop the machine when you have a smooth mixture. 3. Run the gazpacho through a fine strainer into a large bowl. Season with vegan Worcestershire sauce, hot sauce, and black pepper. 4. Store the gazpacho, covered, in the refrigerator until ready to serve with the garnishes. The gazpacho will keep in the refrigerator for up to 5 days.

Per Serving:

calories: 140 | fat: 10g | protein: 4g | carbs: 12g | fiber: 4g

Creamy Corn Chowder

Prep time: 15 minutes | Cook time: 3 to 4 hours |

Serves 4 to 6

1 large onion, diced
4 garlic cloves, minced
4 cups fresh or frozen corn
4 yellow potatoes (about 1⅓ pounds / 590 g), unpeeled and diced
6 cups store-bought low-sodium vegetable broth
1 teaspoon garlic powder

½ teaspoon dried basil
½ teaspoon dried thyme
Ground black pepper
Salt (optional)
3 tablespoons chickpea flour
1 (14½ ounces / 411 g) can white beans, drained and rinsed
1 tablespoon miso paste

1. Combine onion, garlic, corn, potatoes, broth, garlic powder, basil, thyme, pepper, and salt (if using) in a slow cooker. Cover and cook on High for 3 to 4 hours or on Low for 7 to 8 hours. 2. In the last 30 minutes of cooking, remove 3 cups of soup and blend in a blender or food processor with chickpea flour, beans, and miso paste until it becomes thick and creamy. Return the blended mixture to the slow cooker and stir to combine. Serve hot.

Per Serving:

calories: 410 | fat: 2g | protein: 17g | carbs: 88g | fiber: 16g

Asparagus and Leek Soup

Prep time: 15 minutes | Cook time: 35 minutes |

Serves 4

2 leeks
1 tablespoon water
2 garlic cloves, minced
¾ teaspoon dried tarragon (or dried dill or thyme)
1 cup dried red lentils
1 pound (454 g) asparagus, cut

into 1-inch pieces, including the ends
6 cups no-sodium vegetable broth
Juice of 1 lemon
Freshly ground black pepper, to taste

1. Cut off the root ends and dark green portion of the leek stalks. Slit the remaining white and light green portion lengthwise down the center. Rinse the leeks under cool water, using your fingers to remove any dirt between the layers. Thinly slice the leeks. 2. Combine sliced leeks and water in a large pot over medium-high heat. Sauté for 5 minutes. Add garlic and tarragon. Cook for 2 more minutes. 3. Add lentils, asparagus, and vegetable broth. Bring to a boil, cover the pot, reduce heat to medium-low, and cook for 20 to 30 minutes until lentils are tender. 4. Remove some of the cooked lentils, leeks, and asparagus if desired. Use an immersion blender to purée the soup until smooth or slightly chunky. Stir in the ingredients removed, if using.
5. Serve with a light drizzle of fresh lemon juice and season with pepper.

Per Serving:

calories: 243 | fat: 2g | protein: 16g | carbs: 45g | fiber: 8g

Basic Dal

Prep time: 10 minutes | Cook time: 1 hour | Serves 6

1 tablespoon full-fat coconut milk solids, plus more for serving
1 tablespoon minced or grated fresh ginger
4 garlic cloves, minced
1 jalapeño, minced, seeds and ribs removed for less heat
½ teaspoon ground cumin
½ teaspoon ground turmeric

1 cup yellow split peas or brown lentils, soaked overnight and drained
½ cup brown basmati rice
4 cups vegetable broth or water, plus extra as needed
Salt and pepper (optional)
Fresh lime juice
Chopped cilantro

1. Place a large stockpot over medium heat. Melt the milk solids and add the ginger, garlic, jalapeño, cumin, and turmeric. Cook until the spices are fragrant, about 2 minutes. 2. Add the split peas and rice. Stir to combine, then add the broth. Increase the heat to medium-high, bring to a boil, then reduce the heat to low. Cook with the lid slightly ajar until the lentils and rice are tender, about 1 hour. (Add additional broth if you prefer a soup-like consistency.) 3. Season with salt (if desired) and pepper, drizzle with lime juice, sprinkle with cilantro, and serve. (The dal can be refrigerated for up to 5 days.)

Per Serving:

calories: 120 | fat: 1g | protein: 4g | carbs: 23g | fiber: 4g

Roasted Eggplant and Lentil Stew

Prep time: 20 minutes | Cook time: 1 hour 10 minutes | Serves 8

1 large eggplant
4 carrots, coarsely chopped
4 cups no-sodium vegetable broth
1 cup dried brown or green lentils
1 large yellow onion, diced
1 bunch chopped scallions, white and green parts, divided
3 garlic cloves, diced
1 tablespoon water, plus more as needed
1 (14 ounces / 397 g) can full-

fat coconut milk
1 tablespoon red miso paste
1 tablespoon low-sodium soy sauce
1 (28 ounces / 794 g) can diced tomatoes
4 teaspoons ground cumin
1 teaspoon adobo chili powder or smoked paprika
1 celery stalk, coarsely chopped
Fresh cilantro leaves, for serving

1. Preheat the oven to 350°F (180°C). 2. Halve the eggplant lengthwise and place it on a baking sheet, flesh-side up. Spread the carrots around the eggplant on the same baking sheet. 3. Roast for 30 minutes, or until the eggplant and carrots are lightly browned or caramel colored and the carrots are fork-tender. 4. Set the carrots aside. Let the eggplant cool before handling it. Scoop out as much flesh as possible without scooping into the skin and set aside in a bowl. 5. In an 8-quart pot over high heat, bring the vegetable broth to a boil. Lower the heat to maintain a simmer and add the lentils. Cover the pot and cook for 20 to 30 minutes, or until the lentils are soft yet retain their shape. 6. While the lentils cook, in a small sauté pan or skillet over medium heat, cook the onion, white parts of the

scallion, and garlic for 7 to 10 minutes, adding water, 1 tablespoon at a time, to prevent burning, until darkly browned. 7. In a blender, combine the roasted eggplant and onion mixture with the coconut milk, miso paste, and soy sauce. Purée for 2 to 3 minutes until smooth. 8. Once the lentils are finished cooking, add the tomatoes, cumin, chili powder, and celery. Bring the mixture to a simmer. Pour in the eggplant sauce and add the roasted carrots. Cook until warmed to your liking. 9. This stew is best served with a few fresh cilantro leaves and scallion greens on top.

Per Serving:

calories: 259 | fat: 10g | protein: 10g | carbs: 35g | fiber: 9g

Kale and White Bean Soup

Prep time: 10 minutes | Cook time: 2 to 3 hours | Serves 4 to 6

2 medium shallots, finely diced
3 garlic cloves, minced
2 (14½ ounces / 411 g) cans white beans, drained and rinsed
1 pound (454 g) fresh Tuscan or curly kale (about 5 large stalks), chopped

6 cups store-bought low-sodium vegetable broth
Ground black pepper
Salt (optional)
½ bunch fresh flat-leaf parsley, chopped

1. Put the shallots, garlic, beans, kale, broth, pepper, and salt (if using) in the slow cooker. 2. Cover and cook on High for 2 to 3 hours or on Low for 4 to 5 hours. Stir in the parsley just before serving.

Per Serving:

calories: 233 | fat: 2g | protein: 13g | carbs: 42g | fiber: 12g

Broccoli Potato Soup

Prep time: 15 minutes | Cook time: 20 minutes | Serves 8

3 tablespoons water
1 cup diced red, white, or yellow onion
1 teaspoon minced garlic
5 cups vegetable broth
6 cups chopped russet or red

potatoes
1 (10 ounces / 283 g) bag frozen broccoli
Juice of 1 small lemon
Pinch of pepper

1. Heat water in a medium pan over medium-low heat. Add onion and garlic, and sauté for 5 minutes or until the onion becomes tender and translucent.
2. Add broth, potatoes, broccoli, lemon juice, and pepper. 3. Bring to a boil.
4. Boil for 10 to 15 minutes or until the potatoes are fully cooked. 5. Remove from heat. Use an immersion blender to purée half of the soup (or use a regular blender in batches). Return the puréed soup to the pot and combine with the remaining soup.

Per Serving:

calories: 116 | fat: 0g | protein: 4g | carbs: 26g | fiber: 3g

Hearty Black Bean and Corn Soup

Prep time: 10 minutes | Cook time: 30 minutes |
Serves 4

2 tablespoons extra-virgin olive oil (optional)
1 small yellow onion, diced small
2 large carrots, peeled and cut into thin rounds
2 celery stalks, diced small
1 (15 ounces / 425 g) can diced tomatoes, or 2 medium tomatoes, cut into ½-inch pieces
2 small red potatoes, cut into small cubes

2 (15 ounces / 425 g) cans black beans, drained and rinsed
1 cup frozen corn
8 cups water
1 teaspoon smoked paprika
1 teaspoon salt (optional)
1 teaspoon garlic powder
1 small zucchini, cut into small cubes
1 tablespoon finely chopped fresh cilantro

1. In a large saucepan, heat the oil over medium heat. Add the onion, carrots, and celery and cook until the onions are fragrant and the vegetables are starting to get tender, 5 to 7 minutes. 2. Add the tomatoes and cook, stirring occasionally, for 5 minutes. Add the potatoes, beans, corn, and water and stir until combined. Raise the heat to high, bring to a rolling boil, and cook for 5 minutes. 3. Add the smoked paprika, salt (if using), garlic powder, zucchini, and cilantro and stir until combined. Lower the heat to medium-low and simmer the soup until the vegetables are fork-tender, about 15 minutes. Serve hot.

Per Serving:
calories: 380 | fat: 8g | protein: 16g | carbs: 63g | fiber: 16g

Ful Nabed (Egyptian Fava Bean Soup)

Prep time: 25 minutes | Cook time: 40 minutes |
Serves 4 to 6

1 large yellow onion, peeled and diced
1 medium carrot, peeled and diced
1 celery stalk, thinly sliced
4 cloves garlic, peeled
2 teaspoons cumin seeds, toasted and ground
1 tablespoon sweet paprika
2 bay leaves
1 large tomato, finely chopped

6 cups vegetable stock, or low-sodium vegetable broth
3 cups cooked fava beans
¼ teaspoon cayenne pepper, or to taste
¼ cup finely chopped parsley
Zest and juice of 1 lemon
2 tablespoons finely chopped mint
Salt, to taste (optional)

1. Place the onion, carrot, and celery in a large pot and sauté over medium heat for 10 minutes. Add water 1 to 2 tablespoons at a time to keep the vegetables from sticking to the pot. Add the garlic, cumin, paprika, bay leaves, and tomato and cook for 5 minutes. Add the vegetable stock and fava beans and cook, covered, for 20 minutes. 2. Add the cayenne pepper, parsley, lemon zest and juice, and mint. Cook for another 5 minutes and season with salt, if using.

Per Serving:
calories: 99 | fat: 0g | protein: 6g | carbs: 21g | fiber: 6g

Hearty Potato, Tomato, and Green Beans Stufato

Prep time: 10 minutes | Cook time: 3 to 4 hours |
Serves 4 to 6

1 large onion, chopped
4 garlic cloves, minced
3 red or yellow potatoes (about 1 pound / 454 g), unpeeled and cut into 1- to 2-inch chunks
1 pound (454 g) fresh or frozen green beans, cut into bite-size pieces
1 (28 ounces / 794 g) can no-salt-added crushed tomatoes

2 teaspoons dried oregano
2 teaspoons dried basil
1 teaspoon dried rosemary
½ teaspoon red pepper flakes (optional)
Ground black pepper
Salt (optional)
Chopped fresh parsley, for garnish (optional)

1. Put the onion, garlic, potatoes, green beans, tomatoes, oregano, basil, rosemary, red pepper flakes (if using), pepper, and salt (if using) in the slow cooker. 2. Cover and cook on High for 3 to 4 hours or on Low for 6 to 7 hours, until the potatoes are fork tender. Serve garnished with parsley (if using).

Per Serving:
calories: 197 | fat: 1g | protein: 8g | carbs: 40g | fiber: 9g

Hungarian Red Lentil Soup

Prep time: 10 minutes | Cook time: 25 minutes |
Serves 4

1 large yellow onion, diced
3 garlic cloves, minced
3 cups water, plus 1 tablespoon and more as needed
4 ounces (113 g) tomato paste
2 tablespoons Hungarian paprika, plus more for seasoning
1 teaspoon ground mustard
¼ teaspoon freshly ground

black pepper, plus more for seasoning
3 carrots, diced
1 celery stalk, diced
1 cup dried red lentils, rinsed
1 (14 ounces / 397 g) can light coconut milk
Chopped scallions, green parts only, for serving

1. In an 8-quart pot over high heat, combine the onion and garlic. Sauté for 2 to 3 minutes, adding water, 1 tablespoon at a time, to prevent burning, until the onion is translucent but not browned. 2. Add the tomato paste, paprika, mustard, and pepper. Cook, stirring, for 2 minutes. 3. Stir in the remaining 3 cups of water. Add the carrots and celery. Bring the soup to a simmer and add the lentils. Reduce the heat to medium-low, cover the pot, and cook for 10 minutes. 4. Stir in the coconut milk and bring the mixture to a simmer, stirring continuously. Cook for 5 minutes, or until the lentils are tender. 5. Serve topped with scallions and a sprinkle of Hungarian paprika and pepper.

Per Serving:
calories: 309 | fat: 9g | protein: 15g | carbs: 48g | fiber: 10g

Sweet Potato, Red Beans, and Lentil Stew

Prep time: 15 minutes | Cook time: 3 to 4 hours |

Serves 5 to 7

¼ cup chickpea flour
4 medium sweet potatoes (about 1½ pounds / 680 g), peeled and cut into 1½-inch cubes
1 medium onion, diced
1 garlic clove, minced
1 (14½ ounces / 411 g) can red kidney beans, drained and rinsed
1 cup dried brown or green

lentils, rinsed and sorted
4½ cups store-bought low-sodium vegetable broth
1 cup orange juice (from 2 to 3 oranges)
1 teaspoon dried oregano
½ teaspoon celery seed
Ground black pepper
Salt (optional)

1. Place the chickpea flour and sweet potatoes in a gallon-size resealable bag and shake well to coat. 2. Transfer the floured potatoes to the slow cooker. Add the onion, garlic, beans, lentils, broth, orange juice, oregano, celery seed, and pepper. Season with salt (if using). 3. Cover and cook on High for 3 to 4 hours or on Low for 7 to 8 hours.

Per Serving:

calories: 396 | fat: 2g | protein: 18g | carbs: 78g | fiber: 24g

Lemony Herbed Lentil Soup

Prep time: 10 minutes | Cook time: 35 minutes |

Serves 2

1 cup dried brown or green lentils, rinsed
4 cups water
1 teaspoon extra-virgin olive oil (optional)
½ small yellow onion, chopped
2 garlic cloves, minced
1 celery stalk, minced
2 carrots, sliced
1 potato, peeled and diced

1 zucchini, diced
1 (15 ounces / 425 g) can crushed tomatoes
1 teaspoon Italian seasoning
½ teaspoon smoked paprika
2 cups baby spinach
Juice of 1 lemon
1 teaspoon salt, plus more as needed (optional)

1. In a large saucepan, combine the lentils and water and bring to a boil over high heat. Lower the heat to medium and cook until soft, about 25 minutes. 2. Meanwhile, in a large skillet, heat the olive oil over medium heat. Add the onion and garlic and cook until fragrant, about 5 minutes. Add the celery, carrots, and potato and cook for 5 minutes. Add the mixture to the cooked lentils and stir until combined. 3. Add the zucchini, tomatoes, Italian seasoning, and smoked paprika and bring to a boil over medium-high heat. Lower the heat to medium and simmer until the flavors meld, about 10 minutes. 4. Add the spinach, stir, and cook until wilted. Add the lemon juice and salt (if using) and stir until combined. Taste and add more salt if needed.

Per Serving:

calories: 546 | fat: 5g | protein: 31g | carbs: 102g | fiber: 21g

Golden Split Pea Soup

Prep time: 10 minutes | Cook time: 3 to 4 hours |

Serves 5 to 7

1 medium onion, diced
3 carrots, diced
3 celery stalks, diced
3 garlic cloves, crushed
1 cup yellow split peas, rinsed and stones removed
1 yellow potato (about ⅓ pound / 136 g), unpeeled and cubed

4 cups low-sodium vegetable broth or water
1 bay leaf
¾ teaspoon ground cumin
¾ teaspoon ground turmeric
½ teaspoon dry mustard
Ground black pepper
Salt (optional)

1. Put the onion, carrots, celery, garlic, peas, potato, broth, bay leaf, cumin, turmeric, mustard, pepper, and salt (if using) in the slow cooker. Cover and cook on High for 3 to 4 hours or on Low for 7 to 8 hours. 2. Remove and discard the bay leaf. Using an immersion blender or a countertop blender, fully purée the soup before serving.

Per Serving:

calories: 207 | fat: 1g | protein: 11g | carbs: 40g | fiber: 13g

Zucchini Soup

Prep time: 10 minutes | Cook time: 25 minutes |

Makes 2 quarts

2 tablespoons extra-virgin coconut oil (optional)
1 medium yellow onion, diced
2 large garlic cloves, finely chopped
1½ teaspoons fine sea salt, plus

more to taste (optional)
8 medium-large zucchini, cut into 1-inch pieces
3¼ cups filtered water
Freshly ground black pepper
Tamari (optional)

1. Warm the oil in a large pot over medium-high heat. Add the onion and cook for 6 to 8 minutes, until beginning to brown. Stir in the garlic and salt, if using, and cook for 3 to 4 minutes, until the garlic is golden and fragrant. Add the zucchini and water, raise the heat, and bring a boil. Cover the pot, reduce the heat to low, and simmer for 8 to 10 minutes, until the zucchini is tender, pressing it down into the liquid a couple of times during cooking to ensure that it cooks evenly. Test by pressing a piece of zucchini against the side of the pot; it should crush easily. Remove from the heat and set aside to cool slightly. 2. Scoop out 2 cups of the liquid and set aside. Season the soup with pepper. Working in batches, scoop the soup into an upright blender (filling it no more than two-thirds full) and puree on high speed until smooth and velvety, adding some of the reserved cooking liquid if necessary to reach the desired consistency, then pour into a large bowl or another large pot. Season to taste with more salt and pepper, and with tamari, if using, and serve warm. Store leftover soup in jars in the fridge for up to 4 days or freeze for up to 3 months.

Per Serving:(1 quart)

calories: 153 | fat: 14g | protein: 2g | carbs: 8g | fiber: 2g

Creamy Pumpkin and Toasted Walnut Soup

Prep time: 15 minutes | Cook time: 30 minutes |
Makes 4 bowls

1 small pie pumpkin, peeled, seeded, and chopped (about 6 cups)
1 teaspoon olive oil (optional)
¼ teaspoon sea salt (optional)
1 onion, diced
4 cups water or vegetable stock
2 to 3 teaspoons ground sage

2 to 3 tablespoons nutritional yeast
1 cup nondairy milk, or 1 tablespoon nut or seed butter plus 1 cup water or stock
¼ cup toasted walnuts
Freshly ground black pepper, to taste

1. Place a large saucepan on medium and sauté the pumpkin in the oil, seasoning with the salt (if using), until slightly softened, about 10 minutes. Add the onion to the pot and sauté until slightly softened, about 5 minutes. 2. Add the water and bring to a boil. Then turn down to a simmer, cover, and cook 15 to 20 minutes, until the pumpkin is tender when pierced with a fork. 3. Stir in the sage, nutritional yeast, and nondairy milk. Then purée the soup with an immersion blender or in a regular blender until smooth. 4. Garnish with toasted walnuts and pepper.

Per Serving:(1 bowl)

calories: 140 | fat: 5g | protein: 7g | carbs: 20g | fiber: 3g

Minestrone

Prep time: 30 minutes | Cook time: 55 minutes |
Serves 8 to 10

1 large onion, peeled and chopped
2 large carrots, peeled and chopped
2 celery stalks, chopped
4 cloves garlic, peeled and minced
8 cups vegetable stock, or low-sodium vegetable broth
2 tablespoons nutritional yeast (optional)
1 (28 ounces / 794 g) can diced tomatoes

2 teaspoons oregano
2 medium red-skin potatoes, scrubbed and cubed
4 cups packed chopped kale, ribs removed before chopping
½ cup uncooked brown basmati rice
6 cups cooked cannellini beans, or 3 (15 ounces / 425 g) cans, drained and rinsed
Salt and freshly ground black pepper, to taste
1 cup finely chopped basil

1. Place the onion, carrots, and celery in a large saucepan over medium heat and sauté for 10 minutes. Add water 1 to 2 tablespoons at a time to keep the vegetables from sticking to the pan. 2. Add the garlic and cook for another minute. Add the vegetable stock, nutritional yeast (if using), tomatoes, oregano, potatoes, kale, and rice. Bring the pot to a boil over high heat, reduce the heat to medium-low, and simmer for 30 minutes. 3. Add the beans and simmer for 15 minutes, until the rice is tender. Season with salt and pepper and add the basil.

Per Serving:

calories: 118 | fat: 2g | protein: 5g | carbs: 24g | fiber: 7g

Creamy Tomato Soup

Prep time: 10 minutes | Cook time: 35 minutes |
Serves 4

2 carrots, coarsely chopped
½ cup water, plus 1 tablespoon and more as needed
1 yellow onion, coarsely chopped
2 to 4 garlic cloves, coarsely chopped
1 (6 ounces / 170-g) can tomato paste

1 tablespoon Hungarian paprika
1 (28 ounces / 794 g) can diced tomatoes
1 (14 ounces / 397 g) can full-fat coconut milk
1 teaspoon dried thyme
No-sodium vegetable broth or water, for thinning (optional)

1. In an 8-quart pot over medium-high heat, combine the carrots and ½ cup of water. Cover the pot and cook for 10 minutes, or until the carrots can be easily pierced with a fork. Add more water, ¼ cup at a time, if the water evaporates while cooking. Drain and transfer the cooked carrots to a bowl. Set aside. 2. Place the same pot over medium-low heat and combine the onion and garlic. Sauté for 5 to 7 minutes, adding water, 1 tablespoon at a time, to prevent burning, until the onion is fully browned. 3. Turn the heat to medium-high. Add the tomato paste and paprika. Cook, stirring continuously, for 30 seconds to 1 minute. 4. Add the diced tomatoes, coconut milk, thyme, and cooked carrots. Bring the liquid to a simmer. Cover the pot and reduce the heat to medium-low. Cook for 10 minutes, stirring occasionally. 5. Using an immersion blender, blend the soup until smooth. Alternatively, transfer the soup to a standard blender, working in batches as needed, and blend until smooth. 6. Add vegetable broth or water to thin as needed.

Per Serving:

calories: 292 | fat: 19g | protein: 6g | carbs: 28g | fiber: 7g

Chapter 9 Desserts

Sweet Red Beans

Prep time: 10 minutes | Cook time: 30 minutes | Serves 6

1 cup adzuki beans, soaked overnight, drained and rinsed
¼ teaspoon vanilla bean powder or ½ teaspoon vanilla extract

2 cup water
3 tablespoons maple syrup (optional)
⅛ teaspoon salt (optional)

1. In a medium saucepan, place beans and vanilla. Add water and bring to a boil. Cover and continue boiling until tender, about 30 minutes. If the beans are still tough and require more water to cook, add it gradually to avoid soupy beans. 2. Remove from heat and stir in sugar and salt (if desired). Let cool before serving.

Per Serving:
calories: 76 | fat: 0g | protein: 3g | carbs: 16g | fiber: 3g

Chocolate Tahini Muffins

Prep time: 10 minutes | Cook time: 20 minutes | Makes 12 muffins

½ teaspoon plus 2 tablespoons coconut oil, divided (optional)
2 tablespoons ground flaxseeds
6 tablespoons cold water
2 tablespoons tahini
2 tablespoons plain plant-based yogurt
1½ cups unsweetened plant-

based milk
2 teaspoons baking powder
½ cup maple syrup (optional)
¼ cup unsweetened cocoa powder
½ teaspoon salt (optional)
2½ cups whole-wheat flour

1. Preheat the oven to 375ºF (190ºC). Lightly oil a 12-cup muffin tin with ½ tablespoon of coconut oil. 2. In a large bowl, mix together the flaxseed and cold water to make 2 "flax eggs." Let sit for 10 minutes. 3. In a microwave-safe bowl, microwave the remaining 2 tablespoons coconut oil until melted, about 35 seconds. Be careful when removing the bowl so as not to splash hot coconut oil. 4. Add the coconut oil, tahini, yogurt, plant-based milk, baking powder, and maple syrup to the bowl with the flax eggs and mix well with a fork. Add the cocoa powder, salt (if using), and flour and mix until combined. 5. Divide the batter evenly among the 12 muffin cups, filling each about three-fourths full. Put the muffin pan in the oven and lower the heat to 350ºF (180ºC). Bake for 20 minutes, until a toothpick inserted in the middle comes out clean.

Per Serving:
calories: 187 | fat: 6g | protein: 5g | carbs: 31g | fiber: 4g

Chocolate-Peppermint Nice Cream

Prep time: 5 minutes | Cook time: 0 minutes | Serves 2

3 frozen ripe bananas, broken into thirds
3 tablespoons plant-based milk

2 tablespoons cocoa powder
⅛ teaspoon peppermint extract

1. Combine bananas, milk, cocoa powder, and peppermint in a food processor.
2. Process on medium speed for 30 to 60 seconds until the mixture reaches a smooth soft-serve consistency. Serve immediately.

Per Serving:
calories: 173 | fat: 2g | protein: 3g | carbs: 43g | fiber: 6g

Cranberry Orange Biscotti

Prep time: 5 minutes | Cook time: 40 minutes | Makes 18 slices

⅓ cup fresh orange juice
2 tablespoons ground flaxseeds
¾ cup date sugar (optional)
¼ cup unsweetened applesauce
¼ cup almond butter
1 teaspoon pure vanilla extract
1⅔ cups whole wheat pastry

flour
2 tablespoons cornstarch
2 teaspoons baking powder
½ teaspoon ground allspice
½ teaspoon salt (optional)
¾ cup fruit-sweetened dried cranberries

1. Preheat the oven to 350ºF (180ºC) and line a baking sheet with parchment paper or a Silpat baking mat. 2. In a large mixing bowl, vigorously mix orange juice and flaxseeds with a fork until frothy. Mix in date sugar (if using), applesauce, almond butter, and vanilla. 3. Sift in flour, cornstarch, baking powder, and allspice. Add salt (if using) and mix until well combined. Knead in cranberries using your hands since the dough will be stiff. 4. Form the dough into a rectangle about 12 inches long by 3 to 4 inches wide on the prepared baking sheet. Bake for 26 to 28 minutes or until lightly puffed and browned. Let cool for 30 minutes. 5. Increase the oven temperature to 375ºF (190ºC). Using a heavy, sharp knife, slice the biscotti into ½-inch-thick slices in one motion, pushing down. Do not "saw" the slices as they may crumble. Lay the slices on the cookie sheet and bake for 10 to 12 minutes, flipping them halfway through. Allow to cool on the baking sheet before transferring the slices to cooling racks.

Per Serving:
calories: 108 | fat: 2g | protein: 2g | carbs: 19g | fiber: 2g

Chocolate Chip Oat Cookies

Prep time: 10 minutes | Cook time: 15 minutes |
Makes 20 cookies

¾ cup oat flour
¾ cup rolled oats
2 tablespoons hemp hearts or chia seeds
¼ cup pure maple syrup
3 tablespoons unsalted, unsweetened almond butter or

other nut butter
2 tablespoons tahini
1 tablespoon unsweetened soy milk
1 teaspoon vanilla extract
¼ cup vegan mini chocolate chips

1. Line a baking sheet with parchment paper and preheat the oven to 350ºF (180ºC). 2. In a large bowl, combine flour, oats, and hemp hearts. 3. Mix in maple syrup, almond butter, tahini, soy milk, and vanilla until thoroughly combined. 4. Stir in chocolate chips. 5. Drop 20 (1-tablespoon) dough balls evenly spaced on the prepared baking sheet and gently press down to create flat cookies. 6. Bake for 12 minutes or until edges are golden brown. Remove from the oven and let cool on the baking sheet for 10 minutes before transferring to a wire rack to cool completely. Store in an airtight container.

Per Serving:

calories: 151 | fat: 8g | protein: 5g | carbs: 16g | fiber: 3g

No-Bake Mocha Cheesecake

Prep time: 15 minutes | Cook time: 10 minutes |
Makes 1 cake

Crust:
12 chocolate sandwich cookies
Filling:
1 (13½ ounces / 383-g) can full-fat coconut milk
1 tablespoon agar flakes
1 tablespoon plus 1 teaspoon instant coffee

¼ cup maple syrup (optional)
¼ cup water
½ teaspoon vanilla extract
1 cup raw cashews, soaked in hot water for at least 10 minutes, and drained
2 tablespoons unsweetened cocoa powder

1. For the crust, pulse cookies in a food processor until roughly chopped, then process until they resemble crumbs. Pour into a 9-inch pie plate and press to form a crust. Freeze while making the filling. 2. Transfer solids from coconut milk to a high-speed blender. Pour liquid into a small saucepan (solids can be added later). 3. Whisk agar, coffee, maple syrup (if desired), water, and vanilla into the saucepan with liquids. Place over medium heat and allow mixture to come to a simmer with tiny bubbles breaking the surface. Cook for 3 minutes, whisking often, until agar is completely dissolved. 4. Add cashews and cocoa to the blender with the coconut milk solids. Process until smooth, pausing as needed to scrape down the sides. 5. With the blender running on low, pour contents of the saucepan into the blender and process until filling is smooth and thoroughly combined. Pour into the prepared crust and refrigerate until set, at least 30 minutes. Serve chilled.

Per Serving:(⅛ cake)

calories: 325 | fat: 23g | protein: 5g | carbs: 29g | fiber: 3g

Banana Bread Scones

Prep time: 15 minutes | Cook time: 20 minutes |
Makes 10 scones

2 cups whole spelt flour
1 tablespoon aluminum-free baking powder
1 teaspoon ground cinnamon
½ teaspoon fine sea salt (optional)
⅓ cup pure maple syrup (optional)
⅓ cup liquid refined coconut oil, plus extra for greasing the

measuring cup (optional)
2 teaspoons pure vanilla extract
½ cup mashed ripe banana
2 tablespoons hot water
⅓ cup chopped walnuts
⅓ cup Medjool dates, pitted and chopped
Serve:
Coconut butter
Jam

1. Preheat the oven to 350ºF (180ºC) and line a baking sheet with parchment paper. 2. In a large bowl, whisk together spelt flour, baking powder, cinnamon, and sea salt (if using). Make a small well in the center and add maple syrup, coconut oil (if using), vanilla, and mashed banana. Gently stir with a spatula until slightly combined but with jags of flour throughout. 3. Add hot water, chopped walnuts, and dates to the bowl. Stir until everything is evenly combined, being careful not to overmix. 4. Lightly grease a ⅓-cup measuring cup with coconut oil. Scoop scone batter into the measuring cup and drop onto the prepared baking sheet with force to create a puck shape. Repeat with remaining dough, spacing each scone 2 inches apart and re-greasing the measuring cup if necessary. 5. Bake for 20 minutes. Allow the scones to cool slightly on a wire rack before serving with coconut butter and jam.

Per Serving:(2 scones)

calories: 492 | fat: 21g | protein: 11g | carbs: 72g | fiber: 9g

Coconut and Tahini Bliss Balls

Prep time: 10 minutes | Cook time: 0 minutes |
Makes 9 balls

½ cup cashews
½ cups walnuts
½ cup rolled oats
2 tablespoons maple syrup

(optional)
3 tablespoons sesame tahini
½ cup unsweetened shredded coconut, divided

1. Pulse cashews and walnuts in a blender until you have a combination of smaller pieces and nut dust. Transfer to a medium bowl and add oats, maple syrup (if using), tahini, and ¼ cup of coconut, then mix well. The mixture will be sticky. 2. Put the remaining coconut on a plate. Roll the mixture into 9 equal-sized balls and roll each ball in the coconut until evenly coated. Some coconut may stick more than others, resulting in a thin layer of coating. 3. Place the finished balls on a sheet pan or plate and refrigerate for at least 30 minutes to set. Enjoy immediately or store in an airtight container and refrigerate for up to 7 days.

Per Serving:

calories: 419 | fat: 32g | protein: 10g | carbs: 29g | fiber: 6g

Two-Ingredient Peanut Butter Fudge

Prep time: 5 minutes | Cook time: 5 minutes | Serves 8

1 cup chocolate chips
½ cup natural peanut butter

Sea salt (optional)

1. In a small saucepan over medium-low heat, combine chocolate chips and peanut butter. Cook while stirring often until the chocolate is melted and the mixture is thoroughly combined, about 5 minutes. 2. Use a spatula to transfer the mixture into a pie plate or small glass container lined with parchment paper. Sprinkle with sea salt, if desired. Refrigerate for at least 1 hour or overnight until set. Slice into squares and serve, or refrigerate for up to 1 week.

Per Serving:

calories: 194 | fat: 12g | protein: 6g | carbs: 21g | fiber: 2g

Earl Grey Tiramisu

Prep time: 20 minutes | Cook time: 25 minutes | Serves 10

Cookies:
1½ cups almond flour
2 teaspoons loose-leaf Earl Grey tea, ground into a powder
1 teaspoon lemon zest
¼ cup pure maple syrup (optional)
2 tablespoons refined coconut oil, solid (optional)
½ teaspoon pure vanilla extract
Cashew Mascarpone Filling:
2½ cups raw cashews, soaked for at least 6 hours and drained
1¼ cups strong-brewed Earl

Grey tea, divided
½ cup fresh lemon juice
½ cup pure maple syrup (optional)
1 tablespoon pure vanilla extract
½ teaspoon fine sea salt (optional)
⅛ teaspoon nutritional yeast
⅓ cup liquid refined coconut oil (optional)
Cocoa powder or shavings from a vegan dark chocolate bar, for serving

1. Preheat the oven to 350ºF (180ºC) and line a baking sheet with parchment paper. 2. In a medium bowl, mix almond flour, Earl Grey tea, lemon zest, maple syrup, coconut oil (if using), and vanilla with a fork until well combined. 3. Use your hands to bring the dough together and transfer it to the prepared baking sheet. Press and form the dough into an oval-like shape, about 10 × 7 inches and ¼ inch thick. If the dough is sticky, cover it with plastic wrap and roll it out with a rolling pin. 4. Bake for 12 minutes or until the edges are slightly browned. 5. Remove the cookie from the oven and cut it into 1-inch strips along the short side. Separate the cookies and return them to the oven for 8 to 10 more minutes or until evenly golden brown on the sides. Allow the cookies to cool completely. 6. Rinse and drain cashews and place them in a blender with ¼ cup of Earl Grey tea, lemon juice, maple syrup, vanilla, salt (if using), and nutritional yeast. Blend until smooth. 7. With the blender on low, drizzle in coconut oil through the feed hole. Blend again until completely smooth. 8. Pour the remaining Earl Grey tea into a shallow dish and place an 8- × 10-inch serving dish alongside. Break any longer cookies so that they are roughly the same size. 9. Dip each cookie into the Earl Grey tea and arrange them in the serving dish. Pour the cashew mascarpone mixture over the cookies in an even layer. 10. Refrigerate the tiramisu for 8 hours or overnight to set up. Serve with cocoa powder or chocolate shavings on top.

Per Serving:

calories: 212 | fat: 15g | protein: 2g | carbs: 20g | fiber: 1g

Black Sesame–Ginger Quick Bread

Prep time: 20 minutes | Cook time: 50 minutes | Make 12 muffins

⅔ cup black sesame seeds
1 cup candied ginger
1½ cups plus 2 tablespoons whole wheat pastry flour
1 cup almond meal
2½ teaspoons baking powder
½ teaspoon salt (optional)
¾ cup almond milk, room

temperature
¾ cup coconut sugar (optional)
½ cup melted coconut oil (optional)
2 tablespoons chia seeds
1 tablespoon fresh lemon juice
1 tablespoon ginger juice

1. Preheat the oven to 350ºF (180ºC) and adjust an oven rack to the middle position. Line two muffin pans with liners. 2. Pulse sesame seeds in a food processor until ground, then transfer to a large bowl and set aside. 3. Add ginger and 2 tablespoons of flour to the food processor and pulse until ginger is roughly chopped (flour helps keep it suspended in batter as it bakes). 4. In the bowl with the ground sesame seeds, add remaining flour, almond meal, baking powder, and salt (if desired). Stir to combine, then stir in the ginger. Make a well in the center. 5. Process almond milk, sugar, coconut oil (if desired), chia seeds, lemon juice, and ginger juice in the now-empty food processor until completely combined. Fold wet ingredients into dry ingredients until just combined (batter will be thick). 6. Scoop batter into muffin pans and smooth tops with a wet spatula. Bake for 30 minutes or until a toothpick inserted in the center comes out clean. 7. Allow to cool for 10 minutes in the pans, then completely on a rack before slicing or peeling off the liners.

Per Serving:(2 muffins)

calories: 449 | fat: 30g | protein: 9g | carbs: 42g | fiber: 6g

Mango-Peach Sorbet

Prep time: 2 minutes | Cook time: 0 minutes | Serves 4

2 cups frozen mango
2 cups frozen peaches

1 cup fresh orange juice
Pure maple syrup (optional)

1. Combine mango, peaches, and orange juice in a high-powered blender. Purée, scraping down the sides as needed. Add extra liquid if necessary and sweeten with maple syrup to taste. 2. Serve immediately for soft serve sorbet or transfer to an airtight container and freeze until firm enough to scoop for scoopable sorbet. Store any leftovers in the freezer.

Per Serving:

calories: 107 | fat: 0g | protein: 1g | carbs: 26g | fiber: 2g

Golden Banana Bread

Prep time: 5 minutes | Cook time: 50 minutes | Serves 10

Coconut oil, for pan (optional)
Dry Ingredients:
2 cups almond meal (ground almonds)
1 cup certified gluten-free rolled oats
¼ cup ground flaxseeds
2 tablespoons whole psyllium husk
2 teaspoons ground cinnamon
½ teaspoon ground turmeric
½ teaspoon Himalayan pink salt (optional)
Wet Ingredients:

4 very ripe bananas
¼ cup date syrup (optional)
3 tablespoons raw agave nectar (optional)
1 teaspoon vanilla bean powder
Suggested Add-Ins (optional):
½ cup raisins
½ cup chopped walnuts
1 cup diced banana
Garnish (optional):
1 very ripe banana, sliced
¼ cup chopped dark vegan chocolate

1. Coat the bottom and sides of an 8½ × 4½-inch loaf pan with coconut oil (if using) and preheat the oven to 375ºF (190ºC). 2. In a high-speed blender or food processor, combine all dry ingredients and pulse until well mixed, leaving some oats whole. Set aside. 3. In a large bowl, mash 4 bananas with a fork until smooth. Add date syrup, agave (if using), and vanilla bean powder, then mix well. Next, add the dry mixture and mix until well combined, forming a dough-like texture due to ground flaxseeds and psyllium husk. 4. Mix in your choice of add-ins. 5. Scoop the dough mixture into the prepared pan and press firmly down to remove any air pockets. If desired, slice a ripe banana into 4 pieces lengthwise and place them side by side on top of the loaf. 6. Bake for 50 minutes, checking for doneness by poking the center with a toothpick. It should come out clean. 7. Once done, remove from the oven and let it cool in the pan. Garnish with banana slices or chocolate (if using).

Per Serving:
calories: 284 | fat: 15g | protein: 8g | carbs: 39g | fiber: 7g

Fudgy Nut and Seed Butter Brownies

Prep time: 15 minutes | Cook time: 35 minutes | Makes 16 brownies

¾ cup smooth nut or seed butter
¼ cup plus 2 tablespoons pure maple syrup (optional)
¾ cup unsweetened applesauce
1½ teaspoons pure vanilla extract
½ cup unsweetened cocoa powder
3 tablespoons coconut flour

¾ teaspoon baking soda
½ teaspoon fine sea salt (optional)
½ cup vegan chocolate chunks or chopped chocolate from a 70% dark, dairy-free chocolate bar, divided
3 tablespoons whole nuts or seeds, rough-chopped

1.Preheat your oven to 350ºF (180ºC) and line an 8-inch square pan with parchment paper, leaving an overhang on two opposite sides. Set aside.
2. In a medium bowl, whisk together nut or seed butter, applesauce, vanilla, and maple syrup (if using). 3. Add cocoa powder, coconut flour, baking soda, and sea salt (if using) to the nut butter mixture. Whisk until combined, making sure there are no lumps of cocoa in the batter. 4. Melt half of the chocolate chunks in a double boiler, then stir vigorously into the brownie batter until fully incorporated. 5. Pour the brownie batter into the prepared pan and use a spatula to smooth it out evenly, pushing it into the edges and corners of the pan. 6. Sprinkle the reserved chocolate chunks and chopped nuts over the top of the batter. 7. Bake the brownies for approximately 27-30 minutes, until the top is slightly firm and appears dry and lightly cracked.
8. Allow the brownies to cool completely in the pan set on a wire rack. Then, cover them and place in the refrigerator for at least one hour to ensure neat slices when cutting. 9. Before slicing the brownies, run a chef's knife under hot water and dry it off.

Per Serving:(2 brownies)
calories: 255 | fat: 18g | protein: 6g | carbs: 22g | fiber: 4g

Peanut Butter Nice Cream

Prep time: 5 minutes | Cook time: 0 minutes | Serves 2

3 frozen ripe bananas, broken into thirds
3 tablespoons plant-based milk

2 tablespoons defatted peanut powder
1 teaspoon vanilla extract

1. Combine bananas, milk, peanut powder, and vanilla in a food processor.
2. Process on medium speed for 30 to 60 seconds until the mixture reaches a smooth soft-serve consistency. Serve immediately.

Per Serving:
calories: 237 | fat: 3g | protein: 10g | carbs: 45g | fiber: 7g

Triple Chocolate Icebox Cake

Prep time: 10 minutes | Cook time: 0 minutes | Makes 1 cake

1 (13½ ounces / 383-g) can light or full-fat coconut milk
¼ cup unsweetened cocoa powder
2 tablespoons maple syrup (optional)

1 (13 ounces / 369-g) package double chocolate sandwich cookies
2 tablespoons mini chocolate chips (optional)

1. Blend coconut milk, cocoa powder, and maple syrup (if desired) until smooth. 2. In a 9 × 5-inch loaf pan (preferably glass for layer visibility), create a single layer of cookies on the bottom. Spread about a quarter of the filling on top. Repeat with remaining cookies and filling. Cover and refrigerate for at least an hour or overnight. 3. Before serving, use a butter knife to loosen the edges and invert onto a plate. Sprinkle with mini chocolate chips if desired.

Per Serving:(¼ cake)
calories: 272 | fat: 4g | protein: 24g | carbs: 17g | fiber: 4g

Ginger Peach Muffins

Prep time: 10 minutes | Cook time: 27 minutes | Makes 12 muffins

1 cup unsweetened plant-based milk
1 tablespoon ground flaxseeds
1 teaspoon apple cider vinegar
2¼ cups spelt flour
¾ cup date sugar (optional)
1 tablespoon baking powder
½ teaspoon salt (optional)

2 teaspoons ground ginger
1 teaspoon ground cinnamon
¾ cup unsweetened applesauce
1 teaspoon pure vanilla extract
4 medium peaches, peeled, halved, pitted, and cut into ¼-inch slices (about 2 cups)

1. Preheat the oven to 350ºF (180ºC). Line a 12-cup muffin pan with silicone liners or have ready a nonstick or silicone muffin pan. 2. In a large measuring cup, use a fork to vigorously mix together the plant-based milk, flaxseeds, and vinegar. Mix for about a minute, or until it appears foamy. Set aside. 3. In a medium mixing bowl, sift together the flour, date sugar (if using), baking powder, salt (if using), ginger, and cinnamon. Make a well in the center of the mixture and pour in the milk mixture. Add the applesauce and vanilla and stir together with the milk mixture in the well. Incorporate the dry ingredients into the wet ingredients in the well just until the dry ingredients are moistened (do not overmix). Fold in the peaches. 4. Fill each muffin cup all the way to the top. Bake for 24 to 27 minutes, or until a knife inserted through the center comes out clean. 5. Remove the pan from the oven. Let the muffins cool completely, about 20 minutes, then carefully run a knife around the edges of each muffin to remove.

Per Serving:

calories: 146 | fat: 1g | protein: 4g | carbs: 25g | fiber: 3g

Walnut Brownies

Prep time: 10 minutes | Cook time: 20 minutes | Makes 12 brownies

3 ounces (85 g) extra-firm silken tofu, drained
⅓ cup pitted prunes, rough stems removed
½ cup unsweetened plant-based milk, heated until very hot but not boiling
¾ cup 100% pure maple syrup (optional)
½ cup plus 2 tablespoons

unsweetened cocoa powder
¾ cup water, heated until very hot but not boiling
2 teaspoons pure vanilla extract
1 cup whole wheat pastry flour
½ teaspoon baking soda
½ teaspoon salt (optional)
½ cup walnuts, roughly chopped

1. Line an 8 × 8-inch pan with a 10-inch square of parchment paper or have an 8 × 8-inch nonstick or silicone baking pan ready. Preheat the oven to 325ºF (165ºC). 2. Crumble tofu into a blender. Add prunes and hot plant-based milk, then purée for about 30 seconds. Add maple syrup (if using) and purée until relatively smooth, ensuring no chunks of tofu remain. Scrape down the sides of the blender to incorporate all ingredients. 3. Sift cocoa powder into a mixing bowl. Add hot water and mix with a fork until well combined, creating a thick chocolate sauce. 4. Add prune mixture to the chocolate in the mixing bowl and stir to combine. Mix in vanilla. 5. Sift in half of the flour and add baking soda and salt (if using). Mix well. Mix in remaining flour and fold in walnuts. 6. Spread the batter into the prepared baking pan. It will be thick, but it will spread as it bakes, so no need to push it into corners. 7. Bake for 17 to 20 minutes until the top is set and firm to the touch. 8. Let the brownies cool for at least 20 minutes before slicing into 12 squares and serving.

Per Serving:

calories: 148 | fat: 4g | protein: 3g | carbs: 26g | fiber: 2g

Chocolate Microwave Mug Cake

Prep time: 5 minutes | Cook time: 2 minutes | Serves 1

3 tablespoons whole-wheat flour
3 tablespoons unsweetened applesauce
1 tablespoon cocoa powder
1 tablespoon maple syrup

(optional)
1 tablespoon plant-based milk
1 teaspoon vanilla extract
¼ teaspoon baking powder

1. Combine flour, applesauce, cocoa powder, maple syrup (if desired), milk, vanilla, and baking powder in a microwave-safe coffee mug or bowl. Stir until there are no clumps of dry flour left. 2. Microwave on high for 90 seconds or until the cake has risen to the top of the mug. 3. Remove from the microwave and let it cool for at least 5 minutes before serving.

Per Serving:

calories: 185 | fat: 1g | protein: 4g | carbs: 41g | fiber: 3g

Pumpkin Bread Pudding

Prep time: 10 minutes | Cook time: 25 minutes | Serves 8

1¼ cups pumpkin purée (a little over ½ of a 15 ounces / 425 g can)
1 cup unsweetened plant-based milk
½ cup 100% maple syrup (optional)
2 teaspoons pure vanilla extract
2 tablespoons cornstarch
½ teaspoon salt (optional)

½ teaspoon ground cinnamon
¾ teaspoon ground ginger
¼ teaspoon ground nutmeg
¼ teaspoon ground allspice
⅛ teaspoon ground cloves
8 slices stale whole wheat bread, cut into 1-inch cubes (about 6 cups)
½ cup golden raisins

1. Have an 8 × 8-inch nonstick or silicone baking pan ready and preheat the oven to 350ºF (180ºC). 2. In a large bowl, whisk together pumpkin purée, plant-based milk, maple syrup (if using), and vanilla. Add cornstarch, salt (if using), cinnamon, ginger, nutmeg, allspice, and cloves, and whisk well. Stir in bread cubes and raisins, tossing to coat completely. 3. Transfer the mixture to the prepared pan and bake for 25 minutes or until the top is golden brown and firm to the touch. Serve warm.

Per Serving:

calories: 192 | fat: 1g | protein: 4g | carbs: 31g | fiber: 2g

Gluten-Free Vegan Muffins

Prep time: 10 minutes | Cook time: 35 minutes |

Makes 10 muffins

¼ cup ground flaxseeds
1 cup unsweetened almond milk
1 cup millet flour
½ cup gluten-free oat flour
1 tablespoon aluminum-free baking powder
½ cup almond flour
⅓ cup melted extra-virgin

coconut oil (optional)
¼ cup pure maple syrup (optional)
¼ cup freshly squeezed orange juice
1 tablespoon vanilla extract
½ teaspoon fine sea salt (optional)
Fruit, berries, or vegetables

1. Preheat the oven to 375°F (190°C). Line a standard muffin pan with 10 paper liners and set aside. 2. Combine the ground flaxseeds and almond milk in a small bowl and set aside for 10 to 15 minutes to thicken. 3. Sift the millet flour, oat flour, and baking powder into a medium bowl. Add the almond flour and whisk to combine, breaking up any clumps of almond flour. Whisk together the coconut oil, maple syrup, orange juice, vanilla, and salt, if using, in another medium bowl. Add the flax–almond milk mixture and whisk to combine. Add the flour mixture and stir with a rubber spatula until just combined, adding any flavorings, such as fruit, berries, or vegetables. Spoon the batter into the muffin cups and bake for 35 minutes, or until a toothpick inserted in the center of a muffin comes out clean. Remove from the oven and allow the muffins to sit for 5 minutes before transferring them to a wire rack to cool. Be sure to cool completely before serving. Store leftovers in an airtight container at cool room temperature for up to 2 days or in the fridge for up to 4 days; bring to room temperature, warm in the oven, or halve and toast before serving. The muffins can be frozen in an airtight container for up to 3 months. Thaw at room temperature in the container they were frozen in.

Per Serving:

calories: 212 | fat: 10g | protein: 4g | carbs: 27g | fiber: 3g

Homemade Caramel with Dates and Peanut Butter

Prep time: 20 minutes | Cook time: 0 minutes |

Serves 8

5 Medjool dates, pitted
1 tablespoon peanut butter (no sugar or salt added)

2 teaspoons molasses
8 small apples, cored and sliced into 8 wedges

1. Soak the dates in hot water for 10 minutes. 2. Drain the dates and place them in a food processor. Add the peanut butter and molasses and blend to a smooth consistency. 3. Refrigerate the caramel mixture for 20 to 30 minutes. 4. Serve 1 tablespoon of the caramel mixture with each sliced apple. Refrigerate the remaining caramel mixture for up to 5 days.

Per Serving:

calories: 145 | fat: 1g | protein: 1g | carbs: 36g | fiber: 6g

Gooey Bittersweet Chocolate Pudding Cake

Prep time: 15 minutes | Cook time: 3 to 4 hours |

Serves 6 to 8

Cake:
1 cup whole-wheat flour
¼ cup cocoa powder
2 teaspoons baking powder
½ teaspoon ground cinnamon
¼ teaspoon salt (optional)
⅓ cup unsweetened applesauce
2 teaspoons vanilla extract
⅔ cup unsweetened vanilla or plain plant-based milk
2 tablespoons date syrup or

maple syrup (optional)
Nonstick cooking spray (optional)
Pudding:
¼ cup cocoa powder
1 teaspoon instant coffee
½ cup date syrup or maple syrup (optional)
1 teaspoon vanilla extract
1 cup hot water

1. Begin by whisking together the flour, cocoa powder, baking powder, cinnamon, and salt (if desired) in a medium-sized bowl. In another separate medium bowl, combine the applesauce, vanilla, milk, and date syrup (if preferred), then pour this mixture into the flour mixture and stir until fully combined, taking care not to overmix. 2. either coat the inside of your slow cooker with cooking spray or line it with a slow cooker liner before adding the cake batter and spreading it evenly across the bottom of the cooker. To make the pudding, whisk together the cocoa powder, coffee, date syrup (if desired), vanilla, and hot water in a medium-sized bowl, then pour this mixture over the cake ingredients in the slow cooker. The mixture will be watery at this point. Cover and cook on Low for 3 to 4 hours. Once ready to serve, the cake should appear dry on top but possess a pudding-like texture below the surface. For optimal results, enjoy immediately.

Per Serving:

calories: 195 | fat: 2g | protein: 4g | carbs: 44g | fiber: 4g

Pistachio Protein Ice Cream

Prep time: 25 minutes | Cook time: 0 minutes |

Serves 8

1 can low-fat coconut milk
10 pitted Medjool dates
2 scoops organic pea protein
1 tablespoon vanilla extract
½ cup shelled pistachios

Optional Toppings:
Pomegranate seeds
Fresh mint
Chopped dark chocolate

1. Add all ingredients to a blender and blend into a smooth mixture. 2. Alternatively, add all ingredients to a medium bowl, cover it, and process using a handheld blender. 3. Freeze the mixture for 15 minutes, then stir it and freeze for another 10 minutes. 4. Add any desired toppings and freeze for at least 2 hours. 5. Store the ice cream in the freezer for a maximum of 90 days and thaw for 5 minutes at room temperature before serving.

Per Serving:

calories: 115 | fat: 4g | protein: 9g | carbs: 10g | fiber: 2g

Salted Caramel Bites

Prep time: 5 minutes | Cook time: 0 minutes | Makes 18 bites

1 cup raw cashews	½ cup tahini
1 cup soft and sticky Medjool dates, pitted	1 teaspoon pure vanilla extract
	¼ teaspoon sea salt (optional)

1. In the bowl of a food processor fitted with the chopping blade, pulse the cashews until finely chopped. Add the dates and process until a thick, sticky paste forms. Stop to scrape down the sides of the bowl as needed. 2. Add the tahini, vanilla, and salt (if using) and process until the mixture forms a dough. If the mixture isn't sticking together well, add a tiny bit of water and process again. 3. Scoop out a heaping teaspoon of the mixture and roll into a ball about 1½ inches in diameter. Repeat to form approximately 18 balls. Freeze on a baking sheet until firm, then transfer to an airtight container and store at room temperature for up to 5 days.

Per Serving:

calories: 112 | fat: 6g | protein: 2g | carbs: 11g | fiber: 1g

Pineapple Soft-Serve

Prep time: 5 minutes | Cook time: 0 minutes | Serves 2

1 (10 ounces / 283 g) bag frozen pineapple
2 tablespoons to ¼ cup vanilla almond milk

1. In a high-speed blender, process pineapple on high while tamping down for 30 seconds. Add almond milk as needed while processing and tamping for another 30 seconds until the mixture is silky smooth. Serve immediately.

Per Serving:

calories: 80 | fat: 0g | protein: 0g | carbs: 19g | fiber: 2g

Apple-Oat Crisp

Prep time: 10 minutes | Cook time: 25 minutes | Serves 4 to 6

4 medium Granny Smith apples, cored and cut into ½-inch-thick slices	½ teaspoon ground cinnamon
	⅛ teaspoon ground nutmeg
	¼ teaspoon tapioca starch
¾ cup pure maple syrup, divided	⅔ cup rolled oats
	⅔ cup oat flour
1 tablespoon lemon juice	⅓ cup unsweetened applesauce

1. Preheat the oven to 350°F (180°C). 2. In a medium bowl, mix together the apples, ½ cup of maple syrup, the lemon juice, cinnamon, nutmeg, and tapioca starch until the apples are well coated. 3. Spread the apples out in a single layer in an 8-by-8-inch glass baking dish or a 9-inch pie plate. 4. In a medium bowl, mix together the oats, oat flour, remaining ¼ cup of maple syrup, and the applesauce until well combined. Scoop the oat mixture in dollops onto the apples, and spread gently, trying to cover all the apples. 5. Transfer the baking dish to the oven, and bake for 20 to 25 minutes, or until the oat mixture is golden brown. Remove from the oven.

Per Serving:

calories: 344 | fat: 3g | protein: 5g | carbs: 80g | fiber: 9g

Caramel-Coconut Frosted Brownies

Prep time: 10 minutes | Cook time: 25 minutes | Makes 12 brownies

Brownies:
1 (15 ounces / 425 g) can black beans, drained and rinsed	⅓ cup unsweetened applesauce
½ cup rolled oats	2 tablespoons unsalted, unsweetened almond butter
6 tablespoons pure maple syrup	1 teaspoon vanilla extract
⅓ cup cocoa powder	Pinch ground cinnamon

Frosting:
1 cup pitted dates	⅛ teaspoon red miso paste
6 tablespoons unsweetened plant-based milk	¼ cup chopped pecans
2 tablespoons nutritional yeast	3 tablespoons unsweetened coconut flakes
¼ teaspoon vanilla extract	

Make the Brownies: 1. Preheat the oven to 350°F (180°C). Line a 12-cup cupcake tin with liners. 2. In a food processor, combine the beans, oats, maple syrup, cocoa powder, applesauce, almond butter, vanilla, and cinnamon. Process until smooth. 3. Transfer the mixture to the prepared cupcake tin, about 2 tablespoons per cup to start, then evenly divide the remaining mixture. 4. Bake for 20 to 22 minutes, or until the tops are crispy and a toothpick inserted into the center of a cupcake comes out mostly clean. Remove from the oven. Remove the brownies from the tin, and transfer to a wire rack to cool for about 5 minutes. Make the Frosting: 5. Meanwhile, in a food processor, combine the dates, milk, nutritional yeast, vanilla, and miso. Process until mostly smooth. 6. Pulse in the pecans and coconut until well mixed but with some texture remaining. 7. Add 1 heaping tablespoon of the frosting per brownie, and serve.

Per Serving:

calories: 235 | fat: 11g | protein: 10g | carbs: 30g | fiber: 12g

Strawberry Coconut Shake

Prep time: 2 minutes | Cook time: 0 minutes | Serves 2

1 (13 ounces / 369-g) can full-fat coconut milk	1 tablespoon pure maple syrup (optional)
1½ cups frozen strawberries	1 teaspoon pure vanilla extract

1. In a blender, combine the coconut milk, strawberries, maple syrup (if using), and vanilla and purée until smooth. Pour into 2 glasses and serve immediately, or transfer to an airtight container and keep refrigerated for several days or frozen for several weeks.

Per Serving:

calories: 539 | fat: 46g | protein: 5g | carbs: 32g | fiber: 8g

Baked Apples

Prep time: 5 minutes | Cook time: 20 minutes | Serves 4

3 green apples, cored and evenly sliced
¼ cup apple juice

1½ teaspoons cinnamon
Optional Toppings:
1 tablespoon chopped pecans

1. Preheat the oven to 365ºF (185ºC). 2. In a 9 × 9-inch baking pan, spread the apple slices in a single layer. 3. Pour the apple juice over the apples and sprinkle the cinnamon on top. 4. Cover the pan with aluminum foil and bake for 15 to 18 minutes or until the apples are a lighter color and have a soft texture.

Per Serving:

calories: 81 | fat: 0g | protein: 1g | carbs: 21g | fiber: 4g

Apple Crisp

Prep time: 10 minutes | Cook time: 50 minutes | Serves 6 to 8

Filling:
3 pounds (1.4 kg) Granny Smith apples (about 8 apples), peeled, cored, and cut into ¼-inch slices
2 tablespoons cornstarch
Topping:
¼ cup 100% pure maple syrup (optional)
3 tablespoons cashew butter
2 tablespoons unsweetened applesauce

1 teaspoon ground cinnamon
½ teaspoon ground ginger
⅛ teaspoon ground cloves
½ cup 100% pure maple syrup (optional)

1 teaspoon pure vanilla extract
1½ cup rolled oats
½ teaspoon ground cinnamon
¼ teaspoon salt (optional)

1. Preheat the oven to 400ºF (205ºC). Line an 8 × 8-inch pan with parchment paper, making sure that the parchment goes all the way up the sides of the pan, or have ready an 8 × 8-inch nonstick or silicone baking pan. Make the Filling: 2. Place the apples in a large mixing bowl. 3. Sprinkle the cornstarch, cinnamon, ginger, and cloves over the apple slices and toss well to coat. Pour the maple syrup (if using) over the mixture and stir to combine. Place the apple mixture into the prepared baking pan. Make the Topping: 4. In a small bowl, use a fork to stir together the maple syrup (if using), cashew butter, applesauce, and vanilla, until relatively smooth. Add the oats, cinnamon, and salt (if using), and toss to coat. Assemble the Crisp: 5. Spread the topping over the apple mixture. Place the pan in the preheated oven and bake for 20 minutes. Reduce the oven temperature to 350ºF (180ºC) and bake for an additional 30 minutes, or until the topping is golden and filling is bubbly. 6. Remove the pan from the oven and transfer it to a cooling rack. Serve the crisp warm.

Per Serving:

calories: 232 | fat: 4g | protein: 4g | carbs: 45g | fiber: 8g

Mango Sticky Rice

Prep time: 10 minutes | Cook time: 30 minutes | Serves 6

2½ cups water
1 cup short-grain brown rice
½ cup light or full-fat coconut milk
2 tablespoons coconut sugar (optional)

1 to 2 tablespoons fresh lime juice, to taste
2 mangos, peeled and diced
Unsweetened shredded coconut (optional)

1. Bring the water to a boil in a medium saucepan, then lower the heat to medium-low and stir in the rice. Cook, stirring often, until the liquid is absorbed and the rice is tender, about 30 minutes. 2. Remove from the heat and stir in the coconut milk and sugar, if desired. Add lime juice to taste, then pour into a shallow glass dish. Top with mango, garnish with coconut, if desired, and serve. (This dish can also be refrigerated and served cold, but wait to garnish with the coconut until just before serving.)

Per Serving:

calories: 244 | fat: 5g | protein: 4g | carbs: 47g | fiber: 3g

Peach Cobbler

Prep time: 15 minutes | Cook time: 1 to 2 hours | Serves 6 to 8

Filling:
2 (15 ounces / 425 g) cans peaches in juice
½ teaspoon ground cinnamon
½ teaspoon ground ginger
Topping:
1 cup rolled oats
¼ teaspoon ground cinnamon
2 tablespoons coconut cream
1 tablespoon liquid from the

3 tablespoons maple syrup or date syrup (optional)
2 tablespoons cornstarch

canned peaches
4 tablespoons date syrup (optional)

1. Make the filling: Remove the peaches from the cans, reserving the juice. Slice the peaches into bite-size chunks and put them in the slow cooker. Stir in the cinnamon, ginger, syrup (if using), and cornstarch. 2. Make the topping and cook: In a medium bowl, combine the oats, cinnamon, coconut cream, canned peach liquid, and date syrup (if using). Stir together until the oats are wet and crumbly. Sprinkle over the peaches in the slow cooker. 3. To keep the condensation that forms on the inside of the lid away from the topping, stretch a clean dish towel or several layers of paper towels over the top of the slow cooker, but not touching the food, and place the lid on top of the towel(s). If you skip this step, you will have a soggy result. Cook on High for 1 to 2 hours or on Low for 2 to 3 hours.

Per Serving:

calories: 196 | fat: 2g | protein: 3g | carbs: 44g | fiber: 4g

Blueberry Muffin Loaf

Prep time: 25 minutes | Cook time: 1 hour | Makes 1 loaf

Topping:
¼ cup maple sugar or coconut palm sugar (optional)
4 tablespoons whole spelt flour
Small pinch of fine sea salt (optional)
Loaf:
⅓ cup unsweetened almond milk
1 tablespoon fresh orange juice
1½ cups whole spelt flour
½ cup almond flour
2 teaspoons aluminum-free baking powder
¼ teaspoon baking soda
½ teaspoon fine sea salt (optional)

¼ teaspoon ground cinnamon
2 tablespoons coconut oil (optional)

1 teaspoon ground cinnamon
¼ cup unsweetened applesauce
⅓ cup coconut oil, plus extra for greasing the pan
⅓ cup plus 2 tablespoons maple sugar (optional)
1 teaspoon pure vanilla extract
1 cup fresh blueberries or frozen blueberries

1. Preheat the oven to 375ºF (190ºC). Lightly grease an 8- × 4-inch loaf pan with coconut oil. Line the pan with parchment paper, leaving an overhang on the two long sides, and set aside. 2. Make the Crumble Topping: In a small bowl, combine maple sugar, spelt flour, sea salt, cinnamon, and oil, if using. Lightly mix the topping with a fork until it starts clumping. Place the topping in the refrigerator while you make the loaf. 3. Make the Loaf: In a measuring cup, lightly whisk the almond milk with the orange juice, and set aside to curdle. 4. In a large bowl, whisk together the spelt flour, almond flour, baking powder, baking soda, sea salt, and cinnamon. Add the almond milk mixture to the flour mixture. Add the applesauce, oil, maple sugar, if using, and vanilla. Gently mix with a spatula until you have a unified batter, being careful not to overmix. 5. Gently fold the blueberries into the batter. Quickly scrape the batter into the prepared loaf pan, and top it with the crumble mixture. Gently press the crumble mixture into the surface of the loaf with your fingers. The crumble pieces should be surrounded by batter without being submerged. Slide the loaf pan into the oven, and bake for 55 to 60 minutes or until evenly browned on the top and a toothpick inserted into the center of the loaf comes out clean. 6. Cool the loaf completely in the pan before slicing and serving.

Per Serving:(⅛ loaf)
calories: 280 | fat: 11g | protein: 6g | carbs: 42g | fiber: 5g

Coconut Crumble Bars

Prep time: 10 minutes | Cook time: 15 minutes | Makes 8 bars

2 cups raw and unsalted almonds
10 pitted dates
2 scoops soy protein isolate, chocolate flavor

½ cup cocoa powder
½ cup shredded coconut

1. Preheat the oven to 257ºF (125ºC) and line a baking sheet with parchment paper. 2. Put the almonds on the baking sheet and roast them for about 10 to 15 minutes or until they're fragrant. 3. Meanwhile, cover the dates with water in a small bowl and let them sit for about 10 minutes. Drain the dates after soaking and make sure no water is left. 4. Add the almonds, dates, chocolate protein and cocoa powder to a food processor and blend into a chunky mixture. 5. Alternatively, add all ingredients to a medium bowl, cover it, and process using a handheld blender. 6. Line a loaf pan with parchment paper. Add the almond mixture to the loaf pan, spread it out and press it down firmly until it's 1-inch-thick (2.5 cm) all over. 7. Add the shredded coconut in an even layer on top and press it down firmly to make it stick. 8. Divide into 8 bars, serve cold and enjoy! 9. Store the bars in an airtight container in the fridge, and consume within 6 days. Alternatively, store in the freezer for a maximum of 90 days.

Per Serving:
calories: 301 | fat: 21g | protein: 17g | carbs: 9g | fiber: 5g

Chapter 10 Salads

Creamy Fruit Salad

Prep time: 15 minutes | Cook time: 0 minutes |
Serves 4

4 red apples, cored and diced
1 (15 ounces / 425 g) can
pineapple chunks, drained, or 2
cups fresh pineapple chunks
¼ cup raisins

¼ cup chopped pecans or
walnuts
1 cup plain plant-based yogurt
2 teaspoons maple syrup
(optional)

1. Combine the apples and pineapples in a large bowl, ensuring that the apples are fully covered in pineapple juice to prevent browning. 2. Add the raisins, nuts, yogurt, and maple syrup (if desired) to the bowl and mix everything together well. Cover the mixture and refrigerate it for at least two hours to allow the flavors to develop fully.

Per Serving:
calories: 267 | fat: 5g | protein: 6g | carbs: 54g | fiber: 6g

Brussels Sprouts Salad with Lime and Miso

Prep time: 20 minutes | Cook time: 25 minutes |
Serves 4

Dressing:
1½ tablespoons fresh lime juice
½ teaspoon lime zest
2 tablespoons virgin olive oil
(optional)
1 teaspoon Dijon mustard
2 teaspoons mellow or light
miso
1 teaspoon pure maple syrup
(optional)
Salt and pepper, to taste
(optional)
Salad:
1 pound (454 g) Brussels
sprouts, trimmed and quartered

2 teaspoons virgin olive oil
(optional)
½ teaspoon dried chili flakes
Salt and pepper, to taste
(optional)
1 small ripe avocado
Garnishes:
¼ cup chopped fresh mint
leaves
¼ cup chopped fresh basil
leaves
¼ cup toasted sunflower seeds
Minced fresh chili pepper
(optional)

1. Preheat the oven to 400°F (205°C). Line a baking sheet with parchment paper and set aside. 2. Make the Dressing: In a jar with a tight-fitting lid, combine the lime juice, lime zest, olive oil, Dijon mustard, light miso, maple syrup, salt, and pepper, if using. Tightly secure the lid, and shake the jar vigorously to combine. Mash any remaining lumps of miso with a spoon. Set aside. 3. Make the

Salad: Place the quartered Brussels sprouts onto the baking sheet. Drizzle with the olive oil and season with the chili flakes, salt, and pepper, if using. Toss to coat and slide the baking sheet into the oven. Roast the Brussels sprouts for about 20 to 25 minutes, flipping once at the halfway point. Brussels sprouts should appear evenly charred or browned. 4. Transfer the hot Brussels sprouts to a medium bowl. Pour half of the dressing over the Brussels sprouts, and toss to coat. 5. Transfer the Brussels sprouts to a serving platter. Peel the avocado and remove the pit. Roughly dice the avocado and scatter the pieces on top of the Brussels sprouts. Drizzle the remaining half of the dressing over the salad. Garnish with the chopped mint, chopped basil, toasted sunflower seeds, and minced chili, if using. Serve immediately.

Per Serving:
calories: 275 | fat: 21g | protein: 7g | carbs: 19g | fiber: 9g

Dill Potato Salad

Prep time: 15 minutes | Cook time: 20 minutes |
Serves 4

6 medium potatoes, scrubbed
and chopped into bite-size
pieces
1 zucchini, chopped (same size
pieces as the potatoes)
¼ cup chopped fresh dill, or
about 2 tablespoons dried
1 to 2 teaspoons Dijon mustard
⅛ teaspoon sea salt (optional)
Freshly ground black pepper, to

taste
1 tablespoon nutritional yeast
(optional)
Nondairy milk or water
(optional)
3 celery stalks, chopped
1 green or red bell pepper,
seeded and chopped
1 tablespoon chopped chives or
scallions

1. To prepare the dish, begin by filling a large pot about a quarter of the way with water and bringing it to a boil. Add the potatoes and let them boil for 10 minutes. After 10 minutes, add the zucchini to the pot and continue boiling for an additional 10 minutes. 2. remove the pot from the heat and drain the water, reserving about one cup of the cooking liquid. Set the cooked vegetables aside in a large bowl to cool. Next, transfer about half a cup of the cooked potatoes to a blender or food processor, along with the reserved cooking liquid, dill, mustard, salt (if desired), pepper, and nutritional yeast (if using). Purée everything together until smooth. If needed, add a little nondairy milk or water to achieve your desired consistency. 3. Toss the celery, bell pepper, and chives into the bowl with the cooked potatoes and zucchini. 4. Pour the prepared dressing over the mixture and toss everything together well to ensure that the vegetables are evenly coated.

Per Serving:
calories: 264 | fat: 0g | protein: 8g | carbs: 58g | fiber: 8g

Sweet Potato, Kale, and Red Cabbage Salad

Prep time: 10 minutes | Cook time: 20 minutes |

Serves 2

Salad:
1 teaspoon extra-virgin olive oil (optional)
2 medium sweet potatoes, peeled and diced small
Pinch of salt (optional)
Dressing:
1 avocado, peeled and pitted
Juice of 1½ limes
Pinch of salt (optional)
Pinch red pepper flakes

1 cup frozen corn
2 cups stemmed and chopped kale
1 cup shredded red cabbage
¼ cup pepitas
(optional)
3 tablespoons chopped fresh cilantro leaves
½ cup water

1. To prepare the salad, preheat your oven to 425ºF (220ºC) and grease a sheet pan with olive oil. Spread the sweet potato in a single layer on the prepared sheet pan and sprinkle with salt (if desired). Bake for 10 minutes, then use a spatula to turn the potatoes and continue baking for an additional 5 minutes. Add the corn to the sheet pan and bake everything for another 5 minutes. Meanwhile, in a blender, combine the avocado, lime juice, salt, red pepper flakes (if preferred), cilantro, and water, blending until smooth to create the dressing. 2. To assemble the salad, combine the kale and cabbage in a large bowl, adding half of the dressing and tossing gently. Next, add the sweet potatoes, corn, and remaining dressing, tossing until fully combined. The warmth of the corn and sweet potatoes will help soften the kale slightly. Divide the salad between two bowls, top with pepitas, and serve.

Per Serving:

calories: 488 | fat: 25g | protein: 13g | carbs: 64g | fiber: 16g

Mock Tuna Salad

Prep time: 10 minutes | Cook time: 0 minutes |

Serves 4

Salad:
2 cups raw sunflower seeds, soaked in water for 2 hours
3 to 4 ribs celery, diced
2 scallions, diced
2 tablespoons dulse flakes
¼ cup fresh dill
Dressing:

⅔ cup hemp hearts
¼ cup coconut water or purified water
3 cloves garlic, peeled
½ cup fresh lemon juice
1 teaspoon sea salt (optional)
2 tablespoons stone-ground mustard

1. Prepare the salad: In a food processor, purée the sunflower seeds until they are a slightly chunky pâté. Transfer to a bowl. 2. Mix in the celery, scallions, dulse flakes and dill. Stir well and set aside. 3. Prepare the dressing: In a blender, combine all the dressing ingredients and blend until smooth. Pour the dressing over the salad, toss to mix well and serve.

Per Serving:

calories: 403 | fat: 30g | protein: 13g | carbs: 19g | fiber: 9g

Pineapple Quinoa Salad

Prep time: 10 minutes | Cook time: 15 minutes |

Serves 3

2 cups cooked or canned black beans
½ cup dry quinoa
1 cup fresh or frozen pineapple chunks
8 halved cherry tomatoes

1 red onion, minced
Optional Toppings:
Chili flakes
Soy sauce
Shredded coconut

1. If using dry beans, soak and cook ⅔ cup of black beans as needed, then cook the quinoa for approximately 15 minutes. Next, add all of the ingredients to a large bowl and mix everything together thoroughly. Divide the prepared salad evenly between three bowls, serve with optional toppings, and enjoy! 2. If you have any leftover salad, store it in an airtight container in the refrigerator and consume within two days. Alternatively, you may store the salad in the freezer for up to 30 days, thawing it at room temperature before serving. This salad can be served cold.

Per Serving:

calories: 310 | fat: 2g | protein: 16g | carbs: 56g | fiber: 14g

Apple Broccoli Crunch Bowl

Prep time: 20 minutes | Cook time: 0 minutes |

Serves 6

Bowl:
2 medium heads broccoli
3 diced apples
¼ cup diced red onion
½ cup raisins
½ cup sunflower seed kernels
¼ cup raw shelled hempseed
Dressing:
¼ cup cider vinegar

½ cup extra virgin olive oil (optional)
2 cloves garlic, minced
1 tablespoon maple syrup (optional)
½ teaspoon salt (optional)
¼ teaspoon ground black pepper

To create the bowl, begin by cutting the florets from the broccoli stalks and setting the stalks aside. Cut the florets into very small pieces and place them in a large bowl. Next, remove the hard outer skin from the broccoli stalks to reveal the tender inside. Discard the outer skin and cut the inside stems into matchsticks. Alternatively, you may use a mandolin or food processor that has an attachment capable of cutting the stems into long strips (not grated), or even scissors will work. The goal is to have very small sticks of raw broccoli stems that will hold their shape. Add the prepared stems to the large bowl along with the florets, apples, onions, raisins, sunflower seeds, and hempseed. To make the dressing, whisk together all of the dressing ingredients in a medium-sized bowl. Add the prepared dressing to the salad and toss everything together well. Chill the mixture until ready to serve.

Per Serving:

calories: 296 | fat: 24g | protein: 9g | carbs: 18g | fiber: 4g

Greek Salad in a Jar

Prep time: 10 minutes | Cook time: 10 minutes | Serves 4

Salad:
1 cup uncooked quinoa
1 cucumber, diced
2 cups cherry tomatoes, halved
2 bell peppers, seeded and chopped
½ cup walnuts, chopped
¼ cup sun-dried black olives, sliced
4 cups chopped mixed greens (romaine is great, too)
Dressing:
¼ cup extra-virgin olive oil

(optional)
½ cup fresh lemon juice
1 tablespoon Dijon mustard
3 cloves garlic, minced, or 2 teaspoons garlic powder
¼ cup basil, finely chopped, or 1 tablespoon dried
1 tablespoon chopped fresh oregano, or 1 teaspoon dried
Himalayan pink salt and freshly ground black pepper (about ¼ teaspoon each)

1.Cook the quinoa according to the package directions. Once cooked, set it aside to cool. While the quinoa is cooling, prepare the dressing by combining all of the dressing ingredients in a small jar or container with a lid. Securely screw the lid onto the jar and shake everything together until fully combined. 2. Add 1 to 4 tablespoons of the prepared dressing to the bottom of each jar, depending on personal preference. 3. Add the cucumber, cooked quinoa, tomatoes, bell peppers, walnuts, and olives. Finally, add chopped mixed greens to fill the jar completely. Screw the lid onto the jar and store the prepared salad in the refrigerator for up to four days. When ready to eat, unscrew the lid and pour the contents of the jar into a bowl. The dressing will coat the ingredients as you do so, but if not, use your fork to gently toss the salad before enjoying.

Per Serving:

calories: 399 | fat: 24g | protein: 10g | carbs: 39g | fiber: 6g

Peaches, Peas, and Beans Summer Salad

Prep time: 15 minutes | Cook time: 5 minutes | Serves 6

Dressing:
1 tablespoon balsamic vinegar
1 teaspoon Dijon mustard
1 teaspoon gluten-free tamari soy sauce
Salad:
¾ pound (340 g) young green, yellow or burgundy string beans, trimmed
2 ripe and firm peaches
1 small shallot, peeled and sliced paper thin
Large handful of snap peas, trimmed and sliced down the

2 tablespoons coconut oil (optional)
Salt and pepper, to taste (optional)

middle
Salt and pepper, to taste (optional)
¼ cup chopped fresh basil leaves
¼ cup whole toasted almonds, coarsely chopped

1. To prepare the dressing, combine the balsamic vinegar, Dijon

mustard, tamari, oil, salt, and pepper (if desired) in a small jar with a tight-fitting lid. Secure the lid tightly and shake the jar vigorously until the dressing has a smooth consistency. Set the prepared dressing aside. 2. Bring a medium-sized saucepan of water to a boil. Add salt to the water, then add the trimmed green beans. Blanch the beans for three minutes or until tender and crisp. Drain the beans and immediately place them in a bowl of ice water to cool. Remove the pits from the peaches and slice the fruit thinly. In a large bowl, combine the sliced peaches, shallots, and snap peas. Drain the cooled green beans and gently dry them before adding them to the large bowl. Season the salad with salt and pepper (if desired). Pour the prepared dressing over the vegetables and peaches, tossing everything together lightly to fully combine. 3. Scatter chopped basil and almonds over the top of the salad and serve.

Per Serving:

calories: 132 | fat: 8g | protein: 4g | carbs: 13g | fiber: 4g

Vegan "Toona" Salad

Prep time: 10 minutes | Cook time: 0 minutes | Serves 4

3 cups cooked chickpeas
1 avocado, peeled and pitted
½ cup chopped red onion
¼ cup chopped celery
2 tablespoons Dijon mustard

1½ tablespoons freshly squeezed lemon juice
½ tablespoon maple syrup (optional)
1 teaspoon garlic powder

1. Combining the chickpeas and avocado in a large bowl. Using either a fork or potato masher, smash the mixture until most of the chickpeas have been broken apart. 2. Stir in the onion, celery, mustard, lemon juice, maple syrup (if preferred), and garlic powder, ensuring that all ingredients are thoroughly combined. Serve immediately.

Per Serving:

calories: 298 | fat: 10g | protein: 13g | carbs: 42g | fiber: 13g

Detox Salad

Prep time: 10 minutes | Cook time: 0 minutes | Serves 2

2 cups purple sauerkraut
1 bunch flat-leaf parsley, roughly chopped
¼ cup mixed seeds (pumpkin,

sunflower, sesame, hemp)
2 tablespoons raisins, rinsed
1 avocado, peeled, pitted and sliced

1. Combine the sauerkraut, parsley, seeds, and raisins in a large bowl. 2. Toss everything together until thoroughly combined. When ready to serve, transfer the mixture to smaller bowls or plates and top each serving with half of the sliced avocado. This dish will keep well in the refrigerator for up to three days.

Per Serving:

calories: 321 | fat: 23g | protein: 9g | carbs: 25g | fiber: 12g

Blueprint: Lifesaving Bowl

Prep time: 20 minutes | Cook time: 0 minutes |

Makes 1 bowl

1 cup cooked quinoa	2 tablespoons nutritional yeast
1 cup shredded or chopped raw vegetables	1 tablespoon lime juice or vinegar
½ avocado, sliced	Sesame or hemp seeds
¼ cup prepared kimchi	

1. Arrange all of the ingredients in layers within a bowl and enjoy!

Per Serving:(¼ bowl)

calories: 149 | fat: 5g | protein: 6g | carbs: 20g | fiber: 6g

Orange, Fennel and White Bean Salad

Prep time: 15 minutes | Cook time: 0 minutes |

Serves 4

6 large oranges, peeled and segmented	fennel fronds
2 tablespoons fresh lemon juice	2 cups cooked navy beans, or 1 (15 ounces / 425 g) can, drained and rinsed
2 tablespoons balsamic vinegar	
1 medium fennel bulb, trimmed and thinly sliced	Salt, to taste (optional)
2 tablespoons minced fresh	Cayenne pepper, to taste
	4 cups arugula

1. Combine the orange sections, lemon juice, balsamic vinegar, fennel bulb and fronds, beans, salt (if desired), and cayenne pepper in a large bowl, mixing everything together well. 2. Allow the mixture to sit for one hour before serving. When ready to serve, divide the arugula evenly among four individual plates and spoon the prepared salad on top of the greens.

Per Serving:

calories: 267 | fat: 1g | protein: 10g | carbs: 56g | fiber: 18g

Ancient Grains Salad

Prep time: 20 minutes | Cook time: 55 minutes |

Serves 6

¼ cup farro	coarsely chopped
¼ cup raw rye berries	½ cup chopped fresh parsley
2 ripe pears, cored and coarsely chopped	¼ cup golden raisins
	3 tablespoons freshly squeezed lemon juice
2 celery stalks, coarsely chopped	
1 green apple, cored and	¼ teaspoon ground cumin
	Pinch cayenne pepper

1. Combine the farro and rye berries in an 8-quart pot and add enough water to cover the grains by three inches. Bring the mixture to a boil over high heat, then reduce the heat to medium-low, cover the pot, and cook for 45 to 50 minutes or until the grains are firm and chewy but not hard. 2. Drain the grains and set them aside to cool. In a large bowl, gently stir together the cooled grains, pears, celery, apple, parsley, raisins, lemon juice, cumin, and cayenne pepper. You may serve this dish immediately or store it in an airtight container in the refrigerator for up to one week.

Per Serving:

calories: 127 | fat: 1g | protein: 3g | carbs: 31g | fiber: 5g

Succotash Salad

Prep time: 20 minutes | Cook time: 0 minutes |

Serves 4

1½ cups cooked baby lima beans	diced
	¼ cup balsamic vinegar, or to taste
3 ears corn, kernels removed (about 2 cups)	
	¼ cup chopped parsley
2 large tomatoes, chopped	Salt and freshly ground black pepper, to taste
1 medium red onion, peeled and	

1. Mix all of the ingredients together in a large bowl until well combined.

Per Serving:

calories: 221 | fat: 1g | protein: 9g | carbs: 47g | fiber: 9g

Meyer Lemon Romanesco Glow Salad

Prep time: 20 minutes | Cook time: 0 minutes |

Serves 6

Dressing:	
½ teaspoon Meyer lemon zest	2 tablespoons coconut oil (optional)
1 tablespoon fresh Meyer lemon juice	
	Salt and pepper, to taste (optional)
½ teaspoon Dijon mustard	
Salad:	
1 medium head Romanesco broccoli or cauliflower, broken up into florets	3 green onions, thinly sliced
	2 teaspoons minced fresh sage
	⅓ cup walnut halves, toasted and chopped
1 medium sweet apple, cored and chopped	
	Salt and pepper, to taste (optional)
1 stalk celery, small diced	
1 cup seedless grapes, halved	

1. To create the dressing, begin by whisking together the lemon zest, lemon juice, Dijon mustard, coconut oil, and salt (if desired) and pepper in a small bowl until fully combined. Set this mixture aside. Next, use a food processor to blitz the Romanesco florets in batches until they reach a couscous-like size and texture. Place the processed Romanesco into a large bowl. 2. To the same bowl, add the apples, celery, grapes, green onions, sage, and walnuts. Season everything with salt and pepper (if preferred) and toss to combine. Pour the prepared dressing over the salad and toss everything together to fully combine. You may serve the salad immediately or store it in a container in the refrigerator for up to three days.

Per Serving:

calories: 129 | fat: 8g | protein: 3g | carbs: 15g | fiber: 4g

Lemony Kale Salad

Prep time: 10 minutes | Cook time: 0 minutes |
Serves 4

2 tablespoons freshly squeezed
lemon juice
½ tablespoon maple syrup

(optional)
1 teaspoon minced garlic
5 cups chopped kale

1. In a large bowl, whisk together the lemon juice, maple syrup (if desired), and garlic. Add the kale, massage it in the dressing for 1 to 2 minutes, and serve.

Per Serving:
calories: 51 | fat: 0g | protein: 3g | carbs: 11g | fiber: 1g

Mango Black Bean Salad

Prep time: 25 minutes | Cook time: 0 minutes |
Serves 4

4 cups cooked black beans,
or 2 (15 ounces / 425 g) cans,
drained and rinsed
2 mangoes, peeled, halved,
pitted, and diced
1 medium red bell pepper,
seeded and diced small
1 bunch green onions (green

and white parts), thinly sliced
½ cup finely chopped cilantro
1 jalapeño pepper, minced (for
less heat, remove the seeds)
½ cup red wine vinegar
Zest and juice of 1 orange
Zest and juice of 1 lime

1. Combine all ingredients in a large bowl and mix well. Chill for 1 hour before serving.

Per Serving:
calories: 299 | fat: 1g | protein: 16g | carbs: 56g | fiber: 17g

Quinoa, Corn and Black Bean Salad

Prep time: 25 minutes | Cook time: 0 minutes |
Serves 4

2½ cups cooked quinoa
3 ears corn, kernels removed
(about 2 cups)
1 red bell pepper, roasted,
seeded, and diced
½ small red onion, peeled and
diced
2 cups cooked black beans, or 1
(15 ounces / 425 g) can, drained
and rinsed

1 cup finely chopped cilantro
6 green onions (white and green
parts), thinly sliced
1 jalapeño pepper, minced (for
less heat, remove the seeds)
Zest of 1 lime and juice of 2
limes
1 tablespoon cumin seeds,
toasted and ground
Salt, to taste (optional)

1. Combine all ingredients in a large bowl and mix well. Chill for 1 hour before serving

Per Serving:
calories: 366 | fat: 3g | protein: 16g | carbs: 70g | fiber: 14g

Smoky Potato Salad over Greens

Prep time: 25 minutes | Cook time: 15 minutes |
Serves 6

2 pounds (907 g) waxy potatoes
¼ cup apple cider vinegar
2 scallions, sliced
1 teaspoon maple syrup
(optional)
1 teaspoon tomato paste
½ teaspoon gluten-free Dijon
mustard

½ teaspoon salt (optional)
½ teaspoon smoked paprika
¼ teaspoon black pepper
2 drops liquid smoke
12 ounces (340 g) baby greens
¼ cup unsalted, roasted
almonds, chopped

1. Steam or boil the potatoes in a large pot over medium-high heat until fork-tender, about 15 minutes. Drain and let cool in a single layer. 2. Meanwhile, whisk the vinegar, scallions, maple syrup, tomato paste, mustard, salt (if desired), paprika, pepper, and liquid smoke together in a large bowl. 3. Chop the potatoes into bite-size pieces. Add to the bowl and toss gently with the dressing. Serve over the greens and top with almonds if serving immediately. The salad can be refrigerated for up to 5 days (though the oil-free version will only last a day due to the avocado), then combined with the greens and almonds before eating.

Per Serving:
calories: 179 | fat: 3g | protein: 5g | carbs: 34g | fiber: 6g

Bulgur Lettuce Cups

Prep time: 10 minutes | Cook time: 20 minutes |
Serves 2 to 4

Sauce:
½ cup unsweetened natural
peanut butter
¼ cup soy sauce
3 tablespoons seasoned rice
Cups:
1 cup bulgur
½ cup soy sauce
¼ cup seasoned rice vinegar
½ teaspoon garlic powder
½ teaspoon ground ginger
¼ teaspoon red pepper flakes

vinegar
2 tablespoons lime juice
1 teaspoon liquid aminos
1 teaspoon sriracha

1 cup shredded carrots
1 cup shredded cabbage
½ cup sliced scallions, green
and white parts
1 head red leaf lettuce or Bibb
lettuce

Make the Sauce: 1. In a small bowl, combine the peanut butter, soy sauce, vinegar, lime juice, liquid aminos, and sriracha. Whisk until well combined. Make the Cups: 2. In a medium saucepan, cook the bulgur for about 12 minutes. Remove from the heat. Drain any excess water after cooking. 3. In a small bowl, combine the soy sauce, vinegar, garlic powder, ginger, and red pepper flakes. Mix well. 4. Add the carrots, cabbage, scallions, and soy sauce mixture to the cooked bulgur. Mix thoroughly. 5. Serve the filling scooped into individual lettuce leaves, topped with a drizzle of peanut sauce.

Per Serving:
calories: 532 | fat: 17g | protein: 25g | carbs: 79g | fiber: 18g

Blueberry-Walnut Vinaigrette

Prep time: 5 minutes | Cook time: 0 minutes | Serves 4

¼ cup apple cider vinegar
¼ cup blueberries
¼ cup walnut pieces
1 or 2 tablespoons water (optional)
1 tablespoon minced shallot or

red onion
½ teaspoon dried thyme
½ teaspoon sugar or maple syrup (optional)
Salt and black pepper (optional)

1. Purée the vinegar, blueberries, and half of the walnuts in a blender until smooth, thinning it with 1 or 2 tablespoons of water if desired. 2. Finely chop the rest of the walnuts. Transfer to a jar with a tight-fitting lid and add the shallot, thyme, and sugar. Shake to combine and season with salt (if desired) and pepper. Refrigerate for at least a few hours and up to 3 days to allow the flavors to meld.

Per Serving:

calories: 45 | fat: 3g | protein: 1g | carbs: 3g | fiber: 1g

Caramelized Onion Potato Salad

Prep time: 15 minutes | Cook time: 45 minutes |
Serves 6

Dressing:
3 tablespoons virgin olive oil (optional)
1 tablespoon grainy mustard
1 teaspoon prepared horseradish
1 teaspoon raw agave nectar or
Salad:
2 teaspoons virgin olive oil (optional)
1 large onion, cut into ¼-inch slices
1½ pounds (680 g) mini new potatoes
¼ cup chopped fresh dill

pure maple syrup (optional)
1 tablespoon white wine vinegar
Salt and pepper, to taste (optional)

¼ cup lightly packed chopped fresh flat-leaf parsley
2 green onions, finely sliced
⅓ cup chopped dill pickles or bread-and-butter pickles
Salt and pepper, to taste (optional)

1. Make the dressing. Combine the olive oil, grainy mustard, horseradish, agave nectar, white wine vinegar, salt, and pepper (if desired) in a jar with a tight-fitting lid. Shake the jar vigorously to combine everything and set it aside. 2. Heat the olive oil in a large pot over medium-low heat. Add the onions and cook them for about 40 minutes, stirring every few minutes until they are very soft and deep golden brown. Ensure there are no dry or crispy bits of onion and that they have a jammy texture. If necessary, lower the heat slightly and add a splash of water to prevent crisping. Once fully caramelized, scrape the onions into a bowl and allow them to cool. While the onions are cooking, place the potatoes in a large saucepan over medium-high heat, covering them with cold water by one inch. Bring the mixture to a boil, then lower the heat to a simmer and cook the potatoes for 15 minutes or until tender when pricked with a paring knife. Drain the potatoes and run them under cold water to speed up the cooling process. Once cooled, cut the potatoes into quarters, wedges, or bite-sized pieces, and place them in a large bowl. To the potatoes, add the cooled caramelized

onions, chopped dill, parsley, green onions, and chopped pickles. Season the salad with salt and pepper (if desired). Pour the prepared dressing over the potato salad and toss everything together to fully combine. Serve the salad cold or at room temperature.

Per Serving:

calories: 180 | fat: 9g | protein: 3g | carbs: 24g | fiber: 3g

Beet, Cabbage, and Black Bean Salad

Prep time: 2 minutes | Cook time: 20 minutes |
Serves 4 to 6

3 or 4 medium beets, peeled and cut into ½-inch dice
½ cup water
1 (15 ounces / 425 g) can black beans, drained and rinsed
1 cup shredded cabbage
1 cup shredded spinach
1 cup halved grape tomatoes
2 scallions, green and white

parts, thinly sliced
½ cup seasoned rice vinegar
¼ teaspoon freshly ground black pepper
4 to 6 cups cooked brown rice
1 ripe avocado, pitted, peeled, and diced
Fresh cilantro, for garnish

1. Combining the beets and water in a sauté pan or skillet. Bring the mixture to a simmer over high heat. 2. Once simmering, reduce the heat to medium-low, cover the pan, and cook for 10 to 15 minutes, or until the beets are slightly soft. 3. Remove the pan from the heat and stir in the beans, cabbage, spinach, tomatoes, scallions, vinegar, and pepper. 4. Serve the prepared vegetables over rice, then top everything with sliced avocado and garnish with cilantro.

Per Serving:

calories: 179 | fat: 7g | protein: 7g | carbs: 26g | fiber: 10g

You Won't Believe It's Cashew Ranch Dressing

Prep time: 5 minutes | Cook time: 0 minutes | Serves
12

1¼ cups raw cashews
¾ cup water, plus more as needed
1 tablespoon plus 1½ teaspoons fresh lemon juice
1 tablespoon apple cider vinegar

1½ teaspoons onion powder
1 teaspoon dried dill
1 teaspoon salt (optional)
½ teaspoon dried basil
½ teaspoon garlic powder
¼ teaspoon black pepper

1. Process all the ingredients in a high-speed blender until smooth. Adjust the seasoning if necessary, and add additional water, 1 tablespoon at a time, as needed to achieve the desired consistency. Refrigerate in an airtight container up for up to 1 week. (The dressing will thicken in the refrigerator; stir in water as needed to thin before serving.)

Per Serving:

calories: 81 | fat: 6g | protein: 2g | carbs: 5g | fiber: 0g

Crunchy Curry Salad

Prep time: 20 minutes | Cook time: 0 minutes |

Serves 4

1 head napa cabbage
1 cup shredded carrots
1 red bell pepper, julienned
½ cup thinly sliced scallions
½ cup fresh cilantro, roughly chopped
½ cup sunflower seeds
1 jalapeño chile pepper, thickly sliced
½ cup creamy almond butter
¼ cup canned full-fat coconut

milk
¼ cup rice vinegar
¼ cup diced yellow onion
2 tablespoons white miso paste
2 tablespoons pure maple syrup (optional)
1 tablespoon red curry paste
1 garlic clove, minced
½-inch piece fresh ginger, peeled

1. Trim the end of the cabbage, halve and core it, and then cut it into very thin ribbons or shred it. Place the shredded cabbage in a bowl with the carrots, bell pepper, scallions, cilantro, sunflower seeds, and chile pepper, setting the mixture aside. 2. Use a blender to create a curry sauce by combining almond butter, coconut milk, vinegar, onion, miso, maple syrup (if desired), curry paste, garlic, and ginger, blending until the mixture is smooth. Be sure to stop and scrape down the sides as needed. If the mixture is too thick, add a little more coconut milk and blend again. 3. Pour the prepared sauce over the cabbage mixture and toss everything together well to fully combine. You may serve the dish immediately or store it in an airtight container for up to five days.

Per Serving:

calories: 478 | fat: 31g | protein: 16g | carbs: 42g | fiber: 15g

Lentil Cranberry Salad

Prep time: 10 minutes | Cook time: 0 minutes |

Serves 2

2 cups cooked or canned green lentils
1 small red onion, minced
½ cubed cucumber
¼ cup lemon juice

¼ cup dried cranberries
Optional Toppings:
Black pepper
Tahini

1. When using dry lentils, soak and cook ⅔ cup of dry lentils if necessary. 2. Transfer the lentils to a large bowl, and add the minced red onion, cucumber cubes, lemon juice and cranberries. 3. Stir thoroughly using a spatula and make sure everything is mixed evenly. 4. Divide the lentil salad between two bowls, garnish with the optional toppings, serve and enjoy! 5. Store the salad in an airtight container in the fridge, and consume within 2 days. Alternatively, store in the freezer for a maximum of 30 days and thaw at room temperature. The salad can be served cold.

Per Serving:

calories: 268 | fat: 1g | protein: 19g | carbs: 46g | fiber: 17g

Lemon Garlic Chickpeas Salad

Prep time: 10 minutes | Cook time: 0 minutes |

Serves 2

1 cup cooked or canned chickpeas
½ cup fresh spinach
¼ cup lemon juice
¼ cup tahini

1 clove garlic minced
¼ cup water
Optional Toppings:
Fresh cilantro
Raisins

1. When using dry chickpeas, soak and cook ⅓ cup of dry chickpeas if necessary. 2. Meanwhile, add the tahini, minced garlic, lemon juice and water to a small airtight container or bowl. 3. Whisk the tahini, lemon juice, garlic and water in the bowl to form a thinner and smooth dressing, adding more water if necessary. Alternatively, shake the container with tahini, lemon juice, garlic and water until everything is thoroughly mixed, adding more water if you want a thinner and less creamy dressing. 4. Put the spinach in a strainer, rinse well to clean it thoroughly and then drain well. 5. Add the spinach and chickpeas to a large bowl and mix thoroughly. 6. Divide the salad between two bowls, garnish with the tangerines and the optional toppings, serve and enjoy! 7. Store the salad in an airtight container in the fridge, and consume within 2 days. Alternatively, store in the freezer for a maximum of 30 days and thaw at room temperature. The salad can be served cold.

Per Serving:

calories: 406 | fat: 22g | protein: 19g | carbs: 33g | fiber: 11g

Moroccan Aubergine Salad

Prep time: 20 minutes | Cook time: 20 minutes |

Serves 2

1 teaspoon olive oil (optional)
1 eggplant, diced
½ teaspoon ground cumin
½ teaspoon ground ginger
¼ teaspoon turmeric
¼ teaspoon ground nutmeg
Pinch sea salt (optional)
1 lemon, half zested and juiced,

half cut into wedges
2 tablespoons capers
1 tablespoon chopped green olives
1 garlic clove, pressed
Handful fresh mint, finely chopped
2 cups spinach, chopped

1. Heat the oil (if using) in a large skillet on medium heat, then sauté the eggplant. Once it has softened slightly, about 5 minutes, stir in the cumin, ginger, turmeric, nutmeg, and salt (if using). Cook until the eggplant is very soft, about 10 minutes. 2. Add the lemon zest and juice, capers, olives, garlic, and mint. Sauté for another minute or two, to blend the flavors. 3. Put a handful of spinach on each plate, and spoon the eggplant mixture on top. Serve with a wedge of lemon, to squeeze the fresh juice over the greens.

Per Serving:

calories: 111 | fat: 3g | protein: 4g | carbs: 20g | fiber: 9g

Curried Kale Slaw

Prep time: 20 minutes | Cook time: 0 minutes |

Serves 4

Dressing:
⅔ cup water
2 tablespoons apple cider vinegar
2 tablespoons pure maple syrup (optional)
1 garlic clove, minced
1 teaspoon grated peeled fresh ginger
1 teaspoon Dijon mustard
½ teaspoon curry powder
Freshly ground black pepper, to

taste
Slaw:
1 apple, shredded
1 tablespoon freshly squeezed lemon juice
3 cups thinly sliced kale
1 carrot, shredded
1 cup shredded fennel
¼ cup golden raisins
¼ cup sliced almonds, plus more for garnish

Make the Dressing: 1. In a blender, combine the water, vinegar, maple syrup (if using), garlic, ginger, mustard, and curry powder. Season with pepper. Purée until smooth. Set aside. Make the Slaw: 2. In a large bowl, toss together the apple and lemon juice. 3. Add the kale, carrot, fennel, raisins, and almonds and toss to combine the slaw ingredients. 4. Add about three-quarters of the dressing and toss to coat. Taste and add more dressing as needed. Let sit for 10 minutes to allow the kale leaves to soften. Toss again and top with additional sliced almonds to serve.

Per Serving:

calories: 147 | fat: 4g | protein: 3g | carbs: 26g | fiber: 4g

Lentil Salad with Lemon and Fresh Herbs

Prep time: 10 minutes | Cook time: 45 minutes |

Serves 4

1½ cups green lentils, rinsed
3 cups vegetable stock, or low-sodium vegetable broth
Zest of 1 lemon and juice of 2 lemons
2 cloves garlic, peeled and minced
½ cup finely chopped cilantro

2 tablespoons finely chopped mint
4 green onions (white and green parts), finely chopped, plus more for garnish
Salt and freshly ground black pepper, to taste
4 cups arugula

1. Place the lentils in a medium saucepan with the vegetable stock and bring to a boil over high heat. Reduce the heat to medium, cover, and cook for 35 to 45 minutes, or until the lentils are tender but not mushy. 2. Drain the lentils and place them in a large bowl. Add the lemon zest and juice, garlic, cilantro, mint, green onions, and salt and pepper and mix well. 3. To serve, divide the arugula among 4 individual plates. Spoon the lentil salad on top of the greens and garnish with freshly chopped green onions.

Per Serving:

calories: 277 | fat: 0g | protein: 18g | carbs: 51g | fiber: 8g

Slaw Salad and Avocado Dressing

Prep time: 15 minutes | Cook time: 0 minutes |

Serves 6

Salad:
2 cups thinly sliced red cabbage
1 cup grated carrots
Dressing:
1 avocado, peeled and pitted
1 tablespoon lemon juice
¼ cup unsweetened plant-based milk
1 to 2 teaspoons minced garlic
1 to 2 tablespoons Dijon

¼ cup packed chopped cilantro

mustard
½ tablespoon agave syrup (optional)
½ teaspoon salt (optional)
⅛ teaspoon freshly ground pepper

1. In a large bowl, mix the cabbage, carrots, and cilantro. 2. In a food processor or blender, blend together the avocado, lemon juice, milk, garlic, mustard, agave, salt (if desired), and pepper until smooth. 3. Pour the dressing over the salad and toss well to coat.

Per Serving:

calories: 82 | fat: 5g | protein: 2g | carbs: 9g | fiber: 4g

Perfect Potluck Pasta Salad

Prep time: 20 minutes | Cook time: 30 minutes |

Serves 8

1 pound (454 g) bowtie pasta
2 tablespoons olive oil (optional)
¾ cup diced red, white, or yellow onion
1 teaspoon minced garlic
1 (6½ ounces / 184 g) jar

marinated artichoke quarters with their juices
Juice of 1 lemon
½ teaspoon minced lemon zest
¼ teaspoon salt (optional)
Cherry tomatoes, halved
Freshly ground pepper, to taste

1. In a large pot over medium-high heat, boil water and cook the pasta according to the directions on the package. Remove from the heat and drain. 2. While the pasta cools, begin on the veggies. In a large pan over medium-high heat, heat the olive oil (if desired) and sauté the onion and garlic for 3 minutes or until the onion becomes tender and translucent. 3. Add the artichokes and their juices, lemon juice, lemon zest, and salt (if desired) and simmer over medium heat for 5 minutes. 4. Add the drained pasta and mix well. 5. Garnish with the cherry tomatoes and sprinkle with pepper. 6. Serve warm if you're rushed, or serve chilled if you have 30 minutes to spare.

Per Serving:

calories: 122 | fat: 4g | protein: 3g | carbs: 20g | fiber: 5g

Classic French Vinaigrette

Prep time: 5 minutes | Cook time: 0 minutes | Serves 4

3 tablespoons apple cider vinegar
2 tablespoons minced shallot
1 tablespoon balsamic vinegar
1 teaspoon gluten-free Dijon mustard

½ teaspoon dried thyme
2 teaspoons olive oil (optional)
Salt and black pepper (optional)

1. To prepare the dressing, start by combining the apple cider vinegar, shallot, and balsamic vinegar in a medium-sized jar with a tight-fitting lid. Let the mixture sit for five minutes before stirring in the mustard and thyme. 2. Slowly whisk in the oil in a steady stream until fully combined. Season the dressing with salt and pepper to taste, if desired. Once prepared, refrigerate the dressing for up to five days.

Per Serving:
calories: 24 | fat: 2g | protein: 0g | carbs: 2g | fiber: 0g

Tomato, Corn and Bean Salad

Prep time: 20 minutes | Cook time: 10 minutes | Serves 4

6 ears corn
3 large tomatoes, diced
2 cups cooked navy beans, or 1 (15 ounces / 425 g) can, drained
and rinsed

1 medium red onion, peeled and diced small
1 cup finely chopped basil
2 tablespoons balsamic vinegar
Salt and freshly ground black pepper, to taste

1. Bring a large pot of water to a boil. Add the corn and cook for 7 to 10 minutes. Drain the water from the pot and rinse the corn under cold water to cool, then cut the kernels from the cob. 2. In a large bowl, toss together the corn, tomatoes, beans, onion, basil, balsamic vinegar, and salt and pepper. Chill for 1 hour before serving.

Per Serving:
calories: 351 | fat: 2g | protein: 15g | carbs: 66g | fiber: 17g

Chapter 11 Basics

Green on Greens Dressing

Prep time: 10 minutes | Cook time: 0 minutes | Serves 10

¾ cup water, plus extra as needed
½ cup chopped flat-leaf parsley
¼ cup tahini
1 scallion, sliced
1 tablespoon apple cider

vinegar
2 umeboshi plums, pitted and roughly chopped
1 teaspoon reduced-sodium tamari

1. Simply process all of the ingredients in a blender until smooth.
2. Keep in mind that the dressing may thicken upon sitting, so add additional water as needed before serving to achieve your desired consistency. 3. Once prepared, transfer the dressing to an airtight container and refrigerate for up to 2 days.

Per Serving:

calories: 44 | fat: 3g | protein: 2g | carbs: 3g | fiber: 1g

Gut-Healing Sauerkraut

Prep time: 5 minutes | Cook time: 0 minutes | Makes 4 cups

1 medium purple cabbage
1 tablespoon Celtic sea salt (optional)

2 to 4 tablespoons minced fresh ginger, to taste (optional)

1. Peel off and discard any wrinkly, dry or damaged outer leaves from the cabbage. Reserving 1 healthy, pliable leaf for later, cut the cabbage into quarters right through the core. Carefully cut out and discard the tough inner core. Shred the cabbage, using a mandoline, knife or food processor. We prefer using a food processor fitted with the shredding blade. 2. Put the shredded cabbage into a large bowl. Sprinkle the salt (if using) over the cabbage and massage it with your hands until liquid starts to release. Set aside to marinate. 3. Add the minced ginger to the bowl of cabbage. Use your hands to work the ginger through the cabbage evenly, then once again massage the cabbage until it releases plenty of liquid when squeezed in your hands. The released juice will later be used as a brine. 4. Transfer the cabbage to a wide-mouth 1-quart mason jar, packing it down tightly with each handful added to the jar. When the cabbage is tightly packed down, take the cabbage leaf you reserved earlier and gently fold it until it is about the same width all around as the jar. Place the leaf into the jar, on top of the packed cabbage and make sure it covers it completely. 5. Press the cabbage leaf down firmly, then pour enough brine from the mixing bowl to cover all of the cabbage and submerge it in the liquid. The cabbage

must be below the water (brine) level, away from oxygen. Be sure to leave an inch of space between the top of liquid and the top of the jar. Doing this allows for expansion. However, do not leave too much room at the top of the jar as too much oxygen could cause your kraut to go bad. 6. Allow the kraut to ferment in a cool, dark place for at least 3 days and up to 10, depending on your desired degree of sourness. Once the kraut has fermented to your liking, seal the jar and transfer it to the refrigerator. Fermenting will continue to take place in the fridge, but this will be very, very slow. The flavors may change over time.

Per Serving:

calories: 45 | fat: 0g | protein: 2g | carbs: 10g | fiber: 3g

Tahini Dressing

Prep time: 5 minutes | Cook time: 0 minutes | Makes ½ cup

¼ cup tahini
1 teaspoon minced garlic
3 tablespoons lemon juice
1 tablespoon maple syrup (optional)
1 teaspoon soy sauce

1 teaspoon ground cumin
1 tablespoon olive oil (optional)
1 tablespoon hot water
Pinch of salt and pepper (optional)

1. Simply whisk together all of the ingredients in a small bowl until they are well combined. 2. Once done, transfer the sauce to an airtight container and store it in the fridge for up to 7 days.

Per Serving:(½ cup)

calories: 283 | fat: 24g | protein: 6g | carbs: 16g | fiber: 3g

Buckwheat Sesame Milk

Prep time: 5 minutes | Cook time: 0 minutes | Makes 4 cups

1 cup cooked buckwheat
1 tablespoon tahini, or other nut or seed butter
1 teaspoon pure vanilla extract (optional)

2 to 3 dates, or 15 drops pure stevia (or vanilla stevia), or 2 to 3 tablespoons unrefined sugar (optional)
3 cups water

1. Put everything in a blender, and purée until smooth. 2. Strain the fiber through a piece of cheesecloth or a fine-mesh sieve. 3. Keep in an airtight container in the fridge for up to 5 days.

Per Serving:(1 cup)

calories: 76 | fat: 2g | protein: 2g | carbs: 12g | fiber: 1g

Chipotle Peppers in Adobo Sauce

Prep time: 30 minutes | Cook time: 20 minutes |

Makes 20 to 25 peppers

1 (2 ounces / 57 g) package morita chiles (about 17 to 20)
1 (2 ounces / 57 g) package chipotle chiles (about 10 to 12)
1 to 2 cups boiling water
½ onion, chopped
1 garlic clove, crushed
½ teaspoon ground cumin
½ teaspoon dried oregano
½ teaspoon dried marjoram
¼ cup apple cider vinegar
¼ cup rice vinegar
2 tablespoons date syrup (optional)
2 tablespoons tomato paste

1. Preheat the oven to 350ºF (180ºC). Line a baking sheet with aluminum foil. Place the morita and chipotle chiles on the prepared baking sheet and roast for 5 minutes. Then place them in a medium glass bowl and cover with the boiling water. Use a small plate or bowl to submerge the chiles and let them soak to rehydrate for 30 minutes. 2. Meanwhile, in a nonstick skillet over medium-high heat, dry sauté the onion for about 5 minutes, adding 1 teaspoon of water as needed to prevent sticking, until it is translucent. Add the garlic, cumin, oregano, and marjoram and sauté for 1 more minute, until fragrant. Remove from heat. 3. Transfer the onion mixture to a blender. Add the apple cider vinegar, rice vinegar, date syrup (if using), and tomato paste. After the chiles are rehydrated, remove the stem from 6 to 7 of the morita chiles and, using a paring knife, slice them open to scrape out the seeds. Add the scraped chiles to the blender along with ¾ cup of their soaking liquid. Blend well. Discard any leftover liquid. 4. Pour the sauce back into the skillet and add the remaining chiles. Cook over medium heat, stirring occasionally, for 15 minutes, until the sauce is reduced by half.

Per Serving:

calories: 30 | fat: 0g | protein: 1g | carbs: 6g | fiber: 2g

Chili Powder

Prep time: 15 minutes | Cook time: 0 minutes |

Makes about ½ cup

3 arbol chiles
5 guajillo chiles
5 California chiles
2 tablespoons cumin seeds (not
ground)
2 tablespoons garlic powder
1 tablespoon dried oregano
1 tablespoon onion powder

1. Heat a cast-iron skillet over high heat. As the skillet heats up, remove and discard the stems and seeds from the arbol, guajillo, and California chiles. 2. Place the chiles in the hot, dry skillet and roast for 3 to 5 minutes, turning occasionally, until the color slightly changes and the chiles become softer. Transfer the chiles to a blender or food processor. 3. Put the cumin seeds in the hot skillet and toast until they begin popping. Immediately transfer them to the blender, along with the garlic powder, oregano, and onion powder. 4. Cover tightly and blend into a fine powder. Allow the powder to settle for 2 to 3 minutes before removing the lid. Store in a cool, dry location for up to 6 months.

Per Serving:

calories: 7 | fat: 0g | protein: 0g | carbs: 1g | fiber: 0g

Spicy Cilantro Pesto

Prep time: 10 minutes | Cook time: 0 minutes |

Makes about 1 cup

2 cups packed cilantro
¼ cup hulled sunflower seeds, toasted (optional)
1 jalapeño pepper, coarsely chopped (for less heat, remove the seeds)
4 cloves garlic, peeled and chopped
Zest and juice of 1 lime
Salt, to taste (optional)
½ package extra-firm silken tofu (about 6 ounces / 170 g), drained
¼ cup nutritional yeast (optional)

1. Combine the cilantro, sunflower seeds (if using), jalapeño pepper, garlic, lime zest and juice, salt (if using), tofu, and nutritional yeast (if using) in the bowl of a food processor and purée until smooth and creamy.

Per Serving:(¼ cup)

calories: 143 | fat: 8g | protein: 11g | carbs: 10g | fiber: 5g

Fava Bean Spread

Prep time: 15 minutes | Cook time: 0 minutes |

Makes about 3½ cups

4 cups cooked fava beans, or 2 (15 ounces / 425 g) cans, drained and rinsed
8 cloves garlic, peeled and chopped
Zest of 1 lemon and juice of 2 lemons
1 teaspoon cumin seeds, toasted and ground
Salt, to taste (optional)

1. Combine the fava beans, garlic, lemon zest and juice, cumin, salt (if using), and 1 cup of water in the bowl of a food processor and purée until smooth and creamy. Add more water as needed to achieve a smooth consistency.

Per Serving:(½ cup)

calories: 103 | fat: 1g | protein: 5g | carbs: 17g | fiber: 5g

Potatoes

Prep time: 0 minutes | Cook time: 5 minutes | Serves 1

1 medium potato

1. Use a fork to poke holes all over it for ventilation. 2. Place the potato on a microwave-safe plate and microwave it for 2 minutes. Flip the potato over and microwave for an additional 2 minutes. 3. If the potato is not yet soft, continue microwaving it in 1-minute increments until it reaches your desired level of softness. 4. Once cooked, store the potato in an airtight container in the refrigerator for up to 4 days.

Per Serving:

calories: 164 | fat: 0g | protein: 4g | carbs: 37g | fiber: 5g

Date Syrup

Prep time: 30 minutes | Cook time: 0 minutes |

Makes 1⅓ cups

1 cup Medjool dates, pitted
(about 10 large dates)
1¼ cups purified water, for

blending
1½ teaspoons fresh lemon juice

1. Place the dates in a small bowl and covering them with warm water (not purified water). Let them sit for 30 minutes. 2. drain and rinse the dates before placing them in a high-speed blender along with purified water and lemon juice. 3. Blend everything together for 45 to 60 seconds or until you achieve a smooth consistency. Once done, transfer the date paste to an airtight container and store it in the refrigerator for up to 2 weeks.

Per Serving:

calories: 111 | fat: 0g | protein: 1g | carbs: 30g | fiber: 2g

Roasted Red Pepper Sauce

Prep time: 10 minutes | Cook time: 0 minutes |

Makes 2 cups

1 (12 ounces / 340 g) package
extra-firm silken tofu, drained
2 large red bell peppers, roasted
and seeded
3 cloves garlic, peeled and
chopped

2 tablespoons chopped dill
1 teaspoon salt (optional)
½ teaspoon freshly ground
black pepper
zest of 1 lemon

1.Simply combine all of the ingredients in the bowl of a food processor and purée them until smooth and creamy. Once done, transfer the mixture to an airtight container and refrigerate it until you're ready to use it.

Per Serving:(1 cup)

calories: 205 | fat: 11g | protein: 19g | carbs: 14g | fiber: 3g

Pineapple Chutney

Prep time: 25 minutes | Cook time: 15 minutes |

Makes 1½ cups

½ medium yellow onion, peeled
and diced small
1 tablespoon grated ginger
2 jalapeño peppers, seeded and
minced
½ tablespoon cumin seeds,

toasted and ground
½ fresh pineapple, peeled,
cored, and diced
½ cup finely chopped cilantro
Salt, to taste (optional)

1. Place the onion in a large skillet or saucepan and sautéing it over medium heat for 7 to 8 minutes. If needed, add water 1 to 2 tablespoons at a time to prevent the onion from sticking to the pan.

2. Add the ginger, jalapeño peppers, and cumin seeds and continue cooking for an additional 4 minutes. After that, add the pineapple to the pan and remove it from the heat. Finally, stir in the cilantro and salt (if desired) before serving.

Per Serving:(½ cup)

calories: 98 | fat: 0g | protein: 2g | carbs: 24g | fiber: 3g

Piecrust

Prep time: 10 minutes | Cook time: 0 minutes |

Serves 4

1 cup all-purpose flour, plus
more for rolling
½ teaspoon baking powder
¼ teaspoon salt (optional)
2 tablespoons canola oil, plus
more if storing dough for later

(optional)
½ teaspoon lemon juice
3½ tablespoons plant-based
milk
4 tablespoons water

1. To prepare the dough, start by thoroughly mixing all of the ingredients together in a medium-sized bowl using a wooden spoon. Mix everything until a ball of dough forms. Once done, wrap the dough in plastic wrap and refrigerate it for one hour. If you plan to use the dough right away, dust a work surface with flour, place the chilled dough down, and roll it out into a thin, flat 11-inch circle using a lightly floured rolling pin. Transfer the rolled-out dough to a 9-inch pie dish, fill it with your choice of fillings, and bake according to the recipe's instructions. If you don't plan to use the dough immediately, cover the exterior of the dough with 1 teaspoon of oil (if desired) to prevent it from drying out. Place the lightly oiled ball of dough in a medium-sized bowl and tightly cover it with plastic wrap or place it in an airtight container. Refrigerate the dough for up to seven days.

Per Serving:

calories: 183 | fat: 8g | protein: 4g | carbs: 25g | fiber: 1g

Plant-Based Parmesan

Prep time: 5 minutes | Cook time: 0 minutes | Makes

1 heaping cup

1 cup raw cashews
⅓ cup nutritional yeast

¾ teaspoon garlic powder
½ teaspoon salt (optional)

1. Combine the cashews, nutritional yeast, garlic powder, and salt (if desired) in a blender or food processor. 2. Blend everything on medium-high until the mixture has a texture similar to grated parmesan cheese. You may need to stop and start the blender or food processor a few times to ensure that the nuts are not clumping together at the bottom. 3. Once done, store the parmesan substitute in a glass or plastic container in the refrigerator for up to one month.

Per Serving:

calories: 219 | fat: 15g | protein: 11g | carbs: 14g | fiber: 4g

Herbed Millet Pizza Crust

Prep time: 5 minutes | Cook time: 40 minutes |

Makes 1 large thin-crust pizza crust

½ cup coarsely ground millet
1½ cups water
1 tablespoon mixed dried Italian herbs

¼ teaspoon sea salt (optional)
1 to 2 tablespoons nutritional yeast

1. Preheat your oven to 350ºF (180ºC) and line an 8-inch-round pie dish or springform pan with parchment paper so that you can easily lift the crust out after it's cooked. Keep in mind that the crust may be fragile until it cools and tends to stick unless you use a nonstick pan. 2. Put the millet in a small pot with water and a pinch of salt. Bring the mixture to a boil, then cover and simmer for 15 to 20 minutes, stirring occasionally to prevent sticking. 3. You can add dried herbs to cook with the millet for a more intense flavor or stir them in after the millet is cooked. 4. Once the millet is cooked, add salt (if desired) and nutritional yeast. Spread the cooked and seasoned millet out in an even layer in your pan, all the way to the edges. 5. Put the crust in the oven and bake for 20 minutes or until lightly browned around the edges.

Per Serving:(1 crust)

calories: 378 | fat: 4g | protein: 11g | carbs: 72g | fiber: 8g

Lemon-Tahini Dressing

Prep time: 5 minutes | Cook time: 0 minutes | Serves 8

¼ cup fresh lemon juice
1 teaspoon maple syrup (optional)
1 small garlic clove, chopped

½ cup gluten-free tahini
¼ teaspoon salt (optional)
⅛ teaspoon black pepper
¼ to ½ cup water

1. Pulse together the lemon juice, sugar, garlic, tahini, salt (if using), and pepper in a high-speed blender until well combined. 2. Slowly add water, starting with 1/4 cup, until it reaches your desired consistency. Once done, transfer the dressing to an airtight container and refrigerate for up to 5 days.

Per Serving:

calories: 94 | fat: 8g | protein: 3g | carbs: 4g | fiber: 1g

Hemp Mylk

Prep time: 5 minutes | Cook time: 0 minutes | Makes

3 cups

½ cup hemp hearts
3 cups purified water, for blending

½ teaspoon ground cinnamon
2 dates, pitted

1. Simply combine all of the ingredients in a blender and blend until smooth and creamy. 2. Once done, pour the mixture into a glass jar with a tight-fitting lid and refrigerate. Your homemade hemp milk

should last for up to 5 days in the fridge.

Per Serving:

calories: 47 | fat: 0g | protein: 1g | carbs: 11g | fiber: 1g

Not-So-Fat Guacamole

Prep time: 15 minutes | Cook time: 13 minutes |

Makes 2 cups

1 cup shelled edamame
1 cup broccoli florets
Zest of 1 lime and juice of 2 limes
2 Roma tomatoes, diced
½ small red onion, peeled and diced small

¼ cup finely chopped cilantro
1 clove garlic, peeled and minced (about 1 teaspoon)
Salt, to taste (optional)
1 pinch cayenne pepper, or to taste

1. Place the edamame in a medium-sized saucepan and adding enough water to cover them. Bring the water to a boil and cook the edamame for 5 minutes. Once done, drain and rinse the edamame until they have cooled down. 2. Steam the broccoli in a double boiler or steamer basket for about 8 minutes or until it's very tender. 3. Drain and rinse the broccoli until it has cooled down. Add both the edamame and broccoli to a food processor and purée them until smooth and creamy. If needed, add water to achieve a creamy texture. 4. Transfer the puréed mixture to a bowl and add lime zest and juice, tomatoes, onion, cilantro, garlic, salt (if desired), and cayenne pepper. Mix everything together well and chill the mixture until you're ready to serve.

Per Serving:(1 cup)

calories: 136 | fat: 4g | protein: 10g | carbs: 17g | fiber: 6g

Fried Tofu

Prep time: 5 minutes | Cook time: 15 minutes |

Serves 4

1 (14 ounces / 397 g) block extra-firm tofu
1½ tablespoons canola oil (optional)

1. Place the package of tofu in the freezer overnight or for at least 4 hours. When ready to use, bring a pot of water to a boil and remove the completely frozen tofu from its package before adding it to the pot. 2. Boil the tofu for 10 minutes, then remove it from the pot to cool. 3. Once cool enough to handle, gently press the water out of the tofu with a clean kitchen towel, being careful not to break it. 4. Cut the tofu into 1/2-inch cubes. In a large pan, heat canola oil (if desired) over high heat. 5. Once the oil is hot, add the tofu and fry for 1 to 2 minutes on each side or until it turns golden brown. 6. After frying, place the tofu on a plate lined with a kitchen towel or paper towel to soak up any excess oil. Store the tofu in an airtight container in the fridge for up to 5 days.

Per Serving:

calories: 150 | fat: 12g | protein: 11g | carbs: 2g | fiber: 1g

Superfood Salad Topper

Prep time: 5 minutes | Cook time: 0 minutes | Makes

2⅓ cups

½ cup raw cashews
½ cup sprouted or raw pumpkin seeds
1 cup mixed seeds (sunflower, chia, flax, and hemp)
⅓ cup goji berries
2 tablespoons flax oil or extra-

virgin olive oil (optional)
1 teaspoon curry powder
1 teaspoon ground turmeric
½ teaspoon ground cinnamon
Pinch of cayenne pepper
Pinch of sea salt (optional)

1. In a large bowl, combine the nuts, seeds and goji berries and toss with the oil (if using), curry powder, turmeric, cinnamon, cayenne and salt (if using). 2. Ideally, allow the mix to marinate for 15 minutes before serving. 3. Store the mixture in an airtight glass container in the fridge or freezer. It will keep fresh for weeks, ready to quickly nourish your meals.

Per Serving:

calories: 308 | fat: 27g | protein: 10g | carbs: 10g | fiber: 3g

Mango-Orange Dressing

Prep time: 5 minutes | Cook time: 0 minutes | Serves 8

1 cup diced mango
½ cup orange juice
2 tablespoons fresh lime juice
2 tablespoons gluten-free rice
2 tablespoons chopped cilantro

vinegar
1 teaspoon coconut sugar (optional)
¼ teaspoon salt (optional)

1. Process the mango, orange juice, lime juice, rice vinegar, sugar, and salt (if using) in a blender until smooth. Once blended, stir in the cilantro. Transfer the sauce to an airtight container and refrigerate for up to 2 days.

Per Serving:

calories: 23 | fat: 0g | protein: 0g | carbs: 6g | fiber: 0g

Lime-Cumin Dressing

Prep time: 5 minutes | Cook time: 0 minutes | Serves 4

1 teaspoon ground cumin
1 teaspoon coconut sugar (optional)
¼ teaspoon salt (optional)
3 tablespoons fresh lime juice

1 tablespoon apple cider vinegar
2 teaspoons extra virgin olive oil (optional)

1. Combine the cumin, sugar, and salt (if desired) in a medium jar with a tight-fitting lid. Whisk in the lime juice and vinegar. Whisk in the oil in a slow, steady stream, if desired. Refrigerate for up to 4 days. Shake to combine as needed.

Per Serving:

calories: 28 | fat: 2g | protein: 0g | carbs: 2g | fiber: 2g

Cheesy Sprinkle

Prep time: 5 minutes | Cook time: 0 minutes | Makes

½ cup

½ cup ground sunflower seeds, or Brazil nuts, or macadamia nuts
2 teaspoons sea salt (optional)

1 to 2 tablespoons nutritional yeast
1 tablespoon olive oil (optional)

1. Place the sunflower seeds in a small bowl, then add the salt (if using) and nutritional yeast. Mix to combine. 2. Leave as is for a dry sprinkle, or add just enough olive oil (if using) to bring the mixture together into a crumbly texture.

Per Serving:(1 tablespoon)

calories: 284 | fat: 25g | protein: 9g | carbs: 9g | fiber: 4g

Peanut Milk

Prep time: 5 minutes | Cook time: 0 minutes | Makes

3 cups

1 cup unsalted roasted peanuts
¼ cup raisins

3 cups water

1. In a blender pitcher, soak the peanuts and raisins in the water. Let the mixture sit overnight or for at least 6 hours. 2. Blend the water, peanuts, and raisins together on high for 1 to 2 minutes. 3. Using cheesecloth or a mesh nut-milk bag, strain the milk into a pitcher, separating out the liquid from the solids. 4. Store in an airtight container in the fridge for up to 5 days.

Per Serving:(1 cup)

calories: 284 | fat: 24g | protein: 14g | carbs: 9g | fiber: 4g

Mama Mia Marinara Sauce

Prep time: 10 minutes | Cook time: 2 to 3 hours |

Makes about 7 cups

1 medium onion, diced
5 garlic cloves, minced
2 (28 ounces / 794 g) cans no-salt-added crushed tomatoes
½ cup red wine

2 tablespoons Italian seasoning, or 1 tablespoon each dried basil and dried oregano
Ground black pepper
Salt (optional)

1. Put the onion, garlic, and tomatoes in the slow cooker. Swirl the wine in the empty tomato cans and pour everything into the slow cooker. Add the Italian seasoning, pepper, and salt (if using). Stir to combine. 2. Cover and cook on High for 2 to 3 hours or on Low for 4 to 5 hours.

Per Serving:

calories: 30 | fat: 0g | protein: 1g | carbs: 4g | fiber: 1g

Croutons

Prep time: 5 minutes | Cook time: 15 minutes |

Serves 4

½ day-old baguette, sliced
2 tablespoons olive oil
(optional)

½ tablespoon garlic salt
(optional)

1. Preheat the oven to 350ºF (180ºC). 2. Brush the baguette slices with the olive oil and sprinkle with the garlic salt, if desired. 3. Cut the bread into cubes, place on a baking sheet, and bake for 10 to 15 minutes or until golden brown. 4. Allow the croutons to cool before serving. 5. The croutons are best if served immediately after baking.

Per Serving:

calories: 94 | fat: 7g | protein: 1g | carbs: 7g | fiber: 0g

Nitter Kibbeh

Prep time: 20 minutes | Cook time: 25 minutes |

Makes 1½ cups

2 pounds (907 g) yellow onions, peeled and diced small
9 cloves garlic, peeled and minced
1 tablespoon grated ginger

½ tablespoon turmeric
¼ teaspoon ground cardamom
½ teaspoon ground cinnamon
⅛ teaspoon ground cloves
⅛ teaspoon ground nutmeg

1. Place the onions in a large skillet over medium heat. Stir frequently and add water as needed to prevent the onions from sticking to the pan. 2. Cook for approximately 20 minutes or until the onions are browned. Next, add the garlic, ginger, turmeric, cardamom, cinnamon, cloves, and nutmeg to the skillet and cook for an additional 5 minutes. 3. Add 1/4 cup of water to the skillet and use a spatula to scrape the bottom of the pan and incorporate any bits that may have stuck to it. 4. Transfer the mixture to a blender and purée until smooth and creamy, adding water as necessary to achieve the desired consistency. The mixture can be refrigerated for up to 7 days.

Per Serving:(½ cup)

calories: 119 | fat: 0g | protein: 3g | carbs: 27g | fiber: 3g

Sunflower Hemp Milk

Prep time: 5 minutes | Cook time: 0 minutes | Makes

2 cups

2 cups water
3 tablespoons sunflower seeds
2 tablespoons hemp seeds or other seeds
1 to 2 dates, or 10 drops pure

stevia (or vanilla stevia), or 1 to 2 tablespoons unrefined sugar (optional)
¼ teaspoon pure vanilla extract (optional)

1. Simply put all of the ingredients in a blender and purée until they

are smooth. 2. strain the fiber from the mixture using either a piece of cheesecloth or a fine-mesh sieve. 3. Once done, transfer the drink to an airtight container and store it in the fridge for up to 5 days.

Per Serving:(1 cup)

calories: 139 | fat: 11g | protein: 4g | carbs: 7g | fiber: 2g

Maple-Dijon Dressing

Prep time: 5 minutes | Cook time: 0 minutes | Serves 4

¼ cup apple cider vinegar
2 tablespoons maple syrup
2 teaspoons gluten-free Dijon mustard

¼ teaspoon black pepper
2 tablespoons water
Salt (optional)

1. Combine vinegar, maple syrup (if using), mustard, pepper, and water in a small jar with a tight-fitting lid. 2. Add salt to taste, if desired. Once prepared, refrigerate the dressing for up to 5 days.

Per Serving:

calories: 31 | fat: 0g | protein: 0g | carbs: 7g | fiber: 0g

Quinoa

Prep time: 5 minutes | Cook time: 5 minutes | Makes

3 cups

1 cup quinoa

1½ cups vegetable broth

1. Rinse the quinoa in cold water using a fine-mesh strainer. 2. Put the quinoa and broth into the pressure cooker and cook on high pressure for 5 minutes. 3. Let the pressure out, remove the lid, and fluff the quinoa with a fork. 4. Store in an airtight container in the fridge for up to 5 days.

Per Serving:(1 cup)

calories: 214 | fat: 3g | protein: 8g | carbs: 38g | fiber: 4g

Coriander Chutney

Prep time: 15 minutes | Cook time: 0 minutes |

Makes about 1 cup

½ teaspoon cumin seeds, toasted and ground
½ teaspoon yellow mustard seeds, toasted and ground
1 large bunch cilantro
1 small yellow onion, peeled and chopped (about ½ cup)

¼ cup unsweetened coconut
3 tablespoons grated ginger
2 serrano chiles, stemmed (for less heat, remove the seeds)
Zest and juice of 2 lemons
Salt, to taste (optional)

1. Combine all ingredients in a blender and blend on high until smooth. Add water as needed to achieve a thick paste.

Per Serving:(¼ cup)

calories: 38 | fat: 1g | protein: 0g | carbs: 5g | fiber: 1g

Creamy Herbed Hemp Dressing

Prep time: 10 minutes | Cook time: 0 minutes |
Serves 6

½ cup hemp seeds
¼ cup chopped flat-leaf parsley
2 tablespoons raw cashews
1 scallion, sliced
1 tablespoon apple cider vinegar
1 tablespoon fresh lemon juice
2 teaspoons capers, drained
1 teaspoon nutritional yeast
½ teaspoon garlic powder
½ teaspoon coconut sugar (optional)
¼ teaspoon dried dill
Salt and black pepper (optional)
1 or 2 tablespoons water (optional)

1. Process the hemp seeds, parsley, cashews, scallion, vinegar, lemon juice, capers, nutritional yeast, garlic powder, sugar, and dill in a high-speed blender until smooth. Season with salt (if desired) and pepper and add water, 1 tablespoon at a time, as needed to achieve desired consistency. Refrigerate in an airtight container for up to 5 days.

Per Serving:

calories: 106 | fat: 9g | protein: 4g | carbs: 5g | fiber: 2g

20-Minute Cashew Cheese Sauce

Prep time: 5 minutes | Cook time: 15 minutes |
Makes about 3 cups

½ cup raw cashews
1 cup peeled and diced potatoes
¼ cup diced carrots
¼ cup diced onions
3 cups water
4 tablespoons nutritional yeast
1 tablespoon lemon juice
1 teaspoon miso paste
½ teaspoon garlic powder
½ teaspoon dry mustard
Pinch paprika
Ground black pepper
Salt (optional)

1. Soak the cashews in very hot (boiled) water for 30 to 60 minutes before use to ensure a creamy and delicious texture. If you have a high-speed blender, you can skip this step. 2. In a medium pot, combine the potatoes, carrots, and onion and cover with water. 3. Bring the mixture to a boil and cook for approximately 15 minutes or until the vegetables are tender enough to be mashed with a fork. 4. While the vegetables are boiling, drain the cashews if you soaked them, and transfer them to a blender or food processor. 5. Add the nutritional yeast, lemon juice, miso paste, garlic powder, mustard, and paprika. Season with pepper and salt (if desired). 6. Once the vegetables are cooked, reserve 1 cup of cooking water and add it to the blender along with the cooked vegetables. Blend everything together for 30 to 60 seconds or until smooth. The sauce can be stored in the refrigerator for up to 4 days.

Per Serving:

calories: 55 | fat: 3g | protein: 3g | carbs: 6g | fiber: 1g

Plant-Based Fish Sauce

Prep time: 10 minutes | Cook time: 20 minutes |
Makes 3 to 4 cups

4 cups water
1 (4-by-8-inch) sheet of kombu
½ cup dried shiitake mushrooms
¼ cup low-sodium soy sauce,
tamari, or coconut aminos
3 garlic cloves, crushed
2 teaspoons rice vinegar

1. In a medium saucepan, combine the water, kombu, mushrooms, soy sauce, garlic, and vinegar. Bring the mixture to a boil, then reduce the heat to low. 2. Cover and simmer for 15 to 20 minutes. Remove from the heat. Keep covered and allow to steep overnight or for at least 8 hours. 3. Strain and discard any solids. Store the plant-based fish sauce in the refrigerator in a glass bottle for up to 3 weeks, shaking well before each use.

Per Serving:

calories: 4 | fat: 0g | protein: 0g | carbs: 1g | fiber: 0g

Low-Sodium Vegetable Broth

Prep time: 5 minutes | Cook time: 3 hours | Makes
about 3 quarts

4 carrots, chopped
2 medium onions, skins included, quartered
4 celery stalks, chopped
6 garlic cloves, unpeeled and crushed
2 to 3 kale leaves and stems,
chopped
1 sprig fresh rosemary
3 to 5 springs fresh thyme
1 bunch parsley stems
2 bay leaves
2 to 4 black peppercorns
3 quarts water

1. Place a large stock pot over high heat and toss in the carrots, onions, and celery. Dry sauté for 5 minutes, adding a tablespoon or so of water as needed to keep them from sticking. 2. Add the garlic, kale, rosemary, thyme, parsley stems, bay leaves, and peppercorns and stir. Add the water. 3. Cover, bring to a boil, and then lower the heat. Simmer for 2 to 3 hours. Strain the broth and freeze for up to 6 months.

Per Serving:

calories: 11 | fat: 0g | protein: 0g | carbs: 3g | fiber: 1g

Chapter 12 Staples, Sauces, Dips, and Dressings

Cilantro and Lime Chutney

Prep time: 10 minutes | Cook time: 0 minutes |

Makes 1 cup

2 green chiles, stemmed
1 tablespoon grated peeled fresh ginger
1 teaspoon lime zest
Juice of 1 large lime
2 tablespoons water, plus more as needed

2 cups fresh cilantro, washed and shaken dry
1 tablespoon agave syrup, or pure maple syrup (optional)
½ teaspoon ground cumin
¼ teaspoon ground coriander

1. Combine green chiles, ginger, lime zest and juice, and 2 tablespoons of water in a blender. Blend until the mixture is smooth. 2. Add cilantro, agave syrup (if desired), cumin, and coriander to the blender. Blend again until all ingredients are thoroughly combined. If needed, scrape down the sides of the blender and add up to 2 more tablespoons of water to achieve your desired consistency. 3. Store the sauce in an airtight container in the refrigerator for up to 2 weeks or freeze it for up to 6 months.

Per Serving:(1 tablespoon)

calories: 8 | fat: 0g | protein: 0g | carbs: 2g | fiber: 0g

Stuffed Bell Peppers

Prep time: 15 minutes | Cook time: 25 minutes |

Serves 4

4 green or red bell peppers
2 cups cooked quinoa
1 (15 ounces / 425 g) can black or pinto beans, drained and rinsed

1 tablespoon taco seasoning
¼ teaspoon salt (optional)
1 (10 ounces / 283 g) can red enchilada sauce

1. Preheat your oven to 400ºF (205ºC). 2. Cut the bell peppers in half lengthwise and remove the seeds. 3. Place them on a baking sheet. In a medium bowl, combine the quinoa, beans, taco seasoning, and salt (if desired). 4. Spoon the quinoa mixture into the bell peppers. Pour the enchilada sauce onto the baking sheet between the stuffed peppers. Cover everything with aluminum foil and bake for 25 minutes.

Per Serving:

calories: 272 | fat: 3g | protein: 13g | carbs: 49g | fiber: 10g

Toasted Sesame Miso Dressing

Prep time: 5 minutes | Cook time: 0 minutes | Makes

⅓ cup

2 tablespoons miso
2 tablespoons apple cider vinegar or rice vinegar
1 tablespoon tamari or soy sauce
1 tablespoon water
½ teaspoon toasted sesame oil

(optional)
½-inch piece ginger, grated
½ teaspoon maple syrup (optional)
1 tablespoon sesame seeds (optional)

1. Put all the ingredients together in a bowl and stir together until smooth and creamy.

Per Serving:

calories: 79 | fat: 4g | protein: 3g | carbs: 6g | fiber: 1g

Spicy Satay Sauce

Prep time: 5 minutes | Cook time: 10 minutes |

Serves 8

1 cup peanut butter
2 tablespoons lime juice
¼ cup sweet soy sauce
2 small onions, minced
2 cloves garlic, minced

2 cups water
Optional Toppings:
Red chili flakes
Minced ginger
Fresh cilantro

1. Put all ingredients in a food processor and blend until smooth, add more water if the sauce is too thick. Alternatively, mix everything in a medium bowl, using a handheld mixer. 2. Heat up the sauce in a saucepan over a medium heat. Let it cook for about 10 minutes while stirring continuously as the sauce thickens. 3. Turn off the heat and let the sauce cool down for a minute while stirring. 4. Serve warm with the optional toppings and enjoy! 5. Store the satay sauce in an airtight container in the fridge and consume within 4 days. The satay sauce can also be stored in the freezer for a maximum of 90 days. Thaw at room temperature before serving.

Per Serving:

calories: 217 | fat: 15g | protein: 8g | carbs: 10g | fiber: 2g

Potato Wedges

Prep time: 10 minutes | Cook time: 40 minutes | Serves 2 to 4

3 or 4 medium red potatoes, cut into ½-inch wedges (about 1 pound / 454 g)

1. 1. Preheat your oven to 450°F (235°C) and line a baking sheet with parchment paper. 2. Arrange the potatoes in a single layer on the prepared baking sheet. 3. Bake for 15 to 20 minutes until the potatoes are browned and crispy. 4. Flip the potatoes over and bake for an additional 15 to 20 minutes or until they are crispy. Remove from the oven and serve immediately.

Per Serving:

calories: 149 | fat: 0g | protein: 4g | carbs: 34g | fiber: 4g

Nut Milk

Prep time: 5 minutes | Cook time: 0 minutes | Makes 5 cups

| 1 cup raw cashews or almonds, soaked overnight and drained | 1 teaspoon vanilla extract (optional) |
| 3 dates, pitted (optional) | 4 cups water |

1. Combine the soaked nuts, dates (if using), vanilla extract (if using), and water in a blender. Blend on high for 3 to 4 minutes until the nuts are completely pulverized and the liquid has a creamy consistency. 2. Strain the blended mixture through a nut milk bag, cheesecloth, or fine-mesh sieve and transfer it to an airtight storage container. Chill the nut milk and use it within 4 days.

Per Serving:

calories: 25 | fat: 2g | protein: 0g | carbs: 1g | fiber: 0g

Pico de Gallo

Prep time: 15 minutes | Cook time: 0 minutes | Makes 2 cups

4 tomatoes, chopped small	needed
1 medium yellow onion, minced	Pinch of salt, plus more if needed (optional)
1 jalapeño pepper, seeded and minced	3 tablespoons chopped fresh cilantro
Juice of 1 lime, plus more if	

1. Combine the tomatoes, onion, jalapeño, lime juice, salt (if desired), and cilantro in a large bowl. Mix well and taste the salsa. Adjust the seasoning as needed. 2. Store the salsa in an airtight container in the refrigerator for up to 4 days.

Per Serving:

calories: 19 | fat: 0g | protein: 1g | carbs: 4g | fiber: 1g

Perfect Marinara Sauce

Prep time: 10 minutes | Cook time: 20 minutes | Makes 7 cups

2 (28 ounces / 794 g) cans crushed tomatoes in purée	2 teaspoons onion powder
4 garlic cloves, minced	2 teaspoons paprika
2 tablespoons Italian seasoning	¼ teaspoon freshly ground black pepper
2 teaspoons pure maple syrup	

1. In a medium saucepan, stir together the tomatoes, garlic, Italian seasoning, maple syrup, onion powder, paprika, and pepper. Bring to a simmer. 2. Reduce the heat to low. Cover, and simmer for 15 to 20 minutes, or until the sauce is fragrant and the flavors have melded together. Remove from the heat.

Per Serving:

calories: 39 | fat: 0g | protein: 2g | carbs: 8g | fiber: 2g

Harissa

Prep time: 5 minutes | Cook time: 0 minutes | Makes ½ cup

2 tablespoons caraway seeds	2 teaspoons garlic powder
2 tablespoons coriander seeds	1 teaspoon sweet paprika
2 tablespoons cumin seeds	1 teaspoon crushed red pepper (optional)
2 teaspoons dried mint	

1. Grind the caraway, coriander, and cumin in a clean coffee grinder. Transfer to a jar with a tight-fitting lid; add the mint, garlic powder, paprika, and crushed red pepper, if desired; and shake until combined. Store for up to 6 months.

Per Serving:(⅓ cup)

calories: 150 | fat: 7g | protein: 8g | carbs: 24g | fiber: 12g

Chipotle Relish

Prep time: 15 minutes | Cook time: 0 minutes | Makes 1½ cups

½ cup diced Persian cucumber	lime juice
½ cup diced red bell pepper	¼ teaspoon chipotle chili powder
1 small seedless orange, peeled and diced	¼ cup diced jicama (optional)
½ tablespoon freshly squeezed	

1. In a medium bowl, combine the cucumber, bell pepper, orange, lime juice, chili powder, and jicama (if using). 2. Serve immediately with chips, or cover and refrigerate until serving time.

Per Serving:

calories: 17 | fat: 0g | protein: 0g | carbs: 4g | fiber: 1g

Blueberry-Chia Jam

Prep time: 5 minutes | Cook time: 0 minutes | Makes

1 cup

1 cup fresh or thawed frozen blueberries
¼ cup unsweetened raisins
¼ cup water
1 tablespoon chia seeds

1. In a small saucepan, combine the blueberries, raisins, and water. Cook over medium heat, mashing with a fork or potato masher, for about 5 minutes, or until thickened. 2. Reduce the heat to medium-low. Stir in the chia seeds, and continue to mash as the jam thickens slightly. Remove from the heat. Store in an airtight container in the refrigerator for up to 1 week. The jam will thicken in the refrigerator.

Per Serving:

calories: 29 | fat: 1g | protein: 1g | carbs: 6g | fiber: 1g

Quick Mole Sauce

Prep time: 40 minutes | Cook time: 25 minutes |

Makes 4 cups

4 dried pasilla chiles
2 dried ancho chiles
Boiling water, for soaking the peppers
1 yellow onion, cut into slices
6 garlic cloves, coarsely chopped
1 tablespoon water, plus more as needed
2 tablespoons tomato paste
1 jalapeño pepper, seeded and chopped
2 ounces (57 g) vegan dark chocolate
2 tablespoons whole wheat flour
2 tablespoons cocoa powder
2 tablespoons almond butter
2 teaspoons smoked paprika
1 teaspoon ground cumin
1 teaspoon ground cinnamon
½ teaspoon dried oregano
2½ cups no-sodium vegetable broth

1. Remove the stem ends from the pasilla and ancho chiles and discard the seeds. Cut the chiles in half and place them in a medium bowl. Cover with boiling water and let soak for 20 minutes. Drain the water. 2. In a large nonstick sauté pan or skillet over medium-high heat, cook the onion and garlic for 5 to 7 minutes. Add 1 tablespoon of water at a time to prevent burning. The onions should be dark brown but not burnt. Stir in tomato paste and cook for 2 minutes to caramelize. Transfer the mixture to a high-speed blender. 3. Add soaked chiles, jalapeño pepper, chocolate, flour, cocoa powder, almond butter, paprika, cumin, cinnamon, oregano, and vegetable broth to the blender. Blend for about 3 minutes until smooth. 4. Return the sauté pan or skillet to medium-high heat. Pour in the sauce and cover the pan. Cook until the sauce begins to bubble. Reduce the heat to low and simmer, uncovered, for 5 minutes, stirring occasionally. 5. Serve immediately or store in an airtight container in the refrigerator for up to 1 week, or freeze for up to 6 months.

Per Serving:(½ cup)

calories: 114 | fat: 7g | protein: 4g | carbs: 13g | fiber: 4g

Cilantro-Coconut Pesto

Prep time: 5 minutes | Cook time: 0 minutes | Serves 8

1 (13½ ounces / 383-g) can full-fat coconut milk
1 bunch cilantro leaves
2 jalapeños
1 piece ginger, peeled and minced
1 tablespoon white miso
Water, as needed

1. Blend coconut milk, cilantro, jalapeños, ginger, and miso in a blender until the mixture becomes smooth. Add water as necessary to achieve the desired consistency. The pesto can be stored in the refrigerator for up to 2 days, or divided into resealable containers and frozen for up to 6 months.

Per Serving:

calories: 122 | fat: 12g | protein: 2g | carbs: 4g | fiber: 1g

Pomegranate Ginger Sauce

Prep time: 5 minutes | Cook time: 0 minutes | Serves 8

2 cups fresh or frozen pomegranate seeds
10 dried pitted plums
1 (2-inch) piece ginger
1 tablespoon black pepper

1. Combine all the ingredients in a blender or food processor and blend until a smooth sauce is formed. 2. Store the pomegranate sauce in an airtight container in the refrigerator and consume within 3 days. Alternatively, you can freeze the sauce for up to 60 days and thaw it at room temperature before using.

Per Serving:

calories: 65 | fat: 0g | protein: 1g | carbs: 15g | fiber: 3g

Artichoke Dressing

Prep time: 10 minutes | Cook time: 0 minutes |

Makes 1 cup

1 cup drained jarred or canned artichoke hearts
1 (3-inch) piece scallion, white and light green parts only, coarsely chopped
¼ cup extra-virgin olive oil
(optional)
1 tablespoon freshly squeezed lemon juice, plus more to taste
6 tablespoons filtered water
½ teaspoon fine sea salt, plus more to taste (optional)

1. Combine the artichokes, scallion, olive oil, lemon juice, water, and salt (if desired) in an upright blender. 2. Blend everything together until completely smooth. 3. Use a rubber spatula to scrape down the sides of the blender and blend again. 4. Taste the mixture and adjust the seasoning and lemon juice as needed, then blend once more. 5. You can serve the dip immediately or store it in a glass jar in the fridge for up to 3 days. Before using, be sure to shake the jar well to mix everything together.

Per Serving:(¼ cup)

calories: 144 | fat: 14g | protein: 1g | carbs: 6g | fiber: 4g

Spicy Italian Vinaigrette

Prep time: 5 minutes | Cook time: 0 minutes | Makes

1 cup

1 cup apple cider vinegar
½ cup extra-virgin olive oil
(optional)
2 teaspoons maple syrup
(optional)

2 teaspoons Italian seasoning
¼ teaspoon salt (optional)
¼ teaspoon black pepper
½ teaspoon garlic powder
Pinch red pepper flakes

1. In a jar, combine the apple cider vinegar, olive oil, maple syrup, Italian seasoning, salt (if desired), black pepper, garlic powder, and red pepper flakes. Cover the jar and shake well until all ingredients are thoroughly blended.
2. Store the dressing in the refrigerator for up to 2 weeks.

Per Serving:

calories: 131 | fat: 14g | protein: 0g | carbs: 2g | fiber: 0g

Homemade Beans

Prep time: 5 minutes | Cook time: 2 hours | Makes 3

cups

8 ounces (227 g) dried black beans, picked over and rinsed
3½ cups water
Pinch kelp granules

1. Combine beans, water, and kelp in a Dutch oven or saucepan. Bring the mixture to a boil over high heat. 2. Reduce the heat to low, cover the pot, and let it simmer for approximately 1½ hours. Remove from the heat when done.

Per Serving:

calories: 110 | fat: 1g | protein: 11g | carbs: 29g | fiber: 16g

Lentil and Sweet Potato Bowl

Prep time: 25 minutes | Cook time: 30 minutes |

Serves 4

Lentils:
3 tablespoons water
½ cup diced red, white, or yellow onion
1½ teaspoons minced garlic
1 cup uncooked lentils, rinsed
2 cups vegetable broth

1 teaspoon ground cumin
Base:
1 cup chopped kale, steamed
1 cup cooked brown rice or quinoa
1 microwaved sweet potato, diced

1. Heat water in a medium saucepan over medium-high heat. Add onion and garlic and sauté for 3 minutes until the onion becomes tender and translucent.
2. Add lentils, broth, and cumin to the saucepan and mix thoroughly.
3. Bring the mixture to a boil and stir until the bouillon cube is dissolved, approximately 1 to 2 minutes. Reduce the heat to low, cover the saucepan, and let it simmer for 20 minutes or until the lentils are soft.
4. In a pot with a steamer basket, bring water to a boil over medium-high heat. Place kale in the basket and steam for 3 to 4 minutes or until it softens.
5. Layer rice (or quinoa), kale, lentils, and sweet potatoes in bowls.

Per Serving:

calories: 131 | fat: 1g | protein: 4g | carbs: 28g | fiber: 2g

Nut or Seed Butter

Prep time: 5 minutes | Cook time: 0 minutes | Makes

1 cup

2 cups raw whole nuts or seeds, toasted

1 teaspoon flaky sea salt, or to taste (optional)

1. Place the nuts or seeds in a food processor and process for 2 minutes until they form a ball. Break up the ball, scrape down the sides of the processor, and continue blending for an additional 3 to 4 minutes until the butter is completely smooth and liquid. Scrape the sides of the processor again, add the flaky salt, and pulse to combine. 2. Store the nut or seed butter in a sealed glass jar or airtight container at room temperature for up to 1 month. If the weather is hot, store it in the refrigerator instead.

Per Serving:(⅛ cup)

calories: 207 | fat: 18g | protein: 8g | carbs: 8g | fiber: 2g

Oil-Free Sundried Tomato and Oregano Dressing

Prep time: 10 minutes | Cook time: 5 minutes |

Makes 3 cups

2 cups filtered water
½ cup sundried tomato halves
1 clove garlic, chopped
1 small shallot, chopped
2 tablespoons Dijon mustard

2 tablespoons pure maple syrup
(optional)
¼ teaspoon dried oregano
salt and pepper, to taste
(optional)

1. Boil 2 cups of water. In a small bowl, combine the sundried tomatoes with the boiling water. Allow the tomatoes to soften for approximately 10 minutes.
Transfer the softened sundried tomatoes and soaking liquid into a blender. 2. Add garlic, shallots, Dijon mustard, maple syrup, oregano, salt, and pepper (if desired). Blend the mixture on high until it has a smooth and creamy consistency, pausing occasionally to scrape down the sides of the blender. This process typically takes about 3 minutes. 3. Store the dressing in the refrigerator for up to 1 week.

Per Serving:(½ cup)

calories: 37 | fat: 0g | protein: 1g | carbs: 8g | fiber: 1g

Perfect Baked Tofu

Prep time: 5 minutes | Cook time: 40 minutes | Serves 8

2 (14 ounces / 397 g) packages firm tofu, drained
Freshly ground black pepper

1. Preheat your oven to 450ºF (235ºC).
2. Cut each package of tofu into 8 equal slabs, approximately ½ inch thick.
3. Arrange the tofu in a single layer on a baking sheet lined with parchment paper. Season with pepper.
4. Bake for 20 minutes until the tofu starts to dry and become slightly firm to the touch.
5. Carefully flip the tofu over and season with pepper. Bake for an additional 15 to 20 minutes until the tofu is dry, firm, and has slightly crispy edges. Remove from the oven and store in an airtight container in the refrigerator until ready to use.

Per Serving:

calories: 49 | fat: 4g | protein: 8g | carbs: 2g | fiber: 1g

Pineapple Salsa

Prep time: 5 minutes | Cook time: 0 minutes | Serves 8

1 pound (454 g) fresh or thawed frozen pineapple, finely diced, and juices reserved
1 white or red onion, finely diced
1 bunch cilantro or mint, leaves only, chopped
1 jalapeño, minced (optional)
Salt (optional)

1. To prepare the pineapple salsa, combine the pineapple with its juice, onion, cilantro, and jalapeño (if desired) in a medium bowl. Add salt to taste and serve as desired.

Per Serving:

calories: 40 | fat: 0g | protein: 0g | carbs: 10g | fiber: 1g

Italian Seasoning

Prep time: 5 minutes | Cook time: 0 minutes | Makes 9 tablespoons

8 teaspoons dried marjoram
8 teaspoons dried basil
4 teaspoons dried thyme
2 teaspoons dried rosemary
2 teaspoons dried sage
2 teaspoons dried oregano
1 teaspoon garlic powder

1. Combine marjoram, basil, thyme, rosemary, sage, oregano, and garlic powder in an airtight container with a lid, such as a repurposed spice jar. Shake or mix the ingredients well until thoroughly combined.

Per Serving:

calories: 7 | fat: 0g | protein: 0g | carbs: 2g | fiber: 1g

Sour Cream

Prep time: 5 minutes | Cook time: 0 minutes | Serves 10

1 cup coconut cream
2 tablespoons lemon juice
½ teaspoon apple cider vinegar
½ teaspoon salt (optional)

1. Combine all ingredients in a food processor or blender and blend until the mixture is smooth. Alternatively, mix all ingredients in a medium bowl using hand mixers until smooth.
2. Chill the sour cream and use it as a topping or side dish.
3. Store the sour cream in an airtight container in the refrigerator for up to 4 days. Alternatively, freeze the sour cream for up to 60 days and thaw it at room temperature before use.

Per Serving:

calories: 20 | fat: 1g | protein: 0g | carbs: 3g | fiber: 0g

Magic Mineral Dust

Prep time: 1 minute | Cook time: 0 minutes | Makes ⅓ cup

3 tablespoons raw black sesame seeds, toasted
1 tablespoon Kombu Powder

1. Grind the sesame seeds in an electric spice grinder, or use a suribachi or mortar and pestle to crush them until coarsely ground.
2. Transfer the ground sesame seeds to a small bowl or jar and stir in the kombu powder.
3. Store the mixture in a tightly sealed jar for up to 3 months.

Per Serving:(⅓ cup)

calories: 155 | fat: 13g | protein: 5g | carbs: 6g | fiber: 3g

Spicy Tahini Dressing

Prep time: 10 minutes | Cook time: 0 minutes | Serves 8

½ cup tahini
2 tablespoons lemon juice
1 clove garlic, minced
1 tablespoon paprika powder
½ cup water

1. Combine all ingredients in a small bowl or jar and whisk or shake until the mixture is smooth.
2. Chill the tahini dressing and use it as a topping or side dish.
3. Store the tahini dressing in an airtight container in the refrigerator for up to 4 days. Alternatively, freeze the tahini dressing for up to 60 days and thaw it at room temperature before use.

Per Serving:

calories: 102 | fat: 8g | protein: 4g | carbs: 2g | fiber: 1g

Coconut Whipped Cream

Prep time: 5 minutes | Cook time: 0 minutes | Serves 5

1 cup coconut cream
1 teaspoon vanilla extract

2 tablespoons cocoa powder (optional)

1. Combine all the ingredients in a large bowl and mix for approximately 5 minutes using an electric mixer with beaters or a whisk. 2. Chill the whipped cream before serving and enjoy it as a topping or side dish. 3. Store the whipped cream in an airtight container in the refrigerator and consume within 2 days. Alternatively, you can freeze the whipped cream for up to 60 days and thaw it at room temperature when ready to use.

Per Serving:

calories: 40 | fat: 1g | protein: 0g | carbs: 7g | fiber: 0g

Flavorful Vegetable Broth

Prep time: 5 minutes | Cook time: 50 minutes |

Makes 4 quarts

4½ quarts water
2 medium onions, quartered
3 cups chopped celery
3 cups chopped carrots
4 large garlic cloves, minced
1 tablespoon chopped fresh rosemary
2 teaspoons dried thyme

½ teaspoon black peppercorns
4 bay leaves
1 cup chopped fennel bulb (optional)
1 ounce (28 g) dried wild mushrooms (optional)

1. In a large pot, combine water, onions, celery, carrots, garlic, rosemary, thyme, peppercorns, bay leaves, fennel (if desired), and mushrooms (if desired). Cover the pot and bring the mixture to a boil.
2. Reduce the heat to low and let it simmer for 45 minutes.
3. Place a coffee filter or cheesecloth inside a strainer and strain the mixture over a large bowl.
4. Transfer the broth to glass jars, seal them, and refrigerate for up to 7 days or freeze for up to 6 months.

Per Serving:

calories: 15 | fat: 0g | protein: 1g | carbs: 3g | fiber: 1g

Basil Pesto

Prep time: 10 minutes | Cook time: 0 minutes |

Makes about 1½ cups

1 cup fresh basil, chopped
½ cup pine nuts, or walnuts, or sunflower seeds
1 to 2 garlic cloves, pressed
Zest and juice of 1 small lemon

2 tablespoons nutritional yeast (optional)
¼ cup avocado, or 2 tablespoons tahini (optional)
⅛ teaspoon sea salt (optional)

1. To enhance the sweetness of fresh basil, submerge the leaves in a large bowl of ice water for approximately 5 minutes before chopping.
2. For a richer flavor, lightly toast the nuts by placing them in a small skillet on medium heat, stirring often. Alternatively, put them in an oven at 300ºF (150ºC) for 8 to 10 minutes. Be cautious as small nuts and seeds can burn quickly. If preferred, you may skip this step and proceed directly to step 3.
3. Blend all the ingredients in a food processor or blender until smooth. Taste the mixture and add additional salt (if desired) or seasonings as needed.

Per Serving:(1 tablespoon)

calories: 89 | fat: 8g | protein: 1g | carbs: 2g | fiber: 0g

Jalapeño and Tomatillo Salsa

Prep time: 10 minutes | Cook time: 0 minutes |

Makes 3 cups

4 tomatillos, peeled and washed
3 jalapeño peppers, stemmed and seeded
½ medium yellow onion, peeled
1 garlic clove

½ bunch fresh cilantro (about 1 cup leaves and stems)
¼ teaspoon salt, plus more as needed (optional)
1 cup water

1. Combine tomatillos, jalapeños, onion, garlic, cilantro, salt (if desired), and water in a blender. Blend until the mixture is smooth. Taste and add salt if needed.
2. Store the salsa in an airtight container in the refrigerator for up to 10 days.

Per Serving:

calories: 7 | fat: 0g | protein: 0g | carbs: 1g | fiber: 0g

Anytime "Cheese" Sauce

Prep time: 5 minutes | Cook time: 15 minutes |

Makes 6 cups

1 medium Yukon Gold potato, cut into 1-inch cubes
1 medium sweet potato, cut into 1-inch cubes
¼ cup rolled oats
¼ cup nutritional yeast

1 tablespoon freshly squeezed lemon juice
2 teaspoons garlic powder
2 teaspoons onion powder
1 teaspoon smoked paprika

1. Fill a large stockpot with water and bring it to a boil over high heat. Carefully add the Yukon Gold potato and sweet potato to the boiling water. Cook for 12 minutes before straining, reserving 3 cups of cooking liquid.
2. In a blender, combine the reserved cooking liquid, boiled potato, boiled sweet potato, oats, nutritional yeast, lemon juice, garlic powder, onion powder, and paprika. Blend on high for 3 to 5 minutes until smooth, then serve.

Per Serving:(½ cup)

calories: 53 | fat: 1g | protein: 4g | carbs: 10g | fiber: 2g

Spicy Avocado Crema

Prep time: 10 minutes | Cook time: 0 minutes |

Makes about ¾ cup

1 ripe avocado, halved and pitted
¼ cup canned full-fat coconut milk
2 tablespoons fresh lime juice

½ serrano chile pepper, seeds and ribs removed
¼ cup fresh cilantro, chopped
¼ teaspoon sea salt (optional)

1. Combine the avocado, coconut milk, lime juice, chile pepper, cilantro, and salt (if desired) in a blender or food processor.
2. Blend or process the ingredients until they are smooth. Taste the mixture and add additional salt or lime juice as necessary. Transfer the mixture to an airtight container and refrigerate it until you're ready to use it.

Per Serving:

calories: 80 | fat: 7g | protein: 1g | carbs: 4g | fiber: 2g

Italian Spices

Prep time: 5 minutes | Cook time: 0 minutes | Makes

½ cup

¼ cup dried oregano
3 tablespoons fennel seeds

1 tablespoon garlic powder

1. Combine all the ingredients in a jar with a tight-fitting lid and shake well until they are mixed thoroughly. The mixture can be stored for up to 6 months.

Per Serving:(½ cup)

calories: 132 | fat: 3g | protein: 6g | carbs: 26g | fiber: 14g

Savory Chia Crackers

Prep time: 20 minutes | Cook time: 20 minutes |

Makes 36 crackers

½ cup oat flour
½ cup brown rice flour
¼ cup water
2 teaspoons nutritional yeast

1 teaspoon chia seeds
¼ teaspoon freshly ground black pepper
¼ teaspoon onion powder

1. Preheat the oven to 350ºF (180ºC). Cut 2 sheets of parchment paper the size of your baking sheet. Place them on a work surface.
2. In a food processor, combine the oat and brown rice flours, water, nutritional yeast, chia seeds, pepper, and onion powder. Process for 1 to 2 minutes to combine into a dough. You should be able to pinch the dough between two fingers without it sticking to you. 3. Place the dough on one of the sheets of parchment paper. Using your clean hands, press the dough together into a mound, then press to flatten and shape into a thick square. Place the other sheet of parchment paper on top. Using a rolling pin, evenly flatten

the dough to ⅛ inch thick. If your dough is too thick, the crackers won't be crispy. Remove the top sheet of parchment paper and save it for another use. 4. Using a knife or pizza cutter, cut the dough into 36 (1-by-2-inch) rectangles. Using a fork, lightly prick holes in the center of each cracker. Carefully transfer the parchment paper with the dough on it to a baking sheet. 5. Bake for 10 minutes. Carefully flip the crackers and bake for 10 minutes more until golden brown on the edges. Transfer the crackers to a wire rack to cool. They will crisp as they cool. 6. Store in an airtight container at room temperature for up to 1 week or freeze for up to 1 month.

Per Serving:(4 crackers)

calories: 61 | fat: 1g | protein: 2g | carbs: 12g | fiber: 1g

B-Savory Sauce and Marinade

Prep time: 5 minutes | Cook time: 0 minutes | Makes

1¼ cups

½ cup nutritional yeast
¼ cup reduced-sodium, gluten-free tamari
2 tablespoons apple cider vinegar
2 tablespoons balsamic vinegar
2 tablespoons gluten-free

Worcestershire sauce
1 tablespoon plus 1 teaspoon maple syrup (optional)
2 teaspoons gluten-free Dijon mustard
½ teaspoon ground turmeric
¼ teaspoon black pepper

1. Combine all the ingredients in a resealable container. The sauce can be refrigerated for up to 3 weeks, and it yields enough to marinate 4 blocks of tempeh or tofu, or 16 portobello caps.

Per Serving:(¼ cup)

calories: 84 | fat: 0g | protein: 9g | carbs: 11g | fiber: 2g

Easy Guacamole

Prep time: 15 minutes | Cook time: 0 minutes |

Serves 4

2 large Hass avocados, peeled, stoned and halved
¼ cup lemon juice
1 red onion, minced
1 clove garlic, minced

½ cup chopped fresh cilantro
Optional Toppings:
Jalapeño slices
Sweet corn

1. Combine all ingredients in a food processor and blend until the mixture is smooth. Alternatively, for a chunky guacamole, mash the ingredients in a medium-sized bowl with a fork.
2. Serve the guacamole immediately with optional toppings and enjoy!
3. Store the guacamole in an airtight container in the refrigerator and consume within 2 days. Alternatively, freeze the guacamole for up to 90 days and thaw it at room temperature before serving.

Per Serving:

calories: 181 | fat: 14g | protein: 2g | carbs: 11g | fiber: 6g

Cashew Cream Cheese

Prep time: 5 minutes | Cook time: 15 minutes |

Serves 15

2 cups raw and unsalted cashews	¼ cup nutritional yeast
½ tablespoon balsamic vinegar	Salt and pepper, to taste (optional)

1. Half fill a saucepan with water, put it over medium high heat and bring it to a boil. 2. Add the cashews to the saucepan and boil them for 15 minutes. 3. Strain the cashews after boiling them, then discard the water and let them cool down completely. 4. Add all of the ingredients to a food processor and blend until smooth. 5. Serve the cashew cream cheese chilled and enjoy as a topping or a side! 6. Store the cream cheese in the fridge, using an airtight container, and consume within 4 days. Alternatively, store the cream cheese in the freezer for a maximum of 60 days and thaw at room temperature.

Per Serving:

calories: 76 | fat: 6g | protein: 2g | carbs: 4g | fiber: 1g

Lemon Mint Tahini Cream

Prep time: 5 minutes | Cook time: 0minutes | Serves 6

½ cup tahini	¼ cup lemon juice
3 pitted dates	2 cloves garlic
½ cup water	6 leaves mint

1. Add all the ingredients to a blender or food processor and blend to form a thick and smooth sauce. 2. Store the tahini cream in the fridge, using an airtight container, and consume within 3 days. Alternatively, store the tahini cream in the freezer for a maximum of 60 days and thaw at room temperature.

Per Serving:

calories: 141 | fat: 11g | protein: 5g | carbs: 5g | fiber: 1g

Cheesy Vegetable Sauce

Prep time: 10 minutes | Cook time: 25 minutes |

Makes 4 cups

1 cup raw cashews	(or almond or cashew if gluten-free)
1 russet potato, peeled and cubed	1 tablespoon arrowroot powder, cornstarch, or tapioca starch
2 carrots, cubed	1 onion, chopped
½ cup nutritional yeast	3 garlic cloves, minced
2 tablespoons yellow (mellow) miso paste	1 tablespoon water, plus more as needed
1 teaspoon ground mustard	
2 cups unsweetened oat milk	

1. In an 8-quart pot, combine the cashews, potato, and carrots. Add enough water to cover by 2 inches. Bring to a boil over high heat, then reduce the heat to simmer. Cook for 15 minutes. 2. In a blender, combine the nutritional yeast, miso paste, ground mustard, milk, and arrowroot powder. 3. Drain the cashews, potato, and carrot. Add to the blender but don't blend yet. 4. Rinse the pot, place it over high heat, and add the onion and garlic. Cook for 3 to 4 minutes, adding water 1 tablespoon at a time to prevent burning. Transfer to the blender. Purée everything until smooth. Scrape the sides and continue blending as needed. Pour the cheese sauce into the pot and place it over medium heat. Cook, stirring, until the sauce comes to a simmer. 5. Use immediately, or refrigerate in a sealable container for up to 1 week.

Per Serving:(½ cup)

calories: 191 | fat: 10g | protein: 9g | carbs: 20g | fiber: 4g

Fresh Mango Salsa

Prep time: 15 minutes | Cook time: 0 minutes |

Makes 2 cups

1 large mango, diced	1 tablespoon chopped jalapeño pepper (optional)
1 medium tomato, diced	¼ cup fresh cilantro, parsley, mint, and/or basil, chopped
1 garlic clove, pressed	
Juice of ½ lime	Pinch sea salt (optional)
1 scallion, chopped	

1. Mix everything together in a bowl, or pulse in a food processor if you want a smoother texture.

Per Serving:(1 cup)

calories: 129 | fat: 0g | protein: 2g | carbs: 31g | fiber: 4g

Coconut "Bacon" Bits

Prep time: 15 minutes | Cook time: 12 minutes |

Makes 2 cups

2 tablespoons tamari or low-sodium soy sauce	½ teaspoon smoked paprika
1 tablespoon liquid hickory smoke	¼ teaspoon onion powder
	¼ teaspoon ground white pepper
1 tablespoon pure maple syrup (optional)	2 cups unsweetened coconut flakes (not desiccated)

1. Preheat the oven to 350ºF (180ºC). Line a baking sheet with parchment paper or aluminum foil. Avoid using a silicone mat, because the ingredients will stain the surface. 2. In a large bowl, stir together the tamari, liquid smoke, maple syrup (if using), paprika, onion powder, and ground white pepper. Add the coconut flakes. Stir and toss gently to combine until the coconut flakes are thoroughly coated. Let sit for 10 minutes. Stir again, then spread the coconut evenly on the prepared baking sheet. 3. Bake for 12 minutes. The coconut flakes should look dry and golden brown rather than dark. 4. Let cool completely on the baking sheet. 5. Store in an airtight container at room temperature for 2 weeks or freeze for up to 2 months.

Per Serving:(1 tablespoon)

calories: 36 | fat: 3g | protein: 1g | carbs: 2g | fiber: 1g

Strawberry Chia Jam

Prep time: 2 minutes | Cook time: 10 minutes |
Makes 1½ cups

3 cups frozen strawberries
4 dates, pitted and chopped
small

¼ cup water
3 tablespoons chia seeds

1. In a medium saucepan over medium-high heat, combine the strawberries, dates, and water and bring to a boil. Lower the heat to medium-low and simmer, stirring occasionally, for 10 minutes. Remove from the heat. 2. Using a potato masher, mash the mixture until the jam is smooth but with some chunks remaining. Add the chia seeds and stir well. Transfer the mixture to a small jar, cover, and let cool. The jam will thicken as it cools. The jam can be stored in the refrigerator for up to 5 days.

Per Serving:

calories: 43 | fat: 1g | protein: 1g | carbs: 8g | fiber: 3g

Nutty Plant-Based Parmesan

Prep time: 10 minutes | Cook time: 0 minutes |
Makes 1½ cups

1 cup raw cashews
½ cup nutritional yeast

½ teaspoon salt (optional)

1. In a blender, pulse the cashews until they become a fine dust. Transfer the cashew dust to a small bowl and add the nutritional yeast and salt (if using). Mix well with a spoon. Transfer any leftovers to an airtight container and refrigerate for up to 10 days or freeze for up to 3 months.

Per Serving:

calories: 79 | fat: 5g | protein: 3g | carbs: 5g | fiber: 0g

Everyday Pesto

Prep time: 5 minutes | Cook time: 5 minutes | Makes
1 cup

4 cups packed fresh basil leaves
¼ cup raw cashews
2 tablespoons nutritional yeast
1 garlic clove

¼ teaspoon freshly ground
black pepper
3 tablespoons boiling water,
plus more as needed

1. In a food processor, blend the basil, cashews, nutritional yeast, garlic, pepper, and boiling water until smooth. Add more water to thin until you have a smooth, slightly thick mixture. 2. Refrigerate in a sealed jar for up to 1 month.

Per Serving:(2 tablespoons)

calories: 35 | fat: 2g | protein: 3g | carbs: 2g | fiber: 1g

Creamy Balsamic Dressing

Prep time: 10 minutes | Cook time: 0 minutes |
Makes ¾ cup

¼ cup tahini
¼ cup balsamic vinegar
¼ cup fresh basil, minced
⅛ cup water
1 tablespoon maple syrup

(optional)
1 garlic clove, pressed
Pinch sea salt (optional)
Pinch freshly ground black
pepper (optional)

1. Place all the ingredients in a blender or food processor and blend until smooth. If you mince the basil very finely, you could also whisk the ingredients together without using a blender.

Per Serving:(1 tablespoon)

calories: 157 | fat: 10g | protein: 3g | carbs: 12g | fiber: 2g

High Protein Black Bean Dip

Prep time: 10 minutes | Cook time: 0 minutes |
Serves 3

4 cups black beans, cooked,
rinsed, and drained
2 tablespoons minced garlic
2 tablespoons Italian seasoning
2 tablespoons onion powder

1 tablespoon olive oil (optional)
1 tablespoon lemon juice
¼ teaspoon salt, to taste
(optional)

1. Place black beans in a large bowl and mash them with a fork until everything is mostly smooth. Stir in the remaining ingredients and incorporate thoroughly. The mixture should be smooth and creamy. Add some additional salt (if desired) and lemon juice to taste and serve at room temperature.

Per Serving:

calories: 398 | fat: 7g | protein: 21g | carbs: 63g | fiber: 16g

Fall and Winter All-Purpose Seasoning

Prep time: 5 minutes | Cook time: 0 minutes | Makes
½ cup

3 tablespoons dried rosemary
2 tablespoons plus 2 teaspoons
dried sage
2 tablespoons plus 2 teaspoons

dried thyme
1 teaspoon black pepper
¼ teaspoon ground ginger
(optional)

1. Use a mortar and pestle or coffee grinder to roughly grind the rosemary and sage. Transfer to a jar with a tight-fitting lid; add the thyme, pepper, and ginger, if desired; and shake until combined. Store for up to 6 months.

Per Serving:(½ cup)

calories: 26 | fat: 1g | protein: 1g | carbs: 5g | fiber: 3g

Smoky Mushrooms

Prep time: 10 minutes | Cook time: 10 minutes | Makes 2 cups

2 tablespoons soy sauce
2 tablespoons pure maple syrup
1 tablespoon liquid smoke
1 tablespoon liquid aminos
¼ teaspoon freshly ground

black pepper
1 pound (454 g) cremini
mushrooms, cut into ½-inch-
thick slices

1. In a sauté pan or skillet, whisk together the soy sauce, maple syrup, liquid smoke, liquid aminos, and pepper. 2. Add the mushrooms, and cook over medium-high heat, stirring frequently, for about 10 minutes, or until the liquid evaporates but the mushrooms are still tender and glistening. Remove from the heat. Store in an airtight container in the refrigerator until ready to use.

Per Serving:

calories: 45 | fat: 0g | protein: 3g | carbs: 8g | fiber: 1g

Chickenless Bouillon Base

Prep time: 5 minutes | Cook time: 0 minutes | Makes 2 cups

2 cups nutritional yeast
¼ cup sea salt (optional)
2 tablespoons onion powder
1 tablespoon Italian seasoning

2 teaspoons garlic powder
1 teaspoon ground turmeric
1 teaspoon celery salt
1 teaspoon dried thyme

1. Combine nutritional yeast, salt (if desired), onion powder, Italian seasoning, garlic powder, turmeric, celery salt, and thyme in a small blender, food processor, spice grinder, or mortar and pestle. Blend the ingredients until they form a powder.
2. Store the bouillon powder in a sealable jar or container at room temperature. To make a flavorful stock, use 1 tablespoon of the powder per 1 cup of water.

Per Serving:(1 tablespoon)

calories: 23 | fat: 0g | protein: 3g | carbs: 3g | fiber: 1g

Maple Caramel

Prep time: 5 minutes | Cook time: 15 minutes | Makes 1¼ cups

1 cup full-fat coconut milk
¾ cup pure maple syrup
(optional)
1 teaspoon pure vanilla extract

1 teaspoon fresh lemon juice
¾ teaspoon fine sea salt
(optional)

1. Combine the coconut milk and maple syrup, if using, in a medium saucepan over medium-high heat. Once the mixture comes to a boil, lower the heat to a strong simmer. 2. The caramel will be bubbling continuously. Whisk it every couple of minutes. Keep simmering and whisking the caramel for about 15 minutes or until the volume of the liquid has reduced by ⅓. It will have thickened slightly. 3. Stir the vanilla, lemon juice, and sea salt, if using, into the caramel while it's still warm. Scrape the caramel into a bowl or glass jar. Let the caramel come to room temperature before covering and storing in the refrigerator. Caramel is at ideal texture after refrigerating overnight and will keep for 1 week.

Per Serving:(¼ cup)

calories: 256 | fat: 11g | protein: 1g | carbs: 35g | fiber: 1g

Plant-Based Queso Dip

Prep time: 5 minutes | Cook time: 20 minutes | Makes 3 cups

1 cup raw cashews
1 cup cubed butternut squash
1 yellow or orange bell pepper,
seeded and cut into quarters
2 cups plus 1 teaspoon water,
divided
1 cup unsweetened plant-based
milk

1 tablespoon nutritional yeast
½ teaspoon salt (optional)
½ teaspoon onion powder
½ teaspoon garlic powder
¼ teaspoon smoked paprika
½ jalapeño pepper, seeded and
minced (optional)
1 teaspoon tapioca flour

1. In a medium saucepan, combine the cashews, butternut squash, bell pepper, and 2 cups of water and bring to a boil. Lower the heat to medium and cook until the squash and cashews are soft, about 15 minutes. Drain and transfer the ingredients to a blender or food processor. 2. Add the plant-based milk, nutritional yeast, salt (if using), onion powder, garlic powder, and smoked paprika and blend until smooth and creamy. 3. Transfer the mixture back to the saucepan and slowly bring to a boil over medium-high heat, stirring often. Add the jalapeño (if using) and cook for 2 to 3 minutes. 4. In a small bowl, mix together the tapioca flour and the remaining 1 teaspoon water to make a slurry. Add the slurry to the cheese sauce and cook, stirring constantly, until the sauce is thick and creamy, about 2 more minutes. Refrigerate leftovers for up to 4 days.

Per Serving:

calories: 85 | fat: 6g | protein: 3g | carbs: 7g | fiber: 1g

Rice Vinegar and Sesame Dressing

Prep time: 10 minutes | Cook time: 0 minutes | Makes ½ cup

¼ cup rice vinegar
2 tablespoons maple syrup
(optional)
1 tablespoon tahini

2 garlic cloves, minced
½-inch piece fresh ginger,
peeled and grated

1. Combine the vinegar, maple syrup (if using), tahini, garlic, and ginger in a small Mason jar or other airtight container. 2. Cover with a lid and shake until well mixed. Store in the refrigerator for up to 1 week.

Per Serving:

calories: 54 | fat: 2g | protein: 1g | carbs: 8g | fiber: 0g

Chili Spice Blend

Prep time: 5 minutes | Cook time: 0 minutes | Makes 7½ tablespoons

¼ cup chili powder
4 teaspoons onion powder
4 teaspoons ground cumin
1 teaspoon ground coriander
1 teaspoon garlic powder
½ teaspoon cayenne

1. In an airtight container with a lid (or repurposed spice jar), combine the chili powder, onion powder, cumin, coriander, garlic powder, and cayenne. Shake or mix well.

Per Serving:

calories: 24 | fat: 1g | protein: 1g | carbs: 4g | fiber: 2g

Vegan Basil Pesto

Prep time: 5 minutes | Cook time: 0 minutes | Serves 6

2 bunches basil, leaves only
1 cup spinach
¼ cup roasted almonds
¼ cup toasted pine nuts
4 raw Brazil nuts, chopped
2 garlic cloves
¼ cup water
¼ to ½ teaspoon salt (optional)

1. Using a food processor, pulse the basil, spinach, almonds, pine nuts, Brazil nuts, and garlic until they are finely chopped and well-combined. While the food processor is running, slowly stream in the water until the mixture reaches your desired consistency. Add ¼ teaspoon of salt and adjust to taste.
2. The pesto can be stored in an airtight container in the refrigerator for up to 5 days. Alternatively, it can be frozen in single portions for up to 6 months by scooping it into ice cube trays, freezing it, and then transferring it to an airtight container.

Per Serving:

calories: 81 | fat: 8g | protein: 2g | carbs: 2g | fiber: 1g

Roasted Bell Pepper Wedges

Prep time: 5 minutes | Cook time: 25 minutes | Makes 1½ cups

2 large red bell peppers, seeded and cut into wedges
1 tablespoon freshly squeezed lemon juice
Pinch freshly ground black pepper
½ teaspoon garlic powder (optional)
½ teaspoon cumin seeds (optional)

1. Preheat your oven to 425ºF (220ºC).
2. In a large mixing bowl, combine the bell pepper wedges with lemon juice, black pepper, garlic powder (if desired), and cumin seeds (if desired). Toss the ingredients together until well combined.
3. Arrange the bell pepper wedges on a baking sheet lined with nonstick foil or parchment paper, cut-side down.
4. Bake for 20 to 25 minutes, or until the peppers are soft and lightly charred. Remove from the oven and let them cool for up to 20 minutes before storing them in an airtight container in the refrigerator for up to 5 days.

Per Serving:

calories: 53 | fat: 1g | protein: 2g | carbs: 10g | fiber: 4g

Quick Spelt Bread

Prep time: 5 minutes | Cook time: 45 minutes | Makes 1 loaf

420 grams whole-grain spelt flour (about 3¾ cups)
1 teaspoon baking soda
1 teaspoon baking powder
1½ cups unsweetened soy milk
2 tablespoons pure maple syrup
1 tablespoon lemon juice

1. Preheat the oven to 350ºF (180ºC). 2. Cut parchment paper to evenly line a 9-by-5-inch loaf pan by cutting inward to make the corners fit snugly. Allow the parchment paper to pass the top of the loaf pan (you will use these to remove the loaf from the pan in step 7). 3. In a large bowl, mix together the flour, baking soda, and baking powder. 4. In a medium bowl, mix together the soy milk, maple syrup, and lemon juice. 5. Add the soy milk mixture to the flour mixture, and mix well until combined, all the flour has hydrated, gluten has started to form, and the dough gets a little harder to mix. Transfer to the prepared loaf pan. 6. Bake for 45 minutes, or until the loaf is golden brown and a wooden skewer inserted into the center comes out clean. Remove from the oven. 7. Using the parchment paper as a sling, remove the bread from the loaf pan, and let cool completely before cutting.

Per Serving:

calories: 204 | fat: 2g | protein: 8g | carbs: 42g | fiber: 6g

Roasted Beet Dip

Prep time: 5 minutes | Cook time: 30 to 40 minutes | Makes 2 cups

2 medium or 3 small red beets
½ cup sunflower seeds, soaked in water for 8 hours
1 tablespoon hemp oil (optional)
Juice of 1 lemon
2 tablespoons balsamic vinegar
1 teaspoon fennel seeds
½ teaspoon sea salt (optional)
½ teaspoon freshly ground black pepper

1. Preheat the oven to 400ºF (205ºC). Wrap the beets in unbleached parchment paper and place them on a baking sheet. Roast for 30 to 40 minutes, or until the beets are fork-tender. 2. When cool enough to handle, peel away the beet skins, using your hands. Chop the beets and place them in a blender or food processor. Add the remaining ingredients and blend until smooth. 3. Store in an airtight container in the fridge for up to 5 days. Leftovers make the perfect weekday lunch solution or take-along snacks.

Per Serving:

calories: 81 | fat: 6g | protein: 2g | carbs: 4g | fiber: 1g

Spaghetti Squash with Marinara and Veggies

Prep time: 15 minutes | Cook time: 10 minutes | Serves 4

3 tablespoons water
½ green or red bell pepper, diced
½ cup diced red, white, or yellow onion
1 teaspoon minced garlic
2 cups chopped spinach

1 (14½ ounces / 411 g) can diced tomatoes with their juices
½ tablespoon dried oregano
1 (15 ounces / 425 g) can black or pinto beans, drained and rinsed
¼ teaspoon salt (optional)
1 roasted spaghetti squash, cut in half

1. In a large pan over medium-high heat, heat the water. Add the bell pepper, onion, and garlic and sauté for 3 minutes or until the onion is tender and translucent. 2. Add the spinach, tomatoes, oregano, beans, and salt , if desired. Reduce the heat to low and simmer for 5 minutes. 3. While the veggies are cooking, scrape the inside of the roasted spaghetti squash until it resembles spaghetti strands. 4. Pour the pepper and tomato sauce over the spaghetti squash.

Per Serving:
calories: 153 | fat: 1g | protein: 7g | carbs: 32g | fiber: 8g

Dreamy Lemon Curd

Prep time: 10 minutes | Cook time: 5 minutes | Makes 1 cup

¼ cup maple syrup or raw agave nectar (optional)
½ cup full-fat coconut milk
⅓ cup fresh lemon juice
¼ cup room temperature coconut oil (optional)

⅛ teaspoon ground turmeric
⅛ teaspoon sea salt (optional)
2 teaspoons lemon zest
2 tablespoons arrowroot powder

1. In a medium saucepan over medium heat, combine the maple syrup, coconut milk, lemon juice, coconut oil, ground tumeric, sea salt, if using, and lemon zest. Bring the mixture to a light boil, whisking occasionally. 2. When some bubbles start to break the surface, add the arrowroot powder to the saucepan, and whisk constantly as the mixture simmers. After the curd has thickened enough to coat the back of a spoon rather thickly, remove from the heat. 3. Quickly scrape the curd into a jar or bowl. Let it cool slightly at room temperature before pressing a piece of plastic wrap onto the surface of the curd. Store the lemon curd in the refrigerator for up to 1 week.

Per Serving:(¼ cup)
calories: 249 | fat: 20g | protein: 1g | carbs: 17g | fiber: 1g

Sweet Peanut Butter Dipping Sauce

Prep time: 10 minutes | Cook time: 0 minutes | Makes 1 cup

½ cup creamy peanut butter (no added sugar or salt)
2 tablespoons rice vinegar
¼ cup unsweetened coconut milk
1 tablespoon maple syrup (optional)

2 garlic cloves
½-inch piece fresh ginger, peeled and grated
¼ teaspoon red pepper flakes

1. In a food processor, combine the peanut butter, rice vinegar, coconut milk, maple syrup (if using), garlic, ginger, and red pepper flakes. Blend until smooth. 2. Store in an airtight container in the refrigerator for up to 5 days.

Per Serving:
calories: 107 | fat: 8g | protein: 4g | carbs: 6g | fiber: 1g

Made in United States
Troutdale, OR
12/10/2023

15654271R00071